Presented to

Bradford Public Library

in Memory of

Chris Swan

1916 – 1988

✝

— a lover of the colour and of the beauty of life —

by his many friends and admirers

THE
SCENTED
GARDEN

*How to use beautiful plants to create an
intoxicating harmony of fragrances for
garden and home*

D A V I D S Q U I R E
W I T H J A N E N E W D I C K

Doubleday Canada Limited, Toronto

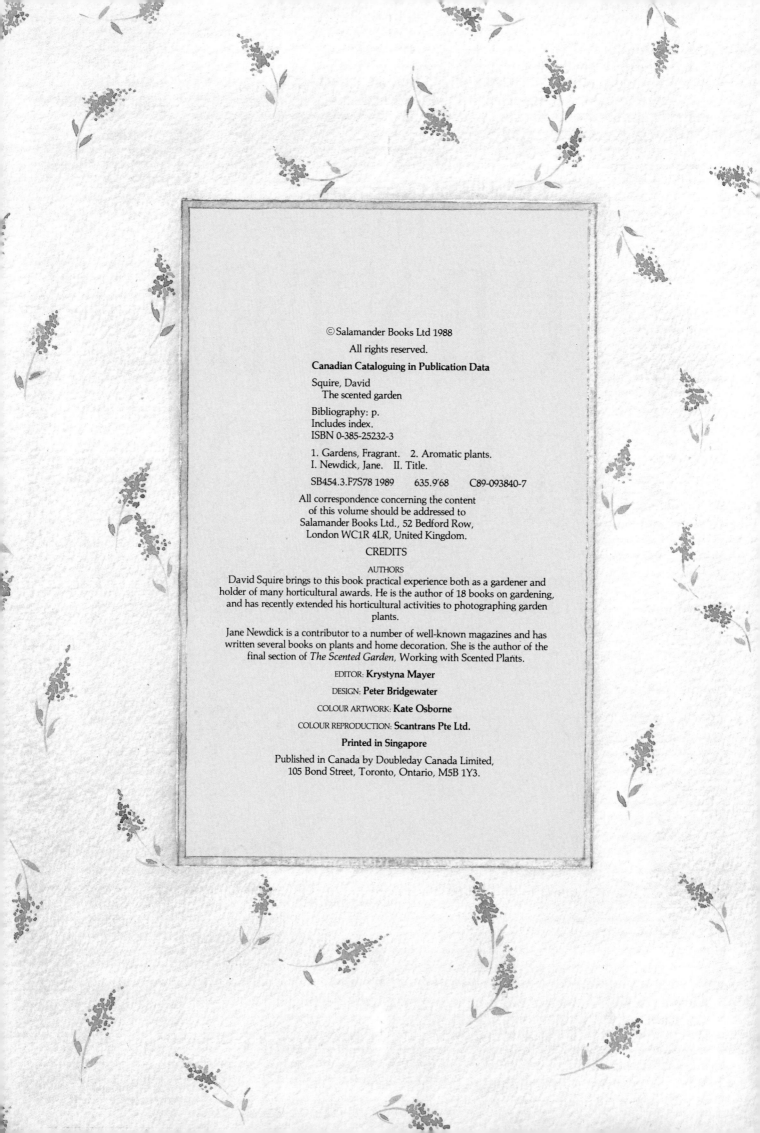

Canadian Cataloguing in Publication Data

Squire, David
  The scented garden

Bibliography: p.
Includes index.
ISBN 0-385-25232-3

1. Gardens, Fragrant.   2. Aromatic plants.
I. Newdick, Jane.   II. Title.

SB454.3.F7S78 1989   635.9'68   C89-093840-7

All correspondence concerning the content
of this volume should be addressed to
Salamander Books Ltd., 52 Bedford Row,
London WC1R 4LR, United Kingdom.

CREDITS

AUTHORS

David Squire brings to this book practical experience both as a gardener and holder of many horticultural awards. He is the author of 18 books on gardening, and has recently extended his horticultural activities to photographing garden plants.

Jane Newdick is a contributor to a number of well-known magazines and has written several books on plants and home decoration. She is the author of the final section of *The Scented Garden*, Working with Scented Plants.

EDITOR: **Krystyna Mayer**

DESIGN: **Peter Bridgewater**

COLOUR ARTWORK: **Kate Osborne**

COLOUR REPRODUCTION: **Scantrans Pte Ltd.**

Printed in Singapore

Published in Canada by Doubleday Canada Limited,
105 Bond Street, Toronto, Ontario, M5B 1Y3.

Contents

Introduction

Smell is probably the least understood of all our five senses, but one that is vitally important. When young, babies find their mother's milk partly through smell, and throughout our lives scent-imprinting occurs through pleasurable or frightening happenings.

Adolescence may be remembered through excesses of aftershave or perfume, or the first introduction to the cool, sparkling freshness of champagne.

Marriage services can frequently be recalled through the sweetness of a bouquet of flowers, while honeymoon locations will be evoked by the tell-tale hint of an aroma: from the resinous scent of pine trees during a warm afternoon, to the spiciness and warm dustiness of a bazaar.

Colors, shapes and sounds can easily be defined, and as one's interest in them develops, so does the vocabulary needed to characterize them. Smells are less easily described, and while we are young we do not generally have the refined and practised vocabulary for them. The sense of smell becomes neglected, and once ignored is often difficult to recapture in all its subtlety.

Appreciating smells, therefore, requires practice and cultivation; connoisseurs of wines can detect even the smallest difference from year to year in a wine by a combination of a great deal of smelling and a little tasting, while cigar experts are even able to determine the vintage of a good cigar.

Likewise, distinctive flavors in food are detected mainly through the sense of smell, and both the bouquet of a wine and the aroma of roast beef are detected and analysed through the olfactory senses. The food industry has long been aware that meals need nose-appeal, as well as the ability to attract the eye and interest the taste-buds.

Everyone – except those who have lost their sense of smell and who are said to be anosmic – is able to appreciate the wonderful range of bouquets that enrich our lives, though proper appreciation does require practice. We do not, however, all have the same ability to detect smells. Women have a keener sense of smell than men, but while pregnant this power diminishes. Nose colds and sinus problems temporarily decrease the ability to detect aromas, while colds and respiratory infections can alter the perceived nature of an aroma.

Perhaps surprisingly, factory workers are often better able to identify odors than people who work outdoors, while people with allergies can smell as well as those without. Young people are much better able to detect smells than the elderly, although the ability still remains at a youthful level right up to late middle age and into early retirement. Dark-haired people are said to have a more sensitive appreciation of smell than those with fair hair, while the total albino is anosmic.

Even if we, as 'higher animals', do not bother to cultivate and use our abilities to detect scents, then insects and animals certainly do. They use scents for many purposes: to attract or find mates, to detect food, to escape being someone else's lunch, and for identification and social purposes.

Many carnivorous animals hunt by scent, while herbivores use the same powers to prevent themselves from becoming the meal. Even humans are said to have a more acute sense of scent detection when they are hungry.

Scents, however, still intrude upon us. We all emit odors, whether or not we wish to acknowledge the fact, and this in turn has generated an enormous industry. The perfumery business is ages old and originated to suppress unwelcome odors – with, perhaps, the addition of a hint of an aphrodisiac.

What does this prove in relation to the wonderful range of scents created by flowers and leaves? It suggests that we are all individual in our detection and appreciation of smells. The sheer range of aromas described in this book, however, is sure to capture the imagination of everyone, and will I hope lead to a greater appreciation and awareness of one of life's more serene pleasures.

DETECTING SCENTS

Smell and taste are closely linked and differ from other senses in as much as they are both chemical reactions. They are, however, fundamentally different. This is because many pure substances that we detect through smell have no taste, and those that we detect through taste frequently have no smell. There are, of course, exceptions and some substances can be detected by both senses. Usually, the substances that are detected through taste are soluble in water, whereas those that we detect through smell are soluble in oil. There are exceptions even to this generality, but it is substantiated by the fact that many of the so-called essential oils have strong odors (the term essential oil is given to any volatile oil derived from a plant and which is used to make perfumes and flavorings).

Our ability to detect smells is said to be 10,000 times more sensitive than that of taste, in spite of the relative inaccessibility of the olfactory organs within

Scented plants have been cultivated in gardens for centuries. This exquisite flower painting is from a 17th century florilegium by Johann Walther. It includes violets, lilies and honeysuckle.

the nose. Such is the sensitivity of these organs that a concentration of ethyl mercaptan – which occurs in rotten meat – of 1/400,000,000th of a milligram per liter of air can be detected.

Temperature and humidity influence the strength and detection of odors: those containing volatile oils become more noticeable in warm weather, while humidity helps to prolong a smell because it reduces the rate at which it evaporates. Hunting dogs, for instance, can follow a trail more easily during periods of high humidity.

CLASSIFYING SMELLS

Attempting to classify the scents of flowers and leaves is like trying to play Vivaldi on a Jew's harp: the subject matter may be known but to give it form and logicality is nearly impossible.

During the 18th century the father of modern botany, the Swedish naturalist Carolus Linnaeus, classified plant odors into seven categories – Aromatic, Fragrant, Ambrosial, Alliaceous (garlic-like), Hircine (goat-like), Foul or Nauseous. Only three of these – Aromatic, Fragrant and Ambrosial – were said to be pleasant. During the early years of this century a test was performed on humans using more than 400 different scents. It concluded that there are only six main smells: Fruity, Flowery, Resinous, Spicy, Foul and Burnt.

When young and starting to enjoy plants our powers of scent description are usually limited, and all we can say is that the bouquet is sweet, or perhaps like that of lily-of-the-valley, reminiscent of a lemon, a pine tree, rosemary or lavender. Often, all we can do is to relate the redolence to another plant or flower that we know well. Even as we age, few descriptive words are added to our vocabulary other than those relating to other plants, and one soon realizes that classifying plant scents is not a science but more a fascinating tapestry of relating one plant aroma to another.

Within each chapter of the book, the many hundreds of scented plants described are grouped into a range of scents. This will enable the reader with a penchant for a particular scent to find a desired plant without delay. Color, height and spread (for trees and shrubs these measurements are those to be expected after 20 years of growth in the right kind of soil), the best situation in a yard and the nature of the plant are also indicated.

The book is divided into a range of chapters, most of them describing types of plants for a particular part of the yard, whether alongside a path, in a rock garden, in or around a water garden, on a patio, in a flower border, and so on.

We all want to get the best out of our yards, creating a treasure-house that will provide plenty of interest throughout the entire year, and if the yard is richly scented with plants of all shapes and sizes, from bulbs to trees, then it is sure to add an extra dimension of surprise and delight.

CHAPTER ONE

Daytime Scents

Gardens rich in scent have a quality
that is nearly indefinable, yet one that
so captivates the mind that they are
among the most memorable.

SCENT can be like the will-o'-the-wisp – here one moment and undetectable the next; dispersed and lost for ever. The scientific element in people invariably strives to analyze and classify whatever they come into contact with, but scents can baffle even the most determined and analytical researcher. Unlike colors, where those people who are fortunate enough to have perfect color vision can accurately label a particular hue they like, scents often baffle attempts at definition.

The sweetness of violets initially captures attention, but if you choose to come back to them, to be enthralled again by their scent, it is seldom detectable. This is not because their exquisite sweetness is any less, but that your sense of detection is exhausted. Usually, however, the inability to detect an aroma is caused by its dissipation into a larger area, or its dispersal by the wind. Therefore, the positioning of a scented garden is all-important.

Few gardeners, though, are able to select their ideal garden; most people have to make do with what they have, creating a garden often under the most difficult of circumstances. Adversity, however, usually generates a determination to succeed seldom aspired to under easier circumstances.

have a superb scent – they are the big brothers of many of the dwarf or slow-growing forms described in Chapters 4 and 6.

Many aromatic conifers can be used to create a windbreak on the windward side of the yard, but make sure that when they mature, their shadow will not create a large sunless area. The line between a garden well protected from strong winds and one that has a balance between areas of sun and shade is a fine one, and as a garden matures, tall trees often have to be removed, thinned out or severely pruned.

Within a yard, aromatic low-growing hedges create interest alongside paths, or as fragrant breaks between one part of the garden and another. A garden that can be seen in its entirety from one position soon loses its appeal, whereas the surprise in turning a corner and being confronted with a fragrant bower abundant with climbers and shrubs, with perhaps a piece of romantic statuary, enriches and excites the mind. A range of plants to create large, aromatic windbreaks, as well as small hedges within the yard, are described at the end of this chapter. In addition, some of the larger trees and shrubs featured in Chapter 9 can be planted to create an attractive screen.

THE PERFECT SITE

The warm stillness of a south- or west-facing slope with shelter from prevailing winds both reduces the risk of scent dispersal and creates the higher temperatures that enable many plants to release their bouquets more readily. Patios in summer especially benefit from warmth, which carries the bouquets of day and afternoon scents into evening, and strengthens those of the evening and night.

Scented plants can, of course, be positioned throughout the yard (those shrubs and trees that create winter color are especially good alongside firm-surfaced paths) but if the yard is large and exposed, an area specifically for scented plants might be the solution. A screen of aromatic conifers in combination with a scented hedge will help to create the necessary stillness. Many large conifers that can be used for screening

SEASONAL SCENTED GARDENS

We all have our favorite times of the year, and perhaps in some way these are influenced by the long days of childhood, or by the season during which birth occurred.

Some of the most memorable scented plants exude their sweetness during winter, when there is usually a dearth of color in yards, which makes them even more welcome. Trees and shrubs known for their winter fragrance are described in detail in Chapter 9, while many smaller plants that are no less welcome include bulbs as well as evergreen perennials.

Not many yards are large enough to enable a complete section to be planted entirely with winter-flowering plants without detracting from a good display in the summer. However, a firm-surfaced pathway partly but generously planted with scented

*T*he apple-like aroma emitted by the bruised foliage of the slow-growing conifer Thuja occidentalis 'Rheingold' is wonderfully refreshing.

winter-flowering plants can be merged into most gardens. Pathways at the sides of the house are good, as long as they are not cold and windy. Avoid places where water can drip on to the plants – they are able to withstand low temperatures, but wetness and searing winds will soon damage them.

Spring brings more bulbs into flower, as it does to many trees and shrubs. The season, according to Lord Tennyson, may be when a young man's fancy lightly turns to thoughts of love, but it is also the time when gardeners stir from their firesides, and venture into the garden for longer periods. Just as an early sunny spell will awaken hibernating animals, so a few scented late winter and early spring plants will quickly activate the gardener.

Scented bulbs are the real gems of spring, whether planted in window boxes, raised beds and tubs or in the ground in formal displays or naturalized around shrubs. The sweetly scented, soldier-like spires of hyacinths create a carpet of color in formal beds, while patches of crocuses highlighted by shafts of sunlight filtering through trees are another delight of spring. Scented bulbs in window boxes bring rich bouquets right up to the house, and in very exposed places this offers some protection from harsh weather. If you do grow bulbs in window boxes, ensure that they are grown in an inner, perhaps plastic, container. This both protects the outer box and allows for quick-change seasonal displays. It also enables the bulbs to die down naturally in their containers rather than being removed from the soil.

Summer brings more scent and color with a super-abundance of shrubs, trees, perennials, annuals and bulbous plants. A patio, tastefully scented and decorated with fragrant lilies – as well as shrubs and herbaceous plants – can successfully compete with other parts of the garden. Scented hanging baskets and wall baskets are unrivalled for bringing eye-height color to walls, patios, garages, bare pergola poles and verandas. Position them carefully, so that when watered they do not drip over other plants, decorative surfaces or wooden floors. Also make sure that wall baskets do not drip excess water over color-washed walls.

The Ramanas Rose (Rosa rugosa) has sweetly scented flowers. The beautiful form 'Roseraie de l'Hay' can be grown in a shrub border or as a large, informal hedge.

*A*ll Lawson Cypress
(Chamaecyparis
lawsoniana) *conifers have foliage
with the bouquet of resin and parsley.
Shown above are the varieties
'Winston Churchill' (left) and
'President Roosevelt' (right).*

The autumn need not be scentless either, even if changing color patterns are slowing. Many of the lilies that enjoy life in pots on patios are still flowering in late summer and autumn – for example, the Gold-banded Lily, *Lilium auratum*, the Easter Lily and the Madonna Lily. Many half-hardy and hardy annuals, such as the sweetly scented nicotiana, continue flowering until the frosts of autumn finish their lives.

The clear blue skies that appear during winter create a superb backdrop for the scented Witch Hazels, some, like the Chinese Witch Hazel, sweetly fragrant. Other winter-flowering shrubs include the heavy and spicy Winter Sweet, the richly scented *Mahonia* 'Charity' and the lily-of-the-valley scented *Mahonia japonica*.

Plants can fill a garden with exciting scents throughout the year. The following chapters describe many of these and how they can be used in the yard and garden.

PLANT	SCENT	COLOR	SITUATION	CULTIVATION
APPLE				
Thuja occidentalis 'Smaragd' American Arborvitae/ White Cedar	Foliage has an apple-like fragrance when crushed.	Deep green foliage.	Ideal as a boundary hedge and, if left unpruned, will reach about 10ft (3m) in 10 years.	Height: 4-7ft (1.2-2.1m) – when clipped Spread: 2-3ft (60-90cm) – when clipped **Evergreen conifer:** Well-drained but moisture-retentive soil, and preferably a sheltered position in light shade. Prune once a year, in late spring.
LAVENDER				
Lavandula 'Hidcote' (syn. *Lavandula nana atropurpurea*) Lavender	Lavender	Deep purple flowers, in 2-inch- (5cm) long spikes, amid silver-green leaves.	Superb as a dwarf hedge alongside a path, and in a cottage-garden type setting.	Height: 1-2ft (30-60cm) Spread: 1½-2ft (45-60cm) **Evergreen shrub:** Well-drained soil and a sunny position.
LEMON				
Cupressus macrocarpa 'Lutea' Monterey Cypress	When crushed, the foliage emits a lemony fragrance.	Soft yellow foliage that becomes a light green with age.	Ideal as a boundary screen.	Height: 20-25ft (6-7.5m) in 15-20 years Spread: 3-4ft (0.9-1.2m) **Evergreen conifer:** Well-drained and slightly sheltered position in full sun.
MUSK				
Rose 'Penelope'	Richly musk-scented	Rich, creamy-pink, semi-double flowers, fading slightly with age.	Creates a superb informal hedge.	Height: 5ft (1.5m) Spread: 4½-5ft (1.3-1.5m) **Deciduous shrub:** Well-drained soil and an open and sunny position.
PINEAPPLE				
Thuja plicata Western Red Cedar/ Giant Arborvitae	When crushed, the foliage has the fragrance of pineapples.	Scale-like, shiny, rich medium-green foliage with white marks underneath.	Ideal as a large boundary hedge, and if left unpruned will reach about 18-25ft (5.4-7.5m) in 10 years. Eventually it reaches over 40ft (12m).	Height: 12-15ft (3.6-4.5m) – when clipped Spread: 3-4ft (0.9-1.2m) – when clipped **Evergreen conifer:** Moisture-retentive deep soil in a sheltered position in full sun.
RASPBERRY				
Rose 'Zephirine Drouhin'	Raspberry-like.	Vivid, cerise-pink flowers.	Creates a superb informal hedge; also a climber or for training into a bush shape.	Height: 5ft (1.5m) Spread: 5ft (1.5m) **Deciduous shrub:** Well-drained soil and an open and sunny position.
RESIN AND PARSLEY				
Chamaecyparis lawsoniana 'Alumii' Lawson Cypress	Crushed foliage emits a fragrance of resin and parsley.	Bluish-gray and sea-green foliage.	As a boundary hedge.	Height: 18-20ft (5.4-6m) – after 15-20 years Spread: 4-5ft (1.2-1.5m) **Evergreen conifer:** Well-drained soil in light shade or full sun.
Chamaecyparis lawsoniana 'Fletcheri' Lawson Cypress	Crushed foliage emits a fragrance of resin and parsley.	Feathery, bluish-gray foliage.	As a boundary hedge.	Height: 18-20ft (5.4-6m) – after 15-20 years Spread: 5-6ft (1.5-1.8m) **Evergreen conifer:** Well-drained soil in light shade or full sun.

PLANT	SCENT	COLOR	SITUATION	CULTIVATION
ROSEMARY				
Rosmarinus officinalis 'Miss Jessop's Upright' Rosemary	Rosemary	Light mauve flowers among medium to dark green leaves.	Superb as a cottage garden hedge. North of zone 7, grow as a pot plant and bring in for the winter.	Height: 5-6ft (1.5-1.8m) Spread: 4-5ft (1.2-1.5m) **Evergreen shrub:** Well-drained soil and a sunny position.
TURPENTINE				
X *Cupressocyparis leylandii* Leyland Cypress	Foliage when crushed emits a slight aroma of turpentine.	Gray-green foliage.	Plant as a boundary screen, but only where a large hedge is required. It is the fastest-growing conifer, and can soon become too large for a small yard.	Height: 25-40ft (7.5-12m) – in 15-20 years Spread: 3½-5ft (1-1.5m) **Evergreen conifer:** Well-drained, deep soil in light shade or full sun
X *Cupressocyparis leylandii* 'Castlewellan' Golden Leyland Cypress	Foliage when crushed emits a slight aroma of turpentine.	New growth is pale yellow, bright gold at its tips.	Eventually forms a large, bright screen. Suitable for a boundary.	Height: 25-35ft (7.5-10.5m) – in 15-20 years Spread: 3½-4½ft (1-1.3m) **Evergreen conifer:** Well-drained, deep soil in light shade or full sun
SWEET				
Rosa rubiginosa Sweet Briar/Eglantine	Very sweet	Clear pink flowers amid deliciously aromatic, apple-scented leaves.	Superb as an informal boundary, especially alongside fields or where grass grows up to the hedge.	Height: 5-7ft (1.5-2.1m) Spread: 5-6ft (1.5-1.8m) **Deciduous shrub:** Well-drained soil and an open and sunny position.
Rosa rugosa 'Frau Dagmar Hastrup'	Sweet	Pale rose-pink flowers with cream stamens, followed by rich crimson hips.	Creates a large, informal hedge. It is also ideal for planting in a border, where it is welcome not only because of its scent but also due to its colorful flowers and round, bright crimson hips (sometimes called heps) which appear later in the year.	Height: 6-7ft (1.8-2.1m) Spread: 5-6ft (1.5-1.8m) **Deciduous shrub:** Well-drained soil and an open and sunny position.
Rosa rugosa 'Roseraie de l'Hay'	Sweet	Rich crimson-purple flowers with cream stamens.	Creates a large, informal hedge.	Height: 6-7ft (1.8-2.1m) Spread: 5-6ft (1.5-1.8m) **Deciduous shrub:** Well-drained soil and an open and sunny position.
Rose 'Felicia'	Very sweet.	Salmon-pink flowers shaded yellow.	Creates a superb informal hedge.	Height: 4-5ft (1.2-1.5m) Spread: 4-5ft (1.2-1.5m) **Deciduous shrub:** Well-drained soil and an open and sunny position.
Rose 'Prosperity'	Very sweet.	Double, creamy-white flowers flushed with gold.	Creates a superb informal hedge.	Height: 5-6ft (1.5-1.8m) Spread: 4-5ft (1.5-1.8m) **Deciduous shrub:** Well-drained soil and an open and sunny position.

CHAPTER TWO

Night-scented Plants

*The tranquility of warm summer
evenings in gardens redolent with
sweet scents soothes and enchants*

*S*UMMER evenings have a quality unsurpassed by any other time of day or year; a warm stillness envelops the garden and romantic, heady scents invade the mind.

Strolls along scented garden paths, perhaps arched with honeysuckle, jasmine or clematis and edged with lavender, are a welcome end to a day's toil. However, it is on patios and terraces that evening fragrances are most appreciated, and many of these scented flowers create a riot of color on walls or cascade generously from window boxes, troughs or hanging baskets. Some plants are better in urns and large tubs, especially those with an upright, woody form.

Having a pleasing scent is important, and if this can be associated with an eye-catching color, especially during half-light at dusk, even more pleasure is created. Fading light has a varying influence on colors; those at the darker end of the spectrum become relatively much darker than lighter ones such as white and yellow. Flowers with these colors, or perhaps dominantly edged or centered with light colors, extend evening color longest. Foliage color is also well worth considering.

Of the shrubs described in Chapter 9, yellow-leaved plants, such as the bright, golden-leaved Mock-Orange, *Philadelphus coronarius* 'Aureus', remain a dominant feature longer than the deep-violet Russian Sage, *Perovskia atriplicifolia* 'Blue Spire'. Both of these superb shrubs have distinctive scents; the Mock-Orange has sweet, orange-blossom flowers during midsummer, while the Russian Sage has coarsely-toothed, gray-green leaves with a sage-like bouquet. Its bonus is tubular, violet-blue flowers during late summer and into autumn.

More than 300 years ago, the world-renowned English herbalist Gerard wrote that the ordinary Mock Orange had such a sweet smell that it troubled and molested his head in a very strange manner. It troubles few minds today, and is well worth planting close to an open window.

Many aromatic plants provide color into late evening through their light-colored foliage. Few shrubs can compete in this respect with the feathery, silvery-gray foliage of artemisia. The shrubby Southernwood, *Artemisia abrotanum*, is known for its invigorating scent and medicinal qualities. It has been used to strew in cupboards to keep moths away. Indeed, its French name Garde-robe, means a protector of clothes.

The White Sage, *Artemisia ludoviciana*, from North America, creates a dominant splash of aromatic white foliage that can be used to harmonize with dark green foliage, as well as acting as an evening lantern in a mixed or herbaceous border. Positioning a dominant clump at the end of the border nearest your house creates a beacon in the darkening shadows.

*T*he sweetly scented Common Soapwort (Saponaria officinalis) creates a dominant display of pink, phlox-like flowers from mid- to late summer.

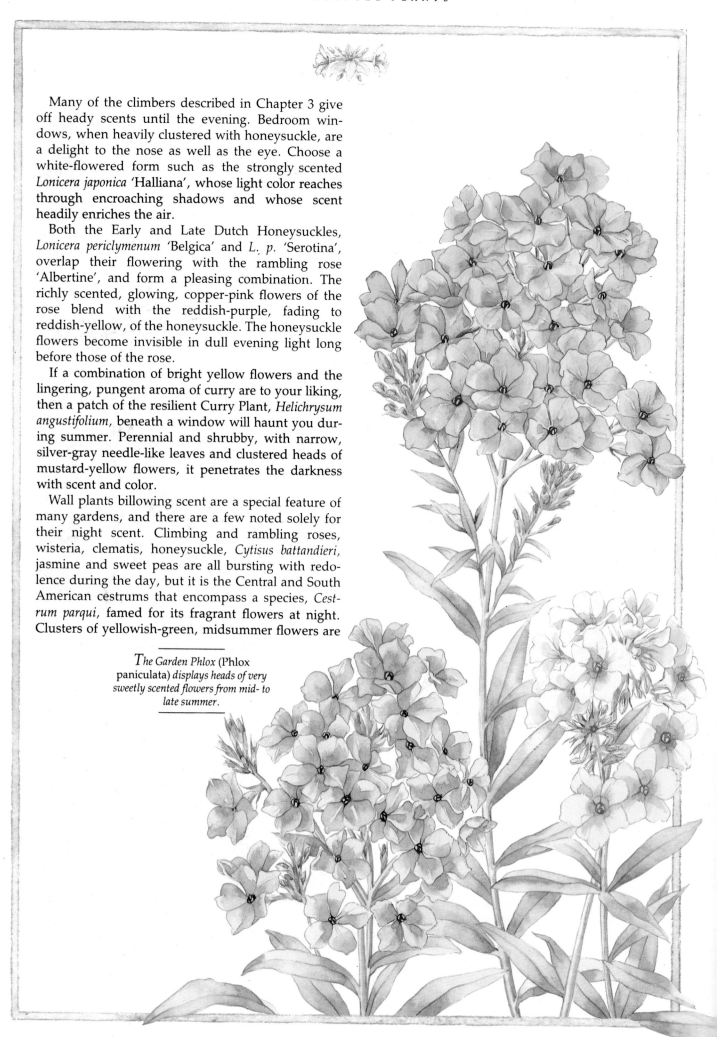

Many of the climbers described in Chapter 3 give off heady scents until the evening. Bedroom windows, when heavily clustered with honeysuckle, are a delight to the nose as well as the eye. Choose a white-flowered form such as the strongly scented *Lonicera japonica* 'Halliana', whose light color reaches through encroaching shadows and whose scent headily enriches the air.

Both the Early and Late Dutch Honeysuckles, *Lonicera periclymenum* 'Belgica' and *L. p.* 'Serotina', overlap their flowering with the rambling rose 'Albertine', and form a pleasing combination. The richly scented, glowing, copper-pink flowers of the rose blend with the reddish-purple, fading to reddish-yellow, of the honeysuckle. The honeysuckle flowers become invisible in dull evening light long before those of the rose.

If a combination of bright yellow flowers and the lingering, pungent aroma of curry are to your liking, then a patch of the resilient Curry Plant, *Helichrysum angustifolium*, beneath a window will haunt you during summer. Perennial and shrubby, with narrow, silver-gray needle-like leaves and clustered heads of mustard-yellow flowers, it penetrates the darkness with scent and color.

Wall plants billowing scent are a special feature of many gardens, and there are a few noted solely for their night scent. Climbing and rambling roses, wisteria, clematis, honeysuckle, *Cytisus battandieri*, jasmine and sweet peas are all bursting with redolence during the day, but it is the Central and South American cestrums that encompass a species, *Cestrum parqui*, famed for its fragrant flowers at night. Clusters of yellowish-green, midsummer flowers are

The Garden Phlox (Phlox paniculata) *displays heads of very sweetly scented flowers from mid- to late summer.*

borne from both the ends of shoots and their leaf-joints. Unfortunately they are not very attractive, but since they flower at night this is unimportant. They are, however, highly fragrant. This is a tender shrub which needs a warm, south-facing wall, where it reaches only 3ft (90cm) or so high and wide.

Honeysuckles carry their wonderful scent over into early evening, and one is especially noted for its night fragrance. This is the sprawling, spreading, shrubby *Lonicera* x *heckrottii*, often known as Gold Flame. The sweetly fragrant yellow flowers, heavily flushed with purple, are borne at the ends of shoots from mid- to late summer.

Warm, south- or west-facing walls that absorb heat during the daytime, enriching the heady and sweet scent of many vines or climbing shrubs, help such plants as the sun-loving and tender Chilean Jasmine, *Mandevilla suaveolens*, to continue the fragrance of its sweet flowers into evening. Its funnel-shaped, periwinkle-like white flowers are borne throughout summer (mainly during early to mid-season) on plants up to 12ft (3.6m) high.

The Banksian Rose or Lady Banks' Rose, *Rosa banksiae*, is a shrub that needs a warm wall richly en-

Phlox paniculata 'Silver Salmon' has restful, soft-colored flowers that with their sweet fragrance create a wonderful cottage-garden aura.

dowed with sun, especially if its shoots are to ripen properly and assure a good display of flowers the following year. Because it needs only the minimal amount of pruning, it is vital that the shoots ripen in full sun and are not damaged by frost. The violet-scented double flowers appear during midsummer. The normal Banksian Rose is white but yellow forms are grown, although the scent is not so noticeable.

In the evening many clematis (see also Chapter 3) are a joy to the weary commuter who arrives home on a hot summer evening to a patio or garden rich in scent. The cowslip bouquet of *Clematis rehderiana* is sufficient to soothe any anxious mind, although it must be said that some admirers of scented plants do not find the mid- to late summer, soft primrose-yellow flowers particularly redolent or as attractive as those of other species. Therefore on small patios or in gardens a more visually attractive climber is better.

The fragrance of many other climbers lingers when

they are growing against a warm and wind-sheltered wall, and in particular the honeysuckles have few equals for scent and color. An arbor woven with stems and leaves and closeted with sweet flowers never fails to create attention, but do be aware that moths attracted by the flowers will also be present.

The Spurge Laurel, *Daphne laureola*, a European native, is a bushy evergreen that bears small, highly fragrant, greenish-yellow flowers during spring. Because the flowers are scented at night, the flowers are pollinated by moths as well as bumblebees. It is a hardy shrub for planting in a border or for setting in a large tub on a patio, and is mainly grown for its handsome, shiny, dark green leaves. Remember that it likes a limestone soil.

For creating evening and night scents in small beds under windows, few plants surpass the Night-scented Stock, *Matthiola bicornis*. This Greek plant is rather straggly, but it does compensate for its sprawling and untidy nature by producing masses of highly scented, lilac-colored flowers during summer. The plants can be clipped back to encourage a neater shape, but as the flowers are borne on 9-inch (23cm) long flower spikes, this does diminish the display.

A better way to make their appearance tolerable during the day is to plant them in combination with Virginia Stock, *Malcolmia maritima*. It is low-growing, up to about 8 inches (20cm) high, creating a mass of sweetly scented red, lilac, rose or white flowers during summer. Each plant flowers for six to eight weeks and as they bloom four weeks after being sown it is not difficult to have them in flower throughout summer.

You will not need a watch or sundial to know the time if you are standing near a bed of *Mirabilis jalapa* in late afternoon. This tropical American plant is known as the Marvel of Peru or the Four o'clock Plant, as the flowers open in late afternoon, remain open at night and fade the following morning. The French know this plant as Belle de Nuit, while in the Malay archipelago it is said to be so punctual in its opening that it is frequently planted in a conspicuous place in gardens so that it can act as a clock. In North America it is known as Beauty of the Night, an indication of the highly fragrant, trumpet-shaped flowers, in colors including red, crimson, rose, yellow and white. It is usually grown as a tender annual, but it is also well disposed to growing in pots in a sunroom or greenhouse.

The sweet and heavy fragrance of the Flowering Tobacco (Nicotiana alata) is particularly intense during warm summer afternoons. On the right is the variety 'Lime Green'.

The Vesper Flower, *Hesperis matronalis*, is scentless during the day but gives out a superb fragrance at evening time. It is no slouch when it comes to gathering names, and is also known as Damask Violet, Sweet Rocket, Dame's Rocket, Purple Rocket, White Rocket, Rucchette, Roiquet and Dame's Violet. Even earlier names include Queen's Gillofers, Summer Lilac, Eveweed, Double Sciney and Close Sciney. It is a short-lived perennial from Southern Europe and Western Asia but is now widely naturalized in many areas, including North America. It is best raised as a biennial by sowing seed one year for flowers during the following one. The long spikes of white, purple or mauve flowers appear amid dark green leaves during midsummer. Unfortunately, it is a difficult plant to blend with others, but nevertheless well worth growing – try it on its own in a narrow bed under a window.

Linnaea borealis is a prostrate evergreen shrub renamed from *Campanula serpyllifolia* by the world-famous botanist Linnaeus. Its size makes it ideal for rock gardens with shady corners, where it soon spreads.

With Evening Primrose as a common name, it is no surprise that *Oenothera biennis* first opens its short-lived, deliciously fragrant, pale yellow, funnel-like flowers in the evening, usually between six and seven o'clock. They appear just in time to be pollinated by twilight-flying insects, but then remain open until they fade a few days later. It is best raised as a biennial and grown against a sunny wall. It comes from North America, where it is known as Evening Primrose or German Rampion. In England it was originally called the Prime-rose Tree or Tree-Primrose of

*The evocatively named Sweet Rocket (*Hesperis matronalis*) can flood a garden with a sweet and penetrating fragrance. The heady fragrance and rich colors of *Nicotiana alata 'Sensation Mixed' (right) create beacons of interest in mixed borders.*

Virginia. The roots – which, when dried, are said to give off a fragrance similar to that of wine – were used by the French as a garnish for salads. The leaves are also edible, and in Germany and the New England area of North America they are eaten cooked or raw.

The Common Mignonette, *Reseda odorata*, with heavily musk-scented, yellowish-brown flowers borne in club-like heads, is superb both in gardens and when grown in pots in a greenhouse. It is also ideal as a cut flower indoors. It is one of those old-fashioned flowers that has fallen out of favor but which richly deserves a wider audience. If you are limited for space in the garden, try several plants in pots on the patio or indoors.

Flowering Tobacco *Nicotiana alata* (syn. *Nicotiana affinis*) is famed for its evening fragrance. The loose, semi-pendulous clusters of white flowers appear from mid- to late summer, opening in evening and drenching the air with a richly sweet scent. Botanically, the inclination of this South American plant is to be a perennial, but it is usually grown as a tender annual and planted outside into beds or pots as soon as all risk of frost has passed. The bushy, well-branched 3ft (90cm) high plants are ideal for growing under a window. Many varieties are available, some opening their flowers during the day. Other flowering tobaccos, *Nicotiana sylvestris* and *Nicotiana suaveolens*, which are described in detail in Chapter 8, also have sweetly scented flowers.

PLANT	SCENT	COLOR	SITUATION	CULTIVATION
FRUITY				
Mirabilis jalapa Four o'clock Plant/ Marvel of Peru	Fruity and sweet.	Trumpet-shaped flowers in a wide color range, including yellow, red, crimson, rose and white, from mid- to late summer. 	As a bedding plant or, if in the smaller variety 'Pygmea', 15–18 inches (38–45cm) high, as a houseplant.	Height: 2ft (60cm) Spread: 12-15 inches (30-38cm) **Tender perennial best grown as an annual:** Light, moisture-retentive and moderately rich soil in full sun.
MAGNOLIA				
Oenothera caespitosa Tufted Evening Primrose	Sweet and magnolia-scented.	White flowers, deepening to rose-pink with age, from early to late summer.	At the front of a border or as a path edging.	Height: 10-12 inches (25-30cm) Spread: 15-18 inches (38-45cm) **Herbaceous perennial:** Well-drained soil in full sun.
SWEET				
Abronia fragrans Sand Verbena	Very sweet.	Pure white flowers which open during summer afternoons.	Plant at the base of south- or west-facing walls.	Height: 6-10 inches (15-25cm) Spread: 8-10 inches (20-25cm) **Tender perennial grown as an annual:** Well-drained, sandy soil and a warm, sheltered position.
Cestrum parqui Willow-leaved Jessamine	Sweet.	Greenish-yellow flowers during late summer and into autumn.	Warm, sheltered, south- or west-facing wall in zone 10.	Height: 3-4ft (0.9-1.2m) Spread: 3-4ft (0.9-1.2m) **Tender, bushy, deciduous shrub:** Well-drained, rich soil and a position in full sun.
Daphne laureola Spurge Laurel	Sweet.	Greenish-yellow flowers in drooping clusters during late winter and early spring.	In woodland borders or the front of shrub borders through zone 7.	Height: 2-4ft (0.6-1.2m) Spread: 3-5ft (0.9-1.5m) **Hardy evergreen shrub:** Well-drained soil, even those containing lime, in light shade or full sun.
Hesperis matronalis Sweet Rocket/ Damask Violet	Sweet and penetrating.	White, purple or mauve flowers in long, loose spikes during early and midsummer.	Perennial and mixed borders, naturalized in woodland borders or as a bold, massed display on its own.	Height: 2-3ft (60-90cm) Spread: 15-18 inches (38-45cm) **Short-lived hardy perennial:** Light, sandy soil in full sun or light shade.
Linnaea borealis Twin Flower	Sweet, resembling meadowsweet.	Trumpet-shaped flesh-pink flowers borne in pairs from the tops of stems from early to midsummer.	Ideal in rock gardens.	Height: 2-3 inches (5-7.5cm) Spread: 1-1½ft (30-45cm) **Hardy evergreen shrub:** Peaty, moisture-retentive soil in sunlight or full shade.
Matthiola bicornis Night-scented Stock	Heavy, sweet and penetrating.	Lilac flowers during July and August.	It is best sown under windows, rather than in window boxes or troughs.	Height: 12-15 inches (30-38cm) Spread: 7-9 inches (18-23cm) **Hardy annual:** Well-drained fertile soil in full sun or light shade.
Nicotiana alata (syn. *Nicotiana affinis*) Nicotiana/Flowering Tobacco	Very sweet and heavy.	Tubular white flowers, 3 inches (7.5cm) long in loose clusters, from mid- to late summer. Range of varieties and colors.	Mixed borders and in containers.	Height: 2-3ft (60-90cm) Spread: 12-15 inches (30-38cm) **Tender annual:** Well-drained, rich soil and a sunny position.
Oenothera acaulis Evening Primrose (syn. *Oenothera* *taraxacifolia*)	Sweet, but faint and demure.	Large white flowers shading to rose from early to late summer. There is also a yellow variety.	In a rock garden or at the edge of a border.	Height: 6 inches (15cm) Spread: 12 inches (30cm) **Hardy perennial, best treated as a biennial:** Well-drained soil and full sun.

PLANT	SCENT	COLOR	SITUATION	CULTIVATION
SWEET				
Oenothera biennis Evening Primrose	Sweet and lingering.	Pale yellow flowers, 1½-2 inches (4-5cm) wide, in clusters on upright stems from early to late summer.	In borders and naturalized in woodland gardens.	Height: 2½-3ft (75-90cm) Spread: 12-15 inches (30-38cm) **Hardy biennial:** Well-drained soil and full sun.
Oenothera missouriensis Missouri Primrose/ Ozark Snowdrops	Sweet, but faint.	Satiny, pale yellow flowers from mid- to late summer.	Rock gardens and the front of borders.	Height: 4-6 inches (10-15cm) Spread: 15-18 inches (38-45cm) **Hardy perennial:** Well-drained soil and full sun.
Oenothera odorata stricta Evening Primrose	Sweet.	Primrose-yellow flowers, becoming slightly red with age, from spring to midsummer.	In borders and naturalized in woodland gardens.	Height: 15-18 inches (38-45cm) Spread: 15-18 inches (38-45cm) **Hardy biennial, best treated as an annual:** Well-drained soil and full sun.
Oenothera trichocalyx Evening Primrose	Sweet.	White, 2½-inch-(6cm) wide flowers during midsummer.	In an annual or mixed border.	Height: 15-18 inches (38-45cm) Spread: 8-10 inches (20-25cm) **Tender bushy deciduous shrub:** Well-drained, rich soil and a position in full sun.
Phlox paniculata (syn. *Phlox decussata*) Garden Phlox/Border Phlox	Very sweet.	Dense heads, 4–6 inches (10-15cm) wide, of purple flowers from mid- to late summer. However, it is mostly grown in one of its many varieties, with a wide color range.	Perennial or mixed border.	Height: 1½-3½ft (0.45-1m) Spread: 1-1½ft (30-45cm) **Herbaceous perennial:** Well-drained but moisture-retentive soil, enriched with compost, and light shade or full sun.
Reseda odorata Sweet Mignonette	Sweet, and attractive to bees.	Loose heads of yellow-white flowers dominated by orange-yellow stamens from early summer to autumn.	Annual borders.	Height: 1-2½ft (30-75cm) Spread: 8-12 inches (20-30cm) **Hardy annual:** Well-drained, slightly limy, compost-rich soil in full sun.
Saponaria officinalis Bouncing Bet/ Common Soapwort/ Fuller's Herb	Sweet.	Single, pink, phlox-shaped flowers from mid- to late summer. Double flowers, in white or pink, are also grown.	Perennial or mixed borders, and for naturalizing in wild gardens. It can be too invasive in a border. It is a European plant that has been cultivated for many centuries in Britain, where it has become naturalized in many places, particularly alongside streams and in damp woods situated in abandoned gardens. It has also become naturalized in North America.	Height: 1-3ft (30-90cm) Spread: 1½-2ft (45-60cm) **Hardy Perennial:** Fertile soil in light shade or full sun.
Silene noctiflora Night-flowering Catchfly/Sticky Cockle	Sweet and rich.	White or pink flowers during summer.	Best when naturalized in a border.	Height: 2-2½ft (60-75cm) Spread: 15-18 inches (38-45cm) **Hardy annual:** Well-drained soil and a sunny or lightly-shaded position.
Silene nutans Nottingham Catchfly/ Dover Catchfly	Sweet and rich.	Whitish or pink drooping flowers from early to midsummer.	Best when naturalized in a border.	Height: 2-2½ft (70-75cm) Spread: 15-18 inches (38-45cm) **Herbaceous perennial:** Well-drained soil and a sunny or lightly shaded position.

CHAPTER THREE

The Scented Pathway

*Functional paths canopied with scented
climbers and edged with a profusion of low-
growing plants are one of the most important
features of a garden.*

*A*LL TOO frequently paths are neglected, considered solely as a way of getting from one part of the yard to another. They can, however, become ribbons of perfume-packed plants that create scent and color both at ground level and around one's head. Few garden features are so distinctive and beautiful as a pergola richly adorned with the vanilla-scented, pea-shaped flowers that hang in glorious bunches from wisterias, or perhaps a scented arch packed with the blazing yellow flowers of laburnum.

Garden paths are often made too narrow for two people to walk comfortably side by side, which is especially annoying when you want to show a friend around your garden. One of the joys of a garden is showing it to other enthusiasts, which is nearly impossible if you have to walk in single file. Wide, firm-surfaced paths that provide access throughout the year give a garden a sense of purpose and permanence. Obviously the path has to match the nature of the garden and the age of the house. A cottage garden never looks right when around an ultra-modern house, and similarly a clinical setting is best kept away from rustic cottages.

Wide gravel paths, with weathered stone slabs set into them to create an all-weather path, are superb alongside rustic poles adorned with climbers, but take care not to use such a path around the house if you shovel snow away every winter – the gravel can get mixed up with the snow and cover a lawn alongside the path, from where it will be difficult to remove. If you are not in the habit of moving snow, but allow it to remain until it melts, then there is no problem.

If you have prostrate and creeping plants meandering between weathered stone paths, do not spread ashes over them when they are covered with snow as a way of providing a grip on the surface – the plants will suffer. Never spread salt over such paths as a quick way to free them of ice, as the plants will not like it and may eventually die.

Visually handicapped people usually enjoy scented gardens and love to walk through them. If a member of your family does have a sight problem, do not plant prickly climbers near the edge of a path as windblown

shoots and branches may hit them in the face. In these circumstances, make any arbor several feet wider than the path and use firm-surfaced slabs in the center with wide strips of gravel along the sides. On solo trips down the path the visually handicapped person will then know where the edges are. It is a good idea in these circumstances for the path to encircle the garden and return to the house, but if space is limited and the path just extends to the end of the garden, ensure that the slabs and gravel do not end abruptly. Give some indication of the end – perhaps a small paved area with the benefit of a seat.

Winter-flowering gardens need a firm-surfaced path through them if they are to be enjoyed without having to resort to boots after even the lightest winter shower. The range of winter-flowering shrubs and trees is wide, and many are included in Chapter 9. Such plants are essential for creating interest along a path during the dull winter months, when fragrant climbers over arches and arbors, as well as more diminutive plants along the edge, are in a dormant state. Remember that most of the climbers that grow on arches and arbors alongside paths are deciduous and will therefore allow winter-fragrant plants to be easily seen. As the season progresses these winter brighteners, which are usually not so attractive in summer, will be cloaked from view by the new foliage on climbers.

To create permanence – and fragrance – alongside a path, you may be wise to consider a conifer. Many are brightly colored, yellow or greenish-yellow, and can act as redolent, year-round focal points alongside a path. Not all conifers, however, are scented – see Chapter 9 for details.

*T*he Mountain Clematis (Clematis montana) *and Wallflowers form a superb duo which brings scent and color to fences and the edges of paths during midsummer.*

For a parsley bouquet enriched with the aroma of resin, choose one of the many forms of the Lawson Cypress, *Chamaecyparis lawsoniana*. The forms 'Lutea', 'Winston Churchill' and 'Stewartii' create dominant shades of yellow, and are wide enough at their base to enable a narrow path to be clipped through their foliage if they are planted 6-7ft (1.8-2.1m) apart. After about 20 years 'Lutea' is about 6ft (1.8m) wide at its base, and 'Stewartii' and 'Winston Churchill' about 8ft (2.4m).

Some fragrant conifers have a pencil-like form

which makes them suitable for planting close to a path, and perhaps the best-known of these is the Incense Cedar, *Calocedrus decurrens,* with its formal, upright stance. Its dark green foliage is arranged in dense, fan-like sprays which have a strong turpentine aroma when bruised. It creates a rather rigid shape that harmonizes best in formal rather than informal and cottage-garden settings. Arbors made of straight, planed wood blend well with it in an uncluttered and rather spacious setting.

Few path edges are as rich in scent and color as those lined with lavender. If this plant is too formal for your yard, then a few rosemary plants here and there will create scent and color, as well as a wonderful cottage-garden aura.

Richly scented, near-prostrate plants that both neatly edge a path and fill gaps between natural stone paving soon create an established look to a path. If a scented lawn sown with Chamomile, *Anthemis nobilis,* borders a path, a wonderful aroma is released underfoot. Select the non-flowering form 'Treneague' if you want a rich, banana-like aroma.

The highly scented Wild Thyme, *Thymus serpyllum,* can also be used to create a lawn, but it will not withstand a great deal of wear and frequently develops patches that need replanting. However, it does form a pleasant surface that is both aromatic and pleasing to the eye. Mother of Thyme, *Thymus praecox,* is superb for filling a bed between an informal path and a garden pond, creating an aromatic carpet of reddish-pink flowers, although often they appear light purple. Its low, carpeting nature gently leads the eye from the path to the pool's edge and does not obscure the view of plants such as water lilies on the water's surface.

Rosa ecae *'Helen Knight', with buttercup-yellow flowers, is a superb scented companion for the lilac-rose* Clematis montana *'Tetrarose', a form of the Mountain Clematis.* Clematis montana *'Elizabeth' (far right) is an ideal pale pink-flowered foil for sun-bleached statuary.*

PERGOLAS, ARCHES AND PILLARS

Pergolas have been in use for many centuries and date back to ancient civilizations. They were most frequently found in warm countries where, together with climbers, they provided shade along a path. They were especially popular in Italy, where they suited the climate wonderfully well. They are invaluable for creating a scented arbor along a path, but do ensure that they are soundly constructed as they have to bear a considerable weight when plants are mature and fully clothed with leaves and flowers.

Climbers planted to ramble over pergolas tend to be those that create a woody framework of stems and remain a permanent feature. The vanilla-scented wisterias are supreme at covering a pergola. The Japanese Wisteria, *Wisteria floribunda,* always creates a more spectacular display when adorning a pergola than when grown against a wall. Brickwork, to my eye, always seems both visually and practically to obstruct the large drooping bunches of flowers, especially those of the form 'Macrobotrys' which frequently has clusters of lilac-blue and purple flowers up to 3ft (90cm) long. Records indicate that these glorious bunches of flowers, correctly known as racemes, reach over 5ft (1.5m) long in their native country.

Many roses can be supported by a pergola, but this never seems wholly successful, as it conflicts with their pruning needs. A single line of supports with a wooden framework between them is better, or just a rustic pole set firmly in the soil with the rose trained and secured to it. When the rose needs to be pruned you can simply lay the whole plant on the ground, remove the shoots and then tie the plant back to the support. The vogue a few years ago was to have brick or wooden pillars with strong, thick rope looped between them. This looked superb on a drawing board, but in practice resulted in the ropes rotting away during midsummer when the plant was heavy with flowers and foliage, and both plant and rope ending up on the ground in a glorious mess. Whether you choose to use a simple wooden framework or a pole as a support, do ensure that it is strong and well anchored.

Rustic arches create a cottage-garden feel and have great charm and visual appeal. Not all climbers are suited to rustic poles, though roses are. For extra scent and color train a late-flowering clematis up the same pole or arch as a rambler rose. The effect is wonderful, and in practical terms the pruning of the rambler can be left until the clematis finishes its display. Their flowering periods will probably overlap, but the clematis will still create a wonderful display when the rose has finished. Clematis can also be cohabited on an arch or pergola with wisteria. If this is your choice, then set the clematis on the cooler and shadier side.

WALLS AND FENCES

Walls and fences alongside paths create a superb backdrop for climbers of all sorts, but especially those that create a dense array of foliage and flowers. Many roses are superb against walls, and create a strong impact of scent and color. A wide range of roses – and their scents – is described at the end of this chapter.

Some climbers, such as the Passion Flower (*Passiflora caerulea*) need a warm, sunny wall and a series of wires up which to climb, whereas the Fragrant Virgin's Bower (*Clematis flammula*) with its sweet, hawthorn-like bouquet, readily clambers over arches and old tree stumps, as well as trailing over tall hedges and shrubs. This clematis has been cultivated for several hundred years and was known as the Biting Clematis or Purging Periwinkle – at one time periwinkles were included in the clematis family.

Some people have detected both vanilla and almond in the fragrance of this flower.

Perhaps the best-known clematis is the Mountain Clematis, *Clematis montana*, with strongly sweet-scented flowers blooming mainly during midsummer. It was earlier known as the Great Indian Virgin's Bower, which reflects its Himalayan origins and ability to cover large walls with flowers. *Clematis rehderiana* has a delicate and slight bouquet akin to that of cowslips, while the herbaceous perennial *Clematis recta*, sometimes known as Upright Virgin's Bower and Flammula Jovis, has sweetly scented, pure white flowers borne on slender, climbing stems. *Clematis heracleifolia* 'Wyevale' also has a herbaceous nature, and both can be grown up twiggy sticks in a herbaceous or mixed border or alongside paths.

The Common White Jasmine, *Jasminum officinale*, creates a mass of richly sweet and jasmine-like

With an exquisite primrose scent, the rambler rose 'Adeläide d'Orleans' can be used to create a scent-soaked framework on walls and around doors. It is ideal in a courtyard garden.

flowers from mid- to late summer and is sufficiently vigorous to swamp a small arbor or wall with scent and color. Other superbly redolent species include *Jasminum* x *stephanense*, which has pale pink flowers in terminal clusters, and Pink Jasmine, *Jasminum polyanthum*, which needs a warm porch or wall. It can also be grown indoors in large pots and trained up a hoop of pliable canes. Outdoors it flowers from late spring to midsummer, and indoors from midwinter to spring.

The honeysuckles need little introduction. Both the Early and Late Dutch Honeysuckles – *Lonicera periclymenum* 'Belgica' and *Lonicera periclymenum* 'Serotina' respectively – develop masses of sweetly scented flowers, while the Goat-leaf Honeysuckle, *Lonicera caprifolium*, reveals its sweet scent particularly during the evenings.

In all but the warmest of areas the Trumpet Honeysuckle, *Lonicera sempervirens*, and the Giant Honeysuckle, *Lonicera hildebrandiana*, need the comfort of a large greenhouse. Both have richly sweet flowers; those of the Trumpet Vine are scarlet and orange-yellow, while the Giant Honeysuckle has creamy-white flowers up to 6 inches (15cm) long. For a sweet and honey-like bouquet try *Lonicera x americana*, which has white or cream flowers that deepen to yellow, with purple tinging on the outside. It is fairly vigorous and ideal for arbors, fences and sprawling in trees.

The sweet pea, *Lathyrus odoratus*, is a well-known, hardy, self-clinging annual climber that can easily be raised from seed to create a wonderful display of fragrant flowers in many colors. For clothing an unsightly fence with flowers and foliage throughout most of summer with little maintenance needed few climbers can rival it. However, it does need some sort of support, whether a wire screen or tall, twiggy sticks. It is also superb in an herbaceous or mixed border.

The almost double flowers of the Rambler rose 'Albertine' have a rich and sweet scent. Here, the rose is partnered with the richly sweet, orange-yellow Trumpet Vine (Lonicera sempervirens) *and the mound-forming* Santolina chamaecyparissus.

The strongly scented modern climbing rose 'Compassion' reveals salmon-pink flowers, flushed with apricot-orange as they open. It is ideal for growing up a pillar.

THE EDGES OF PATHS

Few scented plants used on the edges of paths and flower borders have such a long and fascinating history as dianthus. The carnation, *Dianthus caryophyllus*, also known as the Clove-pink and Gillyflower, is one of our oldest cultivated flowers and was mentioned by the English poet Geoffrey Chaucer as far back as the 14th century. Indeed, in Chaucer's day it was also known as Sops in Wine, referring to its use in flavoring wine. The petals, with their sweet and pleasant odor, were also candied, made into preserves and pickled, when they were served as a sauce with mutton.

The carnation became a symbol of love and was often presented to the object of desire with a message concealed in the calyx – the part that protects the bud and cushions the back of the flower after the petals unfold. A message was passed in this fashion to Marie Antoinette, Queen of France and wife of Louis XVI, when she was imprisoned in 1793. The message was discovered, however, and resulted in stricter conditions and eventually in her execution.

The common name Gilliflower is said to be derived from the Arabic *quaranful*, meaning a clove and referring specifically to the scent of the flower. This led to a wide range of variations, such as Gillyvors, Gillofers, Gely Floures, Gilloflowers and Gilovre. There are many more, including Chaucer's Clove-gilofre and Shakespeare's Gillyvore. The name "Pink" is a relatively recent introduction, rarely used before the 18th century, and not derived from the actual color of many carnations; instead, it is said to come from the Dutch *pink-oog* referring to a twinkling eye. However, it may also be derived from the pinked and scalloped appearance of the petal edges. As soon as the flesh-colored flowers were popularly known as pinks, the word was then used to indicate the color.

The Sweet Violet, *Viola odorata*, has a strong, sweet bouquet that seems to fade after a few minutes, and it is one of the most delicate and memorable plants in a garden. The exquisite perfume remains, of course; it is our noses that fail us. The flowers are full of ionone, a colorless liquid often used in perfumes which has a somewhat soporific effect. The white forms are usually slightly stronger-scented than the purple, but they are all a joy in the garden. The violet is the symbol of humility, often to be found in religious paintings.

Perfume-packed borders alongside paths are particularly welcome in spring. Here, the blue heads of the Grape Hyacinth (Muscari armeniacum) jostle with the primroses.

The sweetness and scent of violets has been used in Turkey and Syria for the preparation of sherbet, a national drink, while only a few generations ago the candying of violets was more popular than it is today. Indeed, candied violets have been eaten as a sweetmeat since medieval times.

Not all violets are scented, and perhaps all others pale into the background beside the highly fragrant Sweet Violet. The Dog, or Heath, Violet, *Viola canina*, which is widely found on dry banks, has scentless flowers. The Hairy Violet, *Viola hirta*, is also scentless. Pansies and violas, nodding cousins of violets, with few exceptions have little scent except when grown *en masse*. *Viola x wittrockiana*, also known as *Viola tricolor hortensis*, the Garden Pansy, is the forefather of many forms and varieties: the summer-flowering variety 'Arkwright Ruby' which is 6 inches (15cm) high with bright crimson flowers, is scented, as is the spring- to autumn-flowering 'Maggie Mott', which has light mauve flowers. Another relative of the Garden Pansy is Heartsease, *Viola tricolor*, frequently known as the Wild Pansy. This slightly scented plant has, among others, the delightful common names Love-in-Idleness (favored by Shakespeare), Call-me-to-you, Jump-up-and-kiss-me, Pink-of-my-John and Three-faces-under-a-hood. There are said to be at least 60 English common names for this pansy, while in North America it is charmingly known as Johnny-jump-up as well as Field Pansy and European Wild Pansy.

A reflection upon violas would not be complete without saying that Napoleon was fond of violets and gave bouquets of them to Josephine on their wedding anniversaries. When banished to Elba he said: 'I will return with the violets in the spring.' Immediately the violet became the symbol of the Bonapartists and he became known as 'Père Violette'. Subsequently, his followers frequently wore the flower as a boutonniere. Before he was exiled to St Helena after his defeat at Waterloo, he is said to have visited the grave of Josephine, where he picked their favorite flower; and when he died the locket he was wearing contained a lock of her hair and a few dried violets.

The Sweet Violet (Viola odorata), *below, is famed for its fragrant flowers, which emerge from late winter to spring. Plant it in containers, as well as along path edges. The Mother-of-Thyme* (Thymus praecox), *right, bears reddish-pink flowers from mid- to late summer.*

VINES				
PLANT	**SCENT**	**COLOR**	**SITUATION**	**CULTIVATION**
COWSLIP				
Clematis rehderiana	Delicate and slight, with a hint of cowslips.	Light, greenish-yellow, small flowers, bell-shaped and nodding in erect heads during late summer and autumn.	It needs a large arbor or wall over which to climb and trail – it is not suited to a small garden.	Height: 20-30ft (6-9m) Spread: 15-20ft (4.5-6m) **Deciduous vine:** As for *C. flammula* (see below).
HAWTHORN				
Clematis flammula Fragrant Virgin's Bower	Richly sweet, resembling the fragrance of hawthorn.	Shining white, small flowers borne in large, loose groups during late summer and into autumn. In autumn it becomes covered with silky seedheads.	Grow over an arch, where the tangled mass of stems and leaves at its top can create a dominant feature. Also suitable for climbing over tree stumps, smothering small arbors, and for scrambling and trailing over tall hedges or other shrubs. It is a superb vine for bringing scent and color to gardens late in the year, and can be used in combination with plants that flower only in midsummer, leaving borders bare of color towards the end of the season.	Height: 10ft (3m) Spread: 6-8ft (1.8-2.4m) **Deciduous vine:** Slightly alkaline, well-drained but moisture-retentive soil, with light shade for the roots and better light for the stems and flowers.
HONEY				
Lonicera x americana	Sweet and honey-like.	White or cream flowers, deepening to yellow with heavily tinged purple on the outside, during midsummer.	Over arbors and fences, and into trees.	Height: 20-25ft (6-7.5m) Spread: 10-15ft (3-4.5m) **Semi-evergreen or deciduous vine:** Well-drained, compost-rich soil in light shade.
Lonicera x heckrottii Goldflame Honeysuckle	Sweet and honey-like.	Yellow flowers, heavily flushed with purple, from mid- to late summer.	Against a wall.	Height: 8-12ft (2.4-3.6m) Spread: 5-10ft (1.5-3m) **Hardy deciduous shrub-like vine:** Well-drained, compost-rich soil in light shade.
JASMINE				
Jasminum officinale Common White Jasmine/Poet's Jessamine	Richly sweet and jasmine-like.	White flowers borne in loose clusters from mid- to late summer.	Best grown over a large arbor; when planted against a wall the roots and shoots have a tendency to penetrate between bricks, especially on old walls where the pointing is in need of attention.	Height: 20-30ft (6-9m) Spread: 12-18ft (3.6-5.4m) **Deciduous vine:** Well-drained soil, in a position against any wall. No regular pruning is needed, but if plants become congested thin out a few shoots as soon as the flowers fade.

VINES				
PLANT	SCENT	COLOR	SITUATION	CULTIVATION
VANILLA				
Wisteria floribunda Japanese Wisteria	Vanilla-like and sweet.	Violet-blue flowers borne in pendulous clusters during early summer.	Over arbors and on south- or west-facing walls. Wisterias can be grown in combination with the delicately fragrant, double-flowered Yellow Banksian Rose (*Rosa banksiae 'Lutea'*). White-flowered forms of the wisteria can also be grown in combinations with other plants, and they contrast well with the dark backgrounds of some old walls.	Height: 20-30ft (6-9m) Spread: 15-20ft (4.5-6m) **Hardy deciduous vine:** Moisture-retentive rich soil in full sun. Prune in early spring.
Wisteria sinensis Chinese Wisteria	Vanilla-like and sweet.	Mauve flowers borne in pendulous clusters during early summer.	Over arbors and on south- or west-facing walls.	Height: 30ft (9m) and more Spread: 20-25ft (6-7.5m) **Hardy deciduous vine:** Moisture-retentive rich soil in full sun. Prune in early spring.
SWEET				
Akebia quinata Fiveleaf Akebia	Sweet and strong.	Reddish-purple flowers during late spring.	On rustic arbors and trellises and twining into trees.	Height: 20-30ft (6-9m) Spread: 12-15ft (3.6-4.5m) **Twining, semi-evergreen vine:** Light but moisture-retentive soil in light shade or full sun.
Clematis armandii	Sweet.	Saucer-shaped white flowers during spring. The variety 'Apple Blossom' has pink and white flowers, while 'Snow Drift' has pure white.	Against a wall.	Height: 12-18ft (3.6-5.4m) Spread: 12-15ft (3.6-4.5m) **Hardy evergreen vine:** As for *C. flammula* (see opposite).
Clematis montana Anemone Clematis/ Mountain Clematis	Strongly sweet.	Pure white, 2-inch-(5cm) wide flowers borne profusely and in large clusters mainly during midsummer. Several varieties also have sweet flowers: 'Elizabeth', which has large, soft pink heads, and 'Alexander', which bears creamy-white blooms.	Superb on large walls and arbors, or where planted to climb up a tree.	Height: 20-30ft (6-9m) Spread: 15-20ft (4.5-6m) **Deciduous vine:** As for *C. flammula* (see opposite).
Clematis orientalis Orange-peel Clematis	Slightly fragrant and sweet.	Yellow, bell-shaped and nodding flowers, 2 inches (5cm) wide, borne amid fern-like leaves during late summer and into autumn. Silky, silvery-gray seedheads appear in autumn.	Ideal for trailing over an arch or against a wall. Its vigorous, scrambling and somewhat sprawling nature makes it perfect for trailing over old fences and into other plants, where it can soon create a cottage-garden atmosphere. A formal setting, frighteningly full of rigidity and straight lines, can be visually disastrous for it.	Height: 12-18ft (3.6-5.4m) Spread: 6-12ft (1.8-3.6m) **Deciduous vine:** As for *C. flammula* (see opposite).

VINES				
PLANT	SCENT	COLOR	SITUATION	CULTIVATION
SWEET				
Clematis recta	Sweet.	Pure-white, star-shaped flowers, about ¾ inch (18mm) wide, borne during midsummer. Flowers followed by fluffy, silky seedheads.	Plant by the side of a path or in a perennial border and support with a cluster of twiggy branches.	Height: 3-4ft (0.9-1.2m) Spread: 2½-3ft (75-90cm) **Hardy herbaceous perennial:** Plant in slightly limy, well-drained but moisture-retentive soil and apply a mulch of peat or compost in spring. Prune the stems back to 6 inches (15cm) above the soil in late autumn (early spring in cold areas).
Jasminum polyanthum Pink Jasmine	Sweet.	White and pale pink flowers from late spring to midsummer.	Ideal over a frame in a porch, where it gains protection. Only suitable outdoors in mild areas; elsewhere it can be grown indoors, where it flowers during winter.	Height: 5-10ft (1.5-3m) Spread: 5-8ft (1.5-2.4m) **Tender, semi-evergreen vine:** Well-drained soil and a sunny, sheltered position.
Jasminum humile 'Revolutum' Italian Jasmine/ Himalayan Jasmine	Sweet.	Small yellow flowers in clusters from mid- to late summer.	Against a warm, south- or west-facing wall.	Height: 6-8ft (1.8-2.4m) Spread: 4-5ft (1.2-1.5m) **Evergreen shrub:** Well-drained soil and a sunny, sheltered position.
Jasminum x stephanense	Sweet.	Pale pink flowers in terminal clusters during midsummer.	Trailing over archways and arbors.	Height: 10-15ft (3-4.5m) Spread: 7-10ft (2.1-3m) **Semi-evergreen or deciduous vine:** Well-drained soil and a sunny, sheltered position.
Lathyrus odoratus Sweet Pea	Richly sweet.	Pink, white or purple, pea-shaped flowers on long stalks from midsummer to autumn.	On wire screens against a wall, over arches or on twiggy sticks in a mixed border. Sweet peas like cool, moist conditions such as those of the West coast and are quickly killed by heat. In mild-winter areas, plant them in late fall for spring bloom.	Height: 6-10ft (1.8-3m) Spread: Sprawling **Hardy self-clinging annual vine:** Well-drained but moisture-retentive, compost-rich, slightly limy soil in full sun or light shade. Plant as soon as the soil can be worked or grow heat-resistant varieties.
Lonicera caprifolium Goat-leaf Honeysuckle/Italian Woodbine	Sweet.	Creamy-white flowers, tinged with pink, during midsummer. The fragrance is at its strongest in the evening and appears to attract long-tongued moths.	Over rustic poles, arbors or fences.	Height: 15-20ft (4.5-6m) Spread: 7-12ft (2.1-3.6m) **Deciduous vine:** Well-drained, compost-rich soil in light shade. Thin out congested shoots after the flowers fade.
Lonicera hildebrandiana Giant Honeysuckle/ Giant Burmese Honeysuckle	Richly sweet.	Creamy-white flowers up to 6 inches (15cm) long from mid- to late summer.	A very warm south-facing wall or a large greenhouse.	Height: 20ft (6m) or more Spread: 10-15ft (3-4.5m) **Tender evergreen or partly deciduous vine:** Only suitable outdoors in the mildest of areas.

VINES				
PLANT	**SCENT**	**COLOR**	**SITUATION**	**CULTIVATION**
SWEET				
Lonicera japonica Japanese Honeysuckle	Sweet.	White to pale yellow flowers from midsummer to autumn.	Over rustic poles and fences.	Height: 25-30ft (7.5-9m) Spread: 7-15ft (2.1-4.5m) **Evergreen vine:** Well-drained, compost-rich soil in light shade. Thin out congested shoots after the flowers fade.
Lonicera periclymenum 'Belgica' Early Dutch Honeysuckle/Dutch Woodbine	Sweet.	Purplish-red and yellow flowers during early and midsummer.	Over rustic poles, arbors and fences.	Height: 15-20ft (4.5-6m) Spread: 7-12ft (2.1-3.6m) **Deciduous vine:** Well-drained, compost-rich soil in light shade. Thin out congested shoots after the flowers fade.
Lonicera periclymenum 'Serotina' Late Dutch Honeysuckle	Sweet.	Flowers with creamy-white inside and reddish-purple exteriors from mid- to late summer.	Over rustic poles, arbors and fences.	Height: 15-20ft (4.5-6m) Spread: 7-12ft (2.1-3.6m) **Deciduous vine:** Well-drained, compost-rich soil in light shade. Thin out congested shoots after the flowers fade.
Lonicera sempervirens Trumpet Honeysuckle/Coral Honeysuckle	Richly sweet.	Narrow, trumpet-like, scarlet and orange-yellow flowers borne in clusters from mid- to late summer.	A very warm south-facing wall or a large greenhouse. This native of the southern states of North America is only evergreen outdoors in the South, though it is hardy through zone 4. In a greenhouse, however, it is one of the best honeysuckles.	Height: 15-20ft (4.5-6m) Spread: 7-12ft (2.1-3.6m) **Tender evergreen or hardy partly deciduous climbing shrub:** Only evergreen in the South.
Passiflora caerulea Common Passion Flower/Blue Passion Flower	Slightly sweet.	Pink-tinged white petals and blue-purple centers.	Trained on supports against a warm, south- or west-facing wall.	Height: 12-15ft (3.6-4.5m) Spread: 8-12ft (2.4-3.6m) **Tender evergreen vine:** Well-drained fertile soil in a sheltered position.
Trachelospermum jasminoides Star Jasmine	Sweet.	White flowers, becoming cream with age, during mid- to late summer.	A warm, south- or west-facing wall.	Height: 10-12ft (3-4.6m) Spread: 8-10ft (2.4-3m) **Evergreen climbing shrub:** Light, well-drained, acid soil. Thin out vigorous and overcrowded shoots in spring.

		CLIMBING AND RAMBLING ROSES		
PLANT	SCENT	COLOR	SITUATION	CULTIVATION
APPLE				
'François Juranville'	Sharp and apple-like.	Glowing pink, flat double flowers with a tint of gold at their centers.	Well suited for covering a large arch or arbor.	Height: 15-18ft (4.5-5.4m) Spread: 12-15ft (3.6-4.5m) Rambler rose (Wichuraiana type).
'Paul Transon'	Strong and apple-like.	Coppery-orange, close-petalled flowers borne in small clusters.	Ideal on a small arbor or arch.	Height: 12-15ft (3.6-4.5m) Spread: 10-12ft (3-3.6m) Rambler rose (Wichuraiana type).
'René André'	Sweet and apple-like.	Soft apricot-yellow, cup-shaped flowers flushed with pink borne on trailing canes.	Vigorous rose, so plant to trail over a large arbor, to climb into a tree or to clamber over a large fence.	Height: 15-20ft (4.5-6m) Spread: 15-18ft (4.5-5.4m) Rambler rose (Wichuraiana type)
'Silver Moon'	Rich and apple-like.	Creamy-white, large, single flowers with golden anthers during midsummer.	Vigorous rose, so plant to clamber over a large arbor or arch.	Height: 20-30ft (6-9m) Spread: 20-25ft (6-7.5m) Rambler rose (Wichuraiana type)
CLOVES				
'Blush Noisette'	Rich and clove-like.	Lilac-pink, semi-double, cupped, small flowers borne in clusters from mid- to late summer.	Grows well against a wall and also forms a beautiful, open shrub in a border.	Height: 8-10ft (2.4-3m) Spread: 10-12ft (3-3.6m) Climbing rose (Noisette type).
FRUITY				
'Leander'	Sharp and fruity.	Small, apricot-yellow, double flowers borne in large clusters.	Ideal for covering a wall or for growing as a shrub in a border.	Height: 10-12ft (3-3.6m) Spread: 8-10ft (2.4-3m) Climber (English rose).
MUSK				
'Paul's Himalayan Musk'	Rich and musk-like.	Blush-pink flowers borne in dainty sprays.	Vigorous rose, so train on a large arbor or plant it so that it climbs and rambles in a tree alongside a path.	Height: 20-30ft (6-9m) Spread: 18-25ft (5.4-7.6m) Rambler rose.
MYRRH				
'Constance Spry'	Strongly myrrh-like.	Clear rose-pink flowers, exceptionally large, cup-shaped and peony-shaped. Each flower has a delicate luminous quality.	Ideal for covering a wall or for growing as a shrub in a border.	Height: 12-15ft (3.6-4.5m) Spread: 10-12ft (3-3.6m) Climber (English rose).
'Cressida'	Strongly myrrh-like.	Apricot-pink, full-petalled flowers.	Ideal for covering a wall or for growing in a shrub border.	Height: 10-12ft (3-3.6m) Spread: 8-10ft (2.4-3m) Climber (English rose).

CLIMBING AND RAMBLING ROSES				
PLANT	SCENT	COLOR	SITUATION	CULTIVATION
ORANGE				
'The Garland'	Rich orange fragrance.	Small, creamy-salmon flowers with narrow, quilted petals producing a daisy-like appearance.	Plant to grow over a small arch or arbor. It can also be grown as a shrub in a border.	Height: 12-15ft (3.6-4.5m) Spread: 10-12ft (3-4.5m) Rambler rose.
'Veilchenblau'	Rich orange scent.	Dark magenta flowers fading to lilac and, occasionally, streaked with white. On occasions the flowers appear almost blue.	Especially suitable for growing over an arch.	Height: 12-15ft (3.6-4.5m) Spread: 10-15ft (3-4.5m) Rambler rose (Multiflora type).
PEONY				
'Gerbe Rose'	Delicious and peony-like.	Soft pink, loose, double flowers tinted with cream. After the first main flush of flowers it continues blooming intermittently over a long period.	Useful for covering an arch.	Height: 10-12ft (3-3.6m) Spread: 8-12ft (2.4-3.6m) Rambler rose (Wichuraiana type).
PRIMROSE				
Adeläide d'Orléans'	Delicate primrose scent.	Small, creamy-pink, semi-double flowers which hang gracefully.	Superb for trailing over arches and arbors over paths.	Height: 12-15ft (3.6-4.5m) Spread: 10-12ft (3-3.6m) Rambler rose (Sempervirens type).
'Débutante'	Primrose scented.	Small, clear rose-pink flowers which fade to blush, borne in dainty sprays.	Ideal for covering small arches.	Height: 12-15ft (3.6-4.5m) Spread: 8-10ft (2.4-3m) Rambler rose (Wichuraiana type).
'Félicité et perpétue'	Delicate and primrose-like.	Creamy-white double flowers, tinted with pink when in bud, borne in large clusters.	A strong-growing rose, ideal for a large arch or arbor. It is one of the hardiest of ramblers, forming a dense mass of growth that is superb in a cottage-garden setting. Ideally, it should be trained upwards and then allowed to sprawl and trail.	Height: 18-20ft (5.4-6m) Spread: 15-18ft (4.5-5.4m) Rambler rose (Sempervirens type).
'Spectabilis'	Primrose-like.	Rose-pink flowers with a tint of lilac.	Small rambler, ideal for a small garden.	Height: 6-8ft (1.8-2.4m) Spread: 5-7ft (1.5-2.1m) Rambler rose (Sempervirens hybrid).
SWEET PEA				
'Mme Grégoire Staechelin'	Delicious sweet pea fragrance.	Glowing coral-pink flowers, splashed and overlaid with crimson.	Vigorous and hardy climber, ideal for a north- or east-facing wall.	Height: 15-20ft (4.5-6m) Spread: 12-18ft (3.6-5.4m) Climbing rose (Large-flowered Climber).

CLIMBING AND RAMBLING ROSES				
PLANT	SCENT	COLOR	SITUATION	CULTIVATION
SWEET				
'Albertine'	Rich and sweet.	Reddish-salmon buds open to reveal large, coppery-pink, almost double flowers.	Ideal for growing on an arbor or arch over a path.	Height: 15-18ft (4.5-5.4m) Spread: 15-18ft (4.5-5.4m) Rambler rose (Wichuraiana type).
'Alexander Girault'	Very sweet.	Profuse reddish-pink flowers that open flat.	Ideal for covering arbors and arches with a mass of flowers. It is a rambler that is best planted in a large area where it can create a dominant display. The beautiful glossy leaves are an additional attraction.	Height: 18-20ft (5.4-6m) Spread: 15-18ft (4.5-5.4m) Rambler rose (Wichuraiana type).
'Céline Forestier'	Strongly tea-rose scented.	Pale yellow, silky, petal-packed during summer.	Plant against a warm wall. It is not an easy rose to grow but is well worth planting.	Height: 8ft (2.4m) Spread: 8-9ft (2.4-2.7m) Climbing rose (Noisette type).
'Château de Clos Vougeot, Climbing'	Strongly sweet.	Dark, rich, velvet-crimson flowers that open wide and flat during sumer. Sometimes it is repeat-flowering after the first flush of blooms.	Ideal against a wall.	Height: 12-15ft (3.6-4.5m) Spread: 10-12ft (3-3.6m) Climbing rose (Hybrid Tea).
'Devoniensis, Climbing'	Richly tea-rose scented.	Creamy-white, large, well-shaped flowers with a flush of apricot at their centers.	Needs a warm south- or west-facing wall.	Height: 10-12ft (3-3.6m) Spread: 10-15ft (3-4.5m) Climbing rose (Tea Rose).
'Dr W. Van Fleet'	Strong and sweet.	Silvery-pink flowers borne in clusters.	Ideal for arches.	Height: 15-20ft (4.5-6m) Spread: 15-18ft (4.5-5.4m) Rambler rose (Wichuraiana type).
'Dreamgirl'	Sharp, piercing scent.	Warm coral-pink flowers borne late in the season.	Ideal against a wall or growing up a pillar.	Height: 8-10ft (2.4-3m) Spread: 8-12ft (2.4-3.6m) Climbing rose (Modern Rose).
'Étoile de Hollande, Climbing'	Strongly fragrant.	Deep crimson, loosely formed, double flowers throughout summer.	Ideal on a large wall.	Height: 10-12ft (3-3.6m) Spread: 10-15ft (3-4.5m) Climbing rose (Climbing Hybrid Tea).
'Gloire de Dijon' The Old Glory Rose	Richly and sweetly scented.	Buff-yellow flowers, sometimes tinted with pink and gold, initially globular then opening to cup-shaped and later flat. Flowers early summer, then continuing.	Ideal for cold walls.	Height: 12-15ft (3.6-4.5m) Spread: 10-12ft (3-3.6m) Climbing rose (Noisette type).
'Guinée'	Richly scented.	Dark, velvety-scarlet, double flowers with black shading. The 4-inch-(10cm) wide flowers are borne throughout most of summer.	Plant against a light-colored wall so that the flowers show up well.	Height: 8-10ft (2.4-3m) Spread: 8-12ft (2.4-3.6m) Climbing rose (Climbing Hybrid Tea).

CLIMBING AND RAMBLING ROSES				
PLANT	SCENT	COLOR	SITUATION	CULTIVATION
SWEET				
'Hero'	Rich and sweet.	Glistening pink, large double flowers in the form of a deep, open cup.	Ideal for covering a small wall or for growing in a shrub border.	Height: 8-9ft (2.4-2.7m) Spread: 7-8ft (2.1-2.4m) Climber (English rose).
'Kathleen Harrop'	Strongly fragrant.	Clear pink, double or semi-double flowers during summer. This is a 'sport' of the well-known 'Zéphirine Drouhin', but less vigorous.	Grow as a climber against a pillar or as a hedge.	Height: 8-10ft (2.4-3m) Spread: 8-12ft (2.4-3.6m) Climbing rose (Climbing Bourbon Rose).
'Lady Hillingdon, Climbing'	Rich, tea rose perfume.	Rich apricot-yellow flowers which open to form large, loosely-formed blooms.	It is especially vigorous when on a warm, south- or west-facing wall.	Height: 10-15ft (3-4.5m) Spread: 10-15ft (3-4.5m) Climbing rose (Tea Rose).
'Lady Waterlow'	Sweetly fresh.	Clear pink, full-petalled flowers shaded with salmon, mainly borne early during the season.	Ideal for creating an early display of scent and color on a wall.	Height: 8-12ft (2.4-3.6m) Spread: 10-12ft (3-3.6m) Climbing rose (Hybrid Tea).
'Lawrence Johnston'	Powerful and very sweet.	Bright, clear yellow, large, semi-double flowers during midsummer and intermittently afterwards.	Ideal for covering a very large wall.	Height: 20-30ft (6-9m) Spread: 15-20ft (4.5-6m) Climbing rose (Foetida, Climber).
'Maigold'	Strong, sweet fragrance.	Bronze-yellow, semi-double flowers with golden stamens during summer.	It tends to be a thorny plant, so take care not to plant it where children may fall against it.	Height: 10-12ft (3-3.6m) Spread: 8-12ft (2.4-3.6m) Climbing rose (Large-flowered Climber).
'Mme Alfred Carrière'	Very sweet.	White flowers slightly tinted with flesh pink. Blooms strongly and freely throughout summer.	Good for covering large walls; very hardy.	Height: 15-20ft (4.5-6m) Spread: 12-15ft (3.6-4.5m) Climbing rose (Noisette type).
'Mme Abel Chantenay, Climbing'	Sweet and delicious.	Bluish-pink buds opening to shapely, quill-petal flowers during midsummer.	Ideal for an east- or north-facing wall.	Height: 10-12ft (3-3.6m) Spread: 10-15ft (3-4.5m) Climbing rose (Hybrid Tea).
'Mary Wallace'	Very sweet.	Rose-pink, semi-double, loosely-formed flowers.	Ideal for covering an arch or arbor.	Height: 15-20ft (4.5-6m) Spread: 15ft (4.5m) Rambler rose (Wichuraiana type).
'Paul's Lemon Pillar'	Strongly sweet.	Waxy, lemon-yellow flowers tinged green at their centers.	Needs a warm south- or west-facing wall if it is to achieve the dimensions suggested. It is an excellent exhibition rose, and is superb for forming a screen of foliage and flowers, although it is summer-flowering only and does not repeat-bloom.	Height: 15-18ft (4.5-5.4m) Spread: 12-15ft (3.6-4.5m) Climbing rose (Hybrid Tea).
'Sander's White'	Deliciously fresh.	Pure white, semi-double, small flowers.	Ideal for clambering over an arbor or large arch.	Height: 15-20ft (4.5-6m) Spread: 15ft (4.5m) Rambler rose (Wichuraiana type).
'Zéphirine Drouhin'	Rich and sweet.	Bright carmine-pink, semi-double flowers borne in great profusion during summer and again in autumn.	Grows well on north- or east-facing walls.	Height: 9-12ft (2.7-3.6m) Spread: 8-10ft (2.4-3m) Climbing rose (Bourbon type).

ALONG THE EDGES OF PATHS				
PLANT	SCENT	COLOR	SITUATION	CULTIVATION
CARAWAY				
Thymus herba-barona Caraway Thyme	Caraway	Dark green leaves and tubular, pale lilac flowers in terminal clusters in midsummer.	Along the edges of paths and as a groundcover.	Height: 3-5 inches (7.5-13cm) Spread: 12-15 inches (30-38cm) **Hardy evergreen dwarf shrub:** Well-drained soil and a sunny position.
CHAMOMILE				
Chamaemelum nobile (syn. *Anthemis nobilis*) 'Treneague' Chamomile	The foliage has a sweet, fruity aroma, especially when crushed. Some say it resembles a mixture of apples and bananas.	Medium-green, moss-like and finely dissected leaves. This variety is non-flowering and is ideal for forming into a lawn.	As a fragrant lawn and at the sides of paths. This variety of chamomile needs less mowing when formed into a lawn than the ordinary type. Set the plants 4-6in (10-15cm) apart in spring. When about 3in (7.5cm) high, 'top' them by cutting off the tips. Gradually reduce the height of the plants to about ¾in (18mm) high. For a flowering variety of chamomile suitable for the sides of paths, choose the common variety.	Height: 6-8 inches (15-20cm) Spread: 8-12 inches (20-30cm) **Hardy perennial:** Well-drained soil and a sunny position.
CLOVES				
Dianthus caryophyllus Carnation/ Gillyflower/Clove-pink	Clove-like and sweet.	The species bears dull purple flowers up to 1½ inches (4cm) wide during midsummer on 2ft-(60cm) long stems. However, this plant is in the parentage of many varieties of border and perpetual-flowering carnations.	Plant the species and border types along path edges and in perennial borders. Perpetual-flowering types (not all scented) need the comfort of a sunroom or greenhouse.	Height: 9 inches (23cm) – foliage height of species Spread: 15 inches (38cm) – foliage spread of species **Hardy perennial:** Well-drained, limy soil and a sunny position.
HAY				
Asperula gussonei Dwarf Woodruff	Fresh and hay-like.	Shell-pink flowers in midsummer amid narrow, white and hairy leaves.	At the edges of paths to soften sharp outlines. Its slightly trailing, sprawling and tufted habit makes it a good choice for cottage gardens, where path edges with soft lines are fundamental to the design. However, if it invades a path too much, it should be gently trimmed back in an informal manner.	Height: 2-3 inches (5-7.5cm) Spread: 6 inches (15cm) **Hardy perennial:** Well-drained, gritty soil and a sunny position.
LEMON				
Thymus x citriodorus Lemon Thyme/ Lemon-scented Thyme	Lemony.	Medium-green leaves and pale pink flowers from mid- to late summer.	Along the edges of paths or in herb gardens.	Height: 10-12 inches (25-30cm) Spread: 9-12 inches (23-30cm) **Hardy evergreen dwarf shrub:** Well-drained soil and a sunny position.
PEPPERMINT				
Mentha requienii Corsican Mint/ Menthella/Crême-de-Menthe plant	Peppermint.	Pale green, aromatic leaves and pale purple flowers from mid- to late summer.	At the edges of paths and for forming aromatic carpets.	Height: 1 inch (2.5cm) Spread: 10-12 inches (25-30cm) **Nearly hardy perennial:** Well-drained but moisture-retentive soil in light shade.

PLANT	SCENT	COLOR	SITUATION	CULTIVATION
ALONG THE EDGES OF PATHS				
PINE NEEDLES AND ORANGE PEEL				
Thymus caespititius	Pine needles blended with orange peel.	Pale purple flowers during midsummer.	Alongside paths or in a rock garden.	Height: 3 inches (7.5cm) Spread: 12 inches (30cm) **Evergreen dwarf shrub:** Well-drained soil and a sunny position.
THYME				
Thymus praecox Mother-of-Thyme	Thyme-like.	Reddish-pink flowers in terminal clusters from mid- to late summer. 	Alongside paths and for creating a groundcover. A large area planted with this thyme is very eye-catching, and the plant is particularly useful for filling areas between gravel or stone paths, and at the edges of ponds. When used near a pond, it has the additional advantage of not blocking the view of aquatic plants close to the surface of the water.	Height: 2-3 inches (5-7.5cm) Spread: 15-18 inches (38-45cm) **Hardy perennial:** Well-drained soil and a sunny position.
Thymus serpyllum Creeping Thyme/ Wild Thyme/English Thyme	Thyme-like, but varieties differ considerably in their aromas.	Deep red through pink to white, in terminal clusters from mid- to late summer. 	Alongside paths and for creating a groundcover. Can also be planted for an aromatic lawn.	Height: 1-3 inches (2.5-7.5cm) Spread: 15-18 inches (38-45cm) **Hardy perennial:** Well-drained soil and a sunny position.
SWEET				
Dianthus x arvernensis	Sweet.	Pink flowers from early to late summer.	Path edges or in a rock garden. This hybrid is often considered to be a form of the Cheddar Pink, *Dianthus gratianopolitanus*, better known as *Dianthus caesins*. However, it is more compact than the normal Cheddar Pink, and better suited for planting along the edges of paths. 	Height: 6 inches (15cm) Spread: 6 inches (15cm) **Hardy perennial:** Well-drained, limy soil in a sunny position.
Dianthus x calalpinus	Sweet.	Pink flowers up to 1½ inches (4cm) wide, with white dots at their centers from mid- to late summer.	Alongside paths and in rock gardens.	Height: 3 inches (7.5cm) Spread: 6 inches (15cm) **Hardy perennial:** Well-drained, limy soil and a sunny position.
Dianthus deltoides Maiden Pink	Sweet and slightly spicy.	Red through to pink and white flowers from midsummer to autumn. Many superb varieties.	Crevices in paving, alongside paths and in rock gardens.	Height: 6-9 inches (15-23cm) Spread: 4-6 inches (10-15cm) **Hardy perennial:** Well-drained, limy soil in a sunny position.

ALONG THE EDGES OF PATHS				
PLANT	SCENT	COLOR	SITUATION	CULTIVATION
SWEET				
Dianthus gratianopolitanus (syn. *Dianthus caesius*) Cheddar Pink	Sweet and slightly spicy.	Pink, 1-inch-(2.5cm) wide, fringed flowers from early to midsummer.	In a rock garden or at the edge of a path.	Height: 4-12 inches (10-30cm) Spread: 10-12 inches (25-30cm) **Hardy perennial:** Well-drained, limy soil in a sunny position.
Dianthus plumarius Grass Pink	Strongly sweet.	Wide color range. The species is seldom grown, but it is, in part, a parent of the well-known garden pinks.	Edges of paths and along borders.	Height: Range from 3-15 inches (7.5-38cm) Spread: 6-9 inches (15-23cm) **Hardy perennial:** Well-drained, limy soil and a sunny position.
Dianthus superbus Fringed Pink/Sweet John	Strongly sweet, with only a hint of spice.	Pale to deep lilac, or occasionally white, flowers 1½ inches (4cm) wide, during late summer.	Low-growing varieties alongside paths and in rock gardens, tall ones in perennial borders.	Height: 9-18 inches (23-45cm) Spread: 6-9 inches (15-23cm) **Short-lived hardy perennial, best treated as a biennial:** Well-drained, limy soil in a sunny position.
Limnanthes douglasii Meadow Foam/Marsh Flower/Poached Egg Flower	Sweet and delicate.	Wide, funnel-shaped, white flowers with yellow centers from mid- to late summer, attractive to bees.	Along path edges and in rock gardens. Its sprawling and rapid groundcovering habit makes it ideal for forming a bright splash of color alongside paths. However, stems which wander too far over path edges will need trimming back.	Height: 4-6 inches (10-15cm) Spread: 4-8 inches (10-20cm) **Hardy annual:** Well-drained fertile soil and a sunny position. It likes cool soil, with its roots able to meander under stones.
Oxalis enneaphylla	Sweet.	White, funnel-shaped flowers during midsummer, amid partly folded gray leaves.	At the edges of paths and in rock gardens. This low-growing plant develops a dense mass of gray leaves which give the edges of a path a soft appearance. Try it in a clinical setting, alongside formal paths. For pale rose-pink flowers in June and July, choose the variety 'Rosea'.	Height: 3 inches (7.5cm) Spread: 6 inches (15cm) **Bulbous-rooted perennial:** Well-drained soil and full sun.
Primula polyantha Polyanthus Primrose	Sweet and demure.	Wide color range, including shades of yellow, red, pink, blue and white, in mixed or separate colors.	Alongside rustic paths, in woodland and in pots indoors.	Height: 6-8 inches (15-20cm) Spread: 8-10 inches (20-25cm) **Perennial:** Fertile, moisture-retentive soil in light shade or full sun.

ALONG THE EDGES OF PATHS				
PLANT	**SCENT**	**COLOR**	**SITUATION**	**CULTIVATION**
SWEET				
Sagina pilifera	Sweet.	White flowers during summer on a tufted, moss-like plant.	Edges of paths and for forming a carpet.	Height: 2 inches (5cm) Spread: 5-8 inches (13-20cm) **Hardy perennial:** Light soil in full sun or partial shade.
Viola blanda Sweet White Violet	Sweet, but faint.	Neat, tufted violet with small, white, purple-veined flowers which appear in early spring. Heart-shaped, slightly downy leaves.	Alongside paths and in rock gardens.	Height: 2-4 inches (5-10cm) Spread: 6-8 inches (15-20cm) **Herbaceous perennial:** Well-drained fertile soil in light shade.
Viola odorata Sweet Violet	Very sweet.	Violet ½-¾-inch-(12-18mm) wide flowers in shades of purple or white from late winter to spring, and occasionally in autumn.	Alongside paths, in rock gardens and containers. Few plants have such a cottage-garden appearance as violets, and this is particularly true of the Sweet Violet. It has a tufted, open habit, so that it never fully covers the soil, which invariably peeps through between the leaves – however, this does not detract from the plant's attractiveness.	Height: 4-6 inches (10-15cm) Spread: 10-12 inches (25-30cm) **Herbaceous perennial:** Well-drained fertile soil in sun or light shade.
Viola tricolor Johnny-jump-up/ Heartsease	Sweet.	Pansy-like flowers, up to 1½ inches (4cm) wide, in a wide color range from cream and yellow to dark blue and purplish-black from late spring to autumn.	Alongside paths, in rock gardens and containers. Due to its pansy-faced flowers, this viola is of a more modern appearance than the Sweet Violet. In fact, many of the large-faced and brightly colored garden pansies such as those described under *Viola x wittrockiana* (below) derive from this species.	Height: 3-6 inches (7.5-15cm) Spread: 6-12 inches (15-30cm) **Herbaceous perennial:** Well-drained fertile soil in sun or light shade.
Viola x wittrockiana (syn. *Viola tricolor hortensis*) Garden Pansy/ Heartsease	Sweet but faint.	Large flowers in wide color range in both summer- and winter-flowering forms. Not all varieties are scented. Also includes tufted pansies that flower from spring to autumn.	Along path edges, in containers and edging borders.	Height: 6-9 inches (15-23cm) Spread: 8-10 inches (20-25cm) **Herbaceous perennial:** Well-drained fertile soil in full sun or light shade.

CHAPTER FOUR

Scented Rock and Water Gardens

*A diverse selection of choice rock and water
garden plants can be used in the scented garden
for their delightful fragrance and original
appearance.*

ATER GARDENS and rock gardens are two facets of gardening that enhance and complement each other. A series of small pools meandering through a rock garden helps to unify the plants and rocks, while aquatic plants create interest throughout the summer, when many rock garden plants have ceased to provide a bright display.

ROCK GARDENS

Rock gardens are usually considered by connoisseurs of alpine plants to be the *crème de la crème* of the garden, with a bounty of small, delicate plants. At one time rock gardens were frequently called rockeries, but this term has long been out of favor – mainly because devotees of alpine plants attractively arranged in a well-designed rock garden formed of natural stone wished to distance themselves from rockeries which were often created from large lumps of broken concrete and arranged in a form that resembled dog food! Such rockeries arose in Britain after the Second World War, when the concrete air-raid shelters in yards were suddenly demolished. Sadly, it has taken many years for most people to realize that, for a rock garden, broken lumps of concrete are simply not suitable.

A rock garden should be a natural phenomenon – an outcrop of rocks which appears to be the work of nature and which harmonizes with the shape and contours of the garden. Superb drainage is vital. Alpine plants in general are able to withstand low temperatures if the soil is well drained, but a combination of very low temperatures and cold, wet soil in the winter months is a recipe for disaster.

Most rock gardens are planted with a liberal range of plants and are not constrained to true alpines which, by definition, are from alpine regions. Dwarf conifers, many bulbs, small shrubs, short-lived perennials and herbaceous plants all combine to create a wealth of color and interest throughout the year. Many of these plants enrich a rock garden with a further quality – scent. These exciting bouquets include the deliciously sweet scent of daphnes; the sweet and fruity bouquet of *Tulipa gesneriana;* the mossy aroma of the Common Snowdrop; the violet scent of *Galanthus*

elwesii, and the honey fragrance of *Crocus chrysanthus.* Dwarf and slow-growing conifers also offer exciting scents, from the resin and parsley bouquet of Lawson cypress cultivars, to the fruity and apple-like aroma of the many varieties of *Thuja occidentalis.*

Snowdrops have been called the morning stars of flowers, as during winter they give some assurance that nature is not dead and that spring is to come. Indeed, the Common Snowdrop, *Galanthus nivalis,* with its mossy bouquet, has been known as Fair Maids of February and Candlemas Bells – the latter because the flowers were once part of an ecclesiastical festival known as the Feast of the Purification of the Virgin which was held on 2 February. When the image of the Virgin was removed from the altar, snowdrops, emblems of purity, were spread over the vacant space. Because of their use in this festival they also gained the name Purification Flower. For a short period they were also called, confusingly, Bulbous Violet, but fortunately this name ceased to be widely used after the mid-1600s.

A similar small bulbous plant, the Snowflake, botanically known as leucojum, is closely related to the galanthus. However, they can be easily distinguished. Snowdrops (galanthus) have three long outer and three short inner petals, whereas Snowflakes (leucojum) have six petals of the same size. The Spring Snowflake, *Leucojum vernum,* has a sweet scent and bears its diminutive white flowers, tipped with green, during late winter and into early spring. There are few people who do not delight in the scents

The combination of deliciously sweet flowers and a low-growing nature makes the evergreen shrub Daphne cneorum 'Variegatum' *ideal for a rock garden.*

of crocuses, and the choice is wide. The well-known *Crocus chrysanthus,* superb in many places in a garden, especially in a rock garden, or in window boxes, has a sweet and honey-like scent. Although *Crocus chrysanthus* has much more to offer in the garden than the Saffron Crocus, *Crocus sativus,* the latter is more famous. The flowers have a sweet and somewhat mossy scent, but it is the female reproductive parts, the stigmas, which yield the saffron that has given the Saffron Crocus such wide acclaim. It takes the dried stigmas of about 4,300 flowers to produce just an ounce of precious saffron.

In medicine it has been used for relieving chronic hemorrhaging and faint-

ing fits, helping digestion and cleansing the lungs; in cooking it acts as a coloring and flavoring agent, and in the arts it is used as a dye. In Imperial Rome it was customary to sprinkle sweet-smelling saffron water in theatres, while banqueting halls and temples were often strewn with crocus flowers and leaves.

The Saffron Crocus also contains an irritant poison which has often proved fatal. In the 1920s, medical testimony in an inquest revealed the custom of administering saffron tea flavored with brandy as a way of alleviating the symptoms of measles. It is sometimes used today as a herbal cure, but the dosage is critical as it can be toxic if taken in excess. An amusing note about it is that it can cause convulsive laughter, and history reveals that a lady was said to have shaken herself to pieces with laughter within three hours.

The Saffron Crocus is steeped in history. As a dye saffron can be traced back to the ancient past, when it was known as *krokos*. In Cilicia, a Roman province in what was then Asia Minor (now Turkey), there was a promontory known as Korykos near to which was grown the finest saffron, and it is natural to suppose that the area took its name from the plant. One legend has it that saffron was taken to England in the reign of Edward III (1312–1377), by a pilgrim who brought a saffron bulb from the Holy Land in the hollow of a stick. Another is that Sir Thomas Smith of Saffron Walden established it in 1330. However, it was probably the Arabs who introduced the bulb to Europe through Spain, and this theory is reinforced by the fact that the word saffron is derived from the Arabic *sahafran*, which has influenced the Italian and Spanish names for this bulb, *zafferano* and *azafran* respectively. Unfortunately, this interesting plant only flowers during warm summers in mild areas; position it in a warm and sheltered place.

Crocus longiflorus, previously and significantly known as *Crocus odorus*, has a sweet and strongly primrose bouquet during late summer and early autumn. *Crocus versicolor* is also primrose-scented.

The diminutive *Iris danfordiae* is ideal for rock gardens, where its honey-scented and sweet flowers fill well-drained pockets with color during mid- and late winter. It is also useful for containers on a patio. Other small irises with pleasing bouquets include the strongly violet-scented *Iris bakeriana*, and the better known and similarly scented Netted Iris, *Iris reticulata*, which flowers during late winter and into spring.

Cyclamen hederifolium, often known as *Cyclamen neopolitanum*, has a sweet but faint bouquet. As well as enriching a rock garden with scent, the corms also have a medicinal value. An ointment made from fresh tubers while the plant is in flower was used to expel worms, while the juice was administered to cure vertigo. An old and more interesting use is that when baked into little flat cakes the ointment apparently

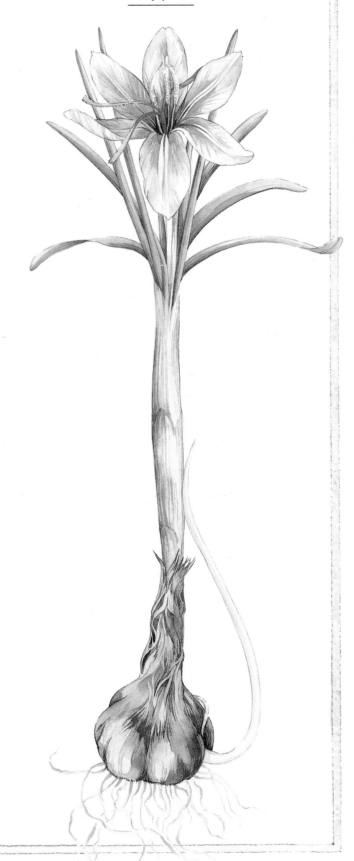

The sweet, somewhat mossy-scented Saffron Crocus (Crocus sativus) is steeped in history: it enriched Roman temples and has been used by the Arabs as a dye for centuries.

causes the eater to fall violently in love! Cyclamen is also known as Sowbread, as the corms were formerly fed to pigs.

Other scented cyclamen include *Cyclamen libanoticum*, which has a sweet but rather musty aroma, *Cyclamen repandum* and *Cyclamen purpurascens* (both sweet).

As well as decorating rock gardens with aromatic small varieties, *Juniperus communis* has been held in great esteem as a medicinal plant. Its properties include an ability to counter poison, cure scurvy and hemorrhoids, kill worms in children and to expel air. There are many others, but more interesting to most people is the inclusion of its berries in several brands of gin, where it adds flavor.

The foliage of *Juniperus communis* and its varieties emits an apple-like scent when crushed, whereas that of *Juniperus virginiana* gives off a soapy smell.

The lightly sweet, mid- to late summer, plume-like flower sprays of Saxifraga cotyledon *are wonderful in a rock garden, where they harmonize well with rocks and a light layer of pebbles over the soil.*

Other conifers with a delightful bouquet include *Chamaecyparis obtusa*, which has a warm and sweet aroma; *Chamaecyparis lawsoniana*, reminiscent of resin and parsley; *Thuja occidentalis*, fruity and apple-like, and *Chamaecyparis pisifera*, which has a resinous scent.

The aroma of garlic is not to everyone's liking. If it is not to yours, steer clear of the Wall Germander, *Teucrium chamaedrys*, with its strong, garlicky smell. This plant has a reputation for relieving gout, and is said to have been used in the 16th century in the treatment of the Holy Roman Emperor Charles V.

ROCK GARDENS				
PLANT	SCENT	COLOR	SITUATION	CULTIVATION
ALMOND				
Galanthus allenii Snowdrop	Almond-scented.	White flowers, with green markings at the tips of the inner petals, during spring.	In a rock garden.	Height: 7-9 inches (18-23cm) Spread: 4-6 inches (10-15cm) **Hardy bulb:** Moisture-retentive soil in light shade.
APPLE				
Juniperus communis 'Compressa'	Apple-like scent when foliage is crushed.	Prickly, light gray-green leaves with a bluish tinge.	In a rock garden, or in small tubs or window boxes.	Height: 1½-2ft (45-60cm) Spread: 6 inches (15cm) **Evergreen conifer:** Well-drained soil in full sun or light shade.
Juniperus communis 'Green Carpet'	Apple-like aroma when the foliage is crushed.	Ground-hugging, with branches densely clothed with dark green leaves that turn bright green in summer.	In a large rock garden, or for planting to hang over walls.	Height: 4-6 inches (10-15cm) Spread: 2½-3ft (75-90cm) **Evergreen conifer:** Well-drained soil in full sun.
Juniperus communis 'Repandum'	Apple-like aroma when the foliage is crushed.	Dwarf, prostrate habit with stems densely packed with gray-blue foliage that becomes slightly bronze during winter.	In a large rock garden or in a tub on a patio.	Height: 12-15 inches (30-38cm) Spread: 3-4ft (1-1.2m) **Evergreen conifer:** Well-drained soil in full sun.
Thuja occidentalis 'Danica'	Foliage emits a fruity, apple-like aroma when crushed.	Slow-growing and bun-shaped with bright green foliage that turns bronze during winter.	In a large rock garden or in a tub on a patio.	Height: 1½-2½ft (45-75cm) Spread: 1½-3ft (45-90cm) **Evergreen conifer:** Well-drained but moisture-retentive soil and a sheltered position in full sun.
Thuja occidentalis 'Hetz Midget'	Foliage emits a fruity, apple-like aroma when crushed.	Globular outline with dark green foliage.	In a rock garden.	Height: 10-12 inches (25-30cm) Spread: 8-12 inches (20-30cm) **Evergreen conifer:** Well-drained but moisture-retentive soil and a sheltered position in full sun.
GARLIC				
Teucrium chamaedrys Wall Germander	Leaves have a strong aroma reminiscent of garlic.	Spikes of bright pink flowers, spotted red and white, from mid- to late summer. Aromatic leaves medium to deep green above, gray beneath.	In a rock garden or in a border at the base of a south- or west-facing wall.	Height: 6-8 inches (15-20cm) Spread: 12-15 inches (30-38cm) **Hardy, sub-shrubby perennial:** Light, well-drained soil in full sun.
HONEY				
Androsace villosa	Honey-like and sweet.	Pure white or pink flowers with yellow eyes during early summer.	A well-prepared pocket in a rock garden, or in a gravel bed or an alpine house.	Height: 2-3 inches (5-7.5cm) Spread: 9-12 inches (23-30cm) **Hardy perennial:** Well-drained, gritty soil and a sunny position.
Crocus chrysanthus	Honey-like and sweet.	Rich golden-yellow flowers during late winter. There are many varieties of it; some, such as 'Snow Bunting', which has white flowers marked with deep purple and with an orange base, are noted for their fragrance.	In rock gardens, window boxes and other containers and in raised beds alongside patios.	Height: 2½-3 inches (6.5-7.5cm) Spread: 2-2½ inches (5-6.5cm) **Hardy bulb:** Well-drained soil and a sheltered position in full sun or light shade.
Iris danfordiae	Honey-like and sweet.	Vivid lemon flowers, lightly blotched with brown, during mid- and late winter.	In a rock garden or in containers on a patio.	Height: 4 inches (10cm) Spread: 3 inches (7.5cm) **Hardy bulb:** light, well-drained and slightly limy soil in full sun.

ROCK GARDENS

PLANT	SCENT	COLOR	SITUATION	CULTIVATION
MOSS				
Galanthus nivalis Common Snowdrop	Mossy fragrance.	White flowers, with green markings on the inner petals, from midwinter to early spring.	In rock gardens or naturalized in woodland.	Height: 4-8 inches (10-20cm) Spread: 4-6 inches (10-15cm) **Hardy bulb:** Moisture-retentive, slightly heavy soil and a position in light shade.
PRIMROSE				
Crocus longiflorus (syn. *Crocus odorus*)	Sweet and strongly primrose-scented.	Deep lilac flowers, with purple-blue insides and purple throats, during late summer and into autumn. It is one of the strongest-scented crocuses.	In rock gardens, window boxes and other containers and in raised beds alongside patios.	Height: 3-4 inches (7.5-10cm) Spread: 3 inches (7.5cm) **Hardy bulb:** Well-drained soil and a sheltered position in full sun or light shade.
Crocus versicolor (syn. *Crocus fragrans*)	Primrose-scented.	Variable color, from white to shades of mauve, during late winter and early spring. It is usually grown in the form 'Picturatus', with white or pale mauve flowers with purple striping.	In rock gardens and along the front of borders.	Height: 4 inches (10cm) Spread: 2½-3 inches (6.5-7.5cm) **Hardy bulb:** Well-drained soil and a position in full sun or light shade.
Tulipa saxatalis	Faintly primrose-like.	Bright pinkish-lilac flowers with deep yellow centers during mid- to late spring.	In a large rock garden or at the base of a warm wall.	Height: 1-1½ft (30-45cm) Spread: 6-8 inches (15-20cm) **Hardy bulb:** Well-drained, slightly alkaline, light and rather poor soil, in full sun.
RESIN				
Chamaecyparis pisifera 'Filifera Nana' Sawara Cypress	Resinous fragrance.	Compact and graceful outline with medium-green foliage.	In a large rock garden or in a large tub on a patio.	Height: 2-3ft (60-90cm) Spread: 2-2½ft (60-70cm) **Evergreen conifer:** Well-drained soil in full sun or light shade.
Chamaecyparis pisifera 'Nana'	Resinous fragrance.	Bun-shaped, with dark green foliage.	In a rock garden.	Height: 6-8 inches (15-20cm) Spread: 10-12 inches (23-30cm) **Evergreen conifer:** Well-drained soil in full sun or light shade.
Chamaecyparis pisifera 'Nana Aureovariegata'	Resinous.	Bun-shaped, with golden variegations to the dark green foliage.	In a rock garden.	Height: 6-8 inches (15-20cm) Spread: 10-12 inches (25-30cm) **Evergreen conifer:** Well-drained soil in full sun or light shade.
Chamaecyparis pisifera 'Sungold'	Resinous.	Mop-head outline, with thread-like, golden-yellow foliage.	In a large rock garden.	Height: 20-24 inches (50-60cm) Spread: 20-24 inches (50-60cm) **Evergreen conifer:** Well-drained soil in full sun or light shade.
RESIN AND PARSLEY				
Chamaecyparis lawsoniana 'Aurea Densa' Lawson Cypress	Crushed foliage emits a fragrance reminiscent of resin and parsley.	Dome-shaped, densely packed with upright fans of bright golden-yellow foliage.	In a large rock garden or in a tub on a patio.	Height: 12-22 inches (30-56cm) Spread: 12-18 inches (30-45cm) **Evergreen conifer:** Well-drained soil in full sun or light shade.
Chamaecyparis lawsoniana 'Gimbornii'	Crushed foliage emits a fragrance reminiscent of resin and parsley.	Neat, compact and rounded outline, with soft blue-green leaves.	In a large rock garden or in a tub on a patio.	Height: 1½-2ft (45-60cm) Spread: 15-18 inches (38-45cm) **Evergreen conifer:** Well-drained soil in full sun or light shade.
Chamaecyparis lawsoniana 'Minima'	Crushed foliage emits a fragrance reminiscent of resin and parsley.	A globular outline with neat sprays of green foliage.	In a large rock garden or in a tub on a patio.	Height: 2½-3ft (75-90cm) Spread: 2½-3ft (75-90cm) **Evergreen conifer:** Well-drained soil in full sun or light shade.

ROCK GARDENS				
PLANT	**SCENT**	**COLOR**	**SITUATION**	**CULTIVATION**
RESIN AND PARSLEY				
Chamaecyparis lawsoniana 'Minima Aurea'	Crushed foliage emits a fragrance reminiscent of resin and parsley.	Conical shape, with nearly vertical sprays of golden-yellow foliage.	In a large rock garden or in a tub on a patio.	Height: 2½-3ft (75-90cm) Spread: 2½-3ft (75-90cm) **Evergreen conifer:** Well-drained soil in full sun or light shade.
Chamaecyparis lawsoniana 'Minima Glauca'	Crushed foliage emits a fragrance reminiscent of resin and parsley.	Globular bush with densely packed sprays of sea-green foliage.	In a large rock garden or in a tub on a patio.	Height: 2½-3ft (75-90cm) Spread: 2½-3ft (75-90cm) **Evergreen conifer:** Well-drained soil in full sun or light shade.
Chamaecyparis lawsoniana 'Nana Lutea'	Crushed foliage emits a fragrance reminiscent of resin and parsley.	Conical outline with sprays of bright yellow foliage that retain their color throughout winter.	In a large rock garden.	Height: 20-24 inches (50-60cm) Spread: 12-18 inches (30-45cm) **Evergreen conifer:** Well-drained soil in full sun or light shade.
Chamaecyparis lawsoniana 'Pygmaea'	Crushed foliage emits a fragrance reminiscent of resin and parsley.	Globular and mounded outline, with gray-green foliage.	In a rock garden or in a tub on a patio.	Height: 12 inches (30cm) Spread: 12 inches (30cm) **Evergreen conifer:** Well-drained soil in full sun or light shade.
Chamaecyparis lawsoniana 'Pygmaea Argentea'	Crushed foliage emits a fragrance reminiscent of resin and parsley.	Conical outline, with bluish-green foliage tipped creamy-white.	In a large rock garden or in a tub on a patio.	Height: 1–1½ft (30-45cm) Spread: 1-1½ft (30-45cm) **Evergreen conifer:** Well-drained soil in full sun or light shade.
SOAP OR PAINT				
Juniperus virginiana 'Globosa' Red Cedar	Soap or paint-like aroma when foliage is crushed.	Rounded and dense habit with scale-like, bright green leaves.	In a large rock garden or in a low tub on a patio.	Height: 2½-3ft (75-90cm) Spread: 2½-3ft (75-90cm) **Evergreen conifer:** Well-drained soil in full sun or light shade.
WARM AND GINGERY				
Chamaecyparis thyoides 'Ericoides' White Cedar	Crushed foliage emits a warm and gingery fragrance.	Conical and compact outline, with sea-green foliage in summer that becomes bronze-purple during winter.	In a large rock garden.	Height: 1½-2ft (45-60cm) Spread: 1½-2ft (45-60cm) **Evergreen conifer:** Well-drained soil in full sun or light shade.
Chamaecyparis thyoides 'Rubicon'	Crushed foliage emits a warm and gingery fragrance.	Compact form, with bronze-green foliage in summer that becomes a rich wine-red in winter.	In a large rock garden.	Height: 1½-2ft (45-60cm) Spread: 1½-2ft (45-60cm) **Evergreen conifer:** Well-drained soil in full sun or light shade.
WARM AND SWEET				
Chamaecyparis obtusa 'Kosteri' Hinoki Cypress	When crushed the foliage emits a warm and sweet aroma.	Dwarf, conical outline with flattened, moss-like sprays of bright green foliage that becomes bronze during winter.	In a large rock garden or in a tub on a patio.	Height: 2½-3ft (75-90cm) Spread: 2ft (60cm) **Evergreen conifer:** Well-drained soil in full sun or light shade.
Chamaecyparis obtusa 'Nana'	When crushed the foliage emits a warm and sweet aroma.	Dwarf, flat-topped dome with flattened sprays of dark green foliage.	In a large rock garden or in a tub on a patio.	Height: 1½-2ft (45-60cm) Spread: 1½-2ft (45-60cm) **Evergreen conifer:** Well-drained soil in full sun or light shade.
Chamaecyparis obtusa 'Nana Aurea'	When crushed the foliage emits a warm and sweet aroma.	Dwarf, flat-topped dome with flattened sprays of golden-tinged foliage.	In a large rock garden or in a tub on a patio.	Height: 1½-2ft (45-60cm) Spread: 1½-2ft (45-60cm) **Evergreen conifer:** Well-drained soil in full sun or light shade.
Chamaecyparis obtusa 'Pygmaea'	When crushed the foliage emits a warm and sweet aroma.	Flat-topped outline with fan-like sprays of bronze-green foliage, tinged reddish-bronze in winter.	In a large rock garden or in a tub on a patio.	Height: 9-12 inches (23-30cm) Spread: 2-3ft (60-90cm) **Evergreen conifer:** Well-drained soil in full sun or light shade.

ROCK GARDENS				
PLANT	SCENT	COLOR	SITUATION	CULTIVATION
VIOLET				
Galanthus elwesii Giant Snowdrop	Violet-scented.	White flowers, with deep green markings on the inner petals, during late winter and early spring.	In a rock garden or in naturalized borders and woodland.	Height: 6-10 inches (15-25cm) Spread: 4-6 inches (10-15cm) **Hardy bulb:** Moisture-retentive soil in light shade.
Iris bakeriana	Strongly violet-scented.	Somewhat variable, but usually available with pale blue standards and dark purple-blue falls, flowering mid- to late winter.	In a rock garden or in containers on a patio.	Height: 5-6 inches (13-15cm) Spread: 3 inches (7.5cm) **Hardy bulb:** Light, well-drained and slightly limy soil in full sun.
Iris reticulata Netted Iris	Violet-scented.	Deep blue-purple flowers, with the falls displaying orange blazes, during late winter and early spring.	In a rock garden or in containers on a patio.	Height: 6 inches (15cm) Spread: 3 inches (7.5cm) **Hardy bulb:** Light, well-drained and slightly limy soil in full sun.
SWEET				
Crocus sativus Saffron Crocus	Sweet and somewhat mossy.	Rich red-purple flowers, with large red stigmas and orange anthers, during late summer. Flowers are usually only produced during warm summers in mild areas.	A warm, sheltered pocket in a rock garden or against a sunny wall.	Height: 4 inches (10cm) Spread: 2½-3 inches (6.5-7.5cm) **Somewhat tender bulb:** Well-drained, rich soil and a sheltered sunny position.
Androsace pubescens	Sweet but light.	White flowers, with faint yellow centers, during early summer.	A well-prepared pocket in a rock garden or in a gravel bed.	Height: 2 inches (5cm) Spread: 6-8 inches (15-20cm) **Hardy perennial:** Well-drained, gritty soil and a sunny position.
Cyclamen hederifolium (syn. *Cyclamen neapolitanum*) Sowbread	Sweet but faint.	Color variable, from mauve to pale pink as well as white, during autumn.	In a rock garden, naturalized on a grassy bank or around shrubs.	Height: 4 inches (10cm) Spread: 4-6 inches (10-15cm) **Hardy corm:** Well-drained, compost-rich soil in light shade and away from drying winds.
Cyclamen libanoticum Sowbread	Sweet but rather musty.	Pale pink, shuttlecock-like flowers during spring.	In a sheltered rock garden in a mild area.	Height: 6 inches (15cm) Spread: 4-6 inches (10-15cm) **Tender corm:** Well-drained, compost-rich soil in light shade and well away from drying winds.
Cyclamen purpurascens (syn. *Cyclamen europaeum*) Sowbread	Sweet.	Rich carmine, shuttlecock-like flowers from midsummer to autumn amid kidney-shaped leaves with silvery markings.	In a rock garden, naturalized on a grassy bank or around shrubs.	Height: 4 inches (10cm) Spread: 4-6 inches (10-15cm) **Hardy corm:** Well-drained, compost-rich soil in light shade and away from drying winds.
Cyclamen repandum Sowbread	Sweet.	Rich pink, shuttlecock-like flowers with twisted petals from spring into summer.	In a rock garden, naturalized on a grassy bank or around shrubs.	Height: 4-6 inches (10-15cm) Spread: 6 inches (15cm) **Hardy corm:** Well-drained, compost-rich soil in light shade and away from drying winds.
Daphne blagayana	Deliciously sweet.	Creamy-white flowers in clustered, upward-facing heads at the ends of shoots during late spring.	Ideal for sprawling between rocks in a large rock garden.	Height: 6 inches (15cm) Spread: 3-5ft (0.9-1.5m) **Low-growing, ground-covering deciduous shrub:** Deep, loam-enriched peat or leafmold in light shade.
Daphne cneorum Garland Flower	Deliciously sweet.	Rose-pink flowers in dense terminal clusters during early summer.	In a rock garden or a narrow border.	Height: 6 inches (15cm) Spread: 2-3ft (60-90cm) **Prostrate evergreen shrub:** Often difficult to establish, but grows in well-drained, moisture-retentive soil.

ROCK GARDENS				
PLANT	SCENT	COLOR	SITUATION	CULTIVATION
SWEET				
Daphne retusa	Richly sweet.	Star-like, deep rose-purple flowers borne in terminal clusters during early and midsummer.	In a small rock garden or raised bed.	Height: 2-3ft (60-90cm) Spread: 1½-3ft (45-90cm) **Slow-growing evergreen shrub:** Well-drained, slightly alkaline soil in full sun.
Dianthus x calalpinus	Sweet.	Pink flowers, up to 1½ inches (4cm) wide and with white dots at their centers, from mid- to late summer.	In a rock garden.	Height: 3 inches (7.5cm) Spread: 6 inches (15cm) **Hardy perennial:** Well-drained, limy soil and a sunny position.
Dianthus x arvernensis	Sweet.	Pink flowers from early to late summer.	In a rock garden or along the edge of a path.	Height: 6 inches (15cm) Spread: 6 inches (15cm) **Hardy perennial:** Well-drained, limy soil in a sunny position.
Dianthus x calalpinus	Sweet.	Pink flowers, up to 1½ inches (4cm) wide and with white dots at their centers, from mid- to late-summer.	In a rock garden.	Height: 3 inches (7.5cm) Spread: 6 inches (15cm) **Hardy perennial:** Well-drained, limy soil and a sunny position.
Dianthus deltoides Maiden Pink	Sweet and slightly spicy.	Red through to pink and white flowers from midsummer to autumn. Many superb varieties.	In a rock garden or in crevices between paving.	Height: 6-9 inches (15-23cm) Spread: 4-6 inches (10-15cm) **Hardy perennial:** Well-drained, limy soil in a sunny position.
Dianthus gratianopolitanus (syn. *Dianthus caesius*) Cheddar Pink	Sweet and slightly spicy.	Pink, 1 inch (2.5cm) wide, fringed flowers from early to midsummer.	In a rock garden or at the edge of a path.	Height: 4-12 inches (10-30cm) Spread: 10-12 inches (20-30cm) **Hardy perennial:** Well-drained, limy soil in a sunny position.
Dianthus plumarius Cottage Pink/ Grass Pink	Strongly sweet.	Wide color range. The species is seldom grown, but it is, in part, a parent of the well-known garden pinks.	In a rock garden or at the edge of a path.	Height: Range from 3-15 inches (7.5-38cm) Spread: 6-9 inches (15-23cm) **Hardy perennial:** Well-drained, limy soil and a sunny position.
Dianthus superbus Fringed Pink/Sweet John	Strongly sweet, with only a hint of spice.	Pale to deep lilac, or occasionally white, flowers 1½ inches (4cm) wide, during late summer.	Low-growing varieties in rock gardens and alongside paths, tall ones in perennial borders.	Height: 9-18 inches (23-45cm) Spread: 6-9 inches (15-23cm) **Short-lived hardy perennial, best treated as a biennial:** Well-drained, limy soil in a sunny position.
Galanthus nivalis reginae-olgae Snowdrop	Sweet and heather-like.	White flowers, with green markings on the inner petals, very similar to *Galanthus nivalis*. However, it flowers much earlier, in autumn, before the leaves appear.	In a rock garden or naturalized in woodland.	Height: 4-8 inches (10-20cm) Spread: 4-6 inches (10-15cm) **Hardy bulb:** Moisture-retentive, light soil in light shade or full sun.
Iris histrioides	Sweet.	Dark blue flowers, with paler and spotted area around an orange crest, during midwinter. Several varieties are available, including 'Major', which has bright royal blue flowers up to 3½ inches (8cm) wide.	In a rock garden.	Height: 4-6 inches (10-15cm) Spread: 3-4 inches (7.5-10cm) **Hardy bulb:** Light, well-drained and slightly limy soil in full sun.
Leucojum vernum Spring Snowflake	Sweet.	White flowers, tipped with green, in late winter and early spring.	In a rock garden or for naturalizing in grass.	Height: 8 inches (20cm) Spread: 3-4 inches (7.5-10cm) **Hardy bulb:** Well-drained but moisture-retentive soil and full sun or light shade.

ROCK GARDENS

PLANT	SCENT	COLOR	SITUATION	CULTIVATION
SWEET				
Linnaea borealis Twin Flower	Sweet, resembling meadowsweet.	Trumpet-shaped, flesh-pink flowers borne in pairs from the tops of stems from early to midsummer.	In a rock garden.	Height: 2-3 inches (5-7.5cm) Spread: 1-1½ft (30-45cm) **Hardy evergreen shrub:** Peaty, moisture-retentive soil in light or full shade.
Narcissus calcicola	Sweet.	Deep yellow flowers with flattened cups during mid-spring.	In a rock garden or a cool greenhouse.	Height: 6 inches (15cm) Spread: 3-4 inches (7.5-10cm) **Hardy bulb:** Well-drained but moisture-retentive, rich soil in light shade.
Narcissus juncifolius Rush-leaved Jonquil	Sweet.	Deep yellow flowers with flattened cups during late spring and early summer.	In a rock garden or a cool greenhouse.	Height: 3-6 inches (7.5-15cm) Spread: 3-4 inches (7.5-10cm) **Somewhat hardy bulb:** Well-drained but moisture-retentive, rich soil in light shade.
Narcissus minor	Sweet.	Variable species, but usually with pale petals and deeper yellow trumpets, during early spring.	In a rock garden.	Height: 8 inches (20cm) Spread: 3-4 inches (7.5-10cm) **Hardy bulb:** Well-drained but moisture-retentive, rich soil in light shade.
Narcissus triandrus var. *concolor* Angel's-Tears	Sweet.	Golden-yellow flowers during spring.	In a rock garden.	Height: 3-4 inches (7.5-10cm) Spread: 2½-3 inches (6.5-7.5cm) **Hardy bulb:** Well-drained but moisture-retentive, rich soil in light shade.
Primula auricula Auricula Primrose/ Common Auricula	Slightly sweet.	Yellow or purple flowers, ¾ inch (18mm) wide, during mid-spring and into early summer. Varieties are available in many other colors, including blue and dark red.	In a rock garden.	Height: 6 inches (15cm) Spread: 6 inches (15cm) **Hardy perennial:** Well-drained, compost-rich soil in full sun or light shade.
Saxifraga cotyledon	Lightly sweet.	Plume-like sprays of white flowers from mid- to late summer. 'Southside Seedling' is especially attractive.	In a rock garden.	Height: 15-18 inches (38-45cm) Spread: 12-15 inches (30-38cm) **Evergreen perennial:** Well-drained, slightly limy soil in full sun or slight shade.
Tulipa aucherana (syn. *Tulipa aucheriana*)	Very sweet.	Pink flowers with yellow centers during mid- to late spring. This species is often considered to be a form of *Tulipa humilis*.	In a rock garden.	Height: 3-5 inches (7.5-13cm) Spread: 3-4 inches (7.5-10cm) **Hardy bulb:** Well-drained, light and slightly alkaline soil.
Tulipa gesnerana	Sweet and fruity fragrance.	Variable species, with bell-shaped, bright scarlet flowers with black centers and purple stamens, during late spring and early summer.	In a rock garden.	Height: 5-8 inches (13-20cm) Spread: 4-5 inches (10-13cm) **Hardy bulb:** Well-drained, light and slightly alkaline soil.
Tulipa sylvestris	Lightly sweet.	Yellow flowers, 2 inches (5cm) long with reflexed outer petals, during mid- to late spring.	In a rock garden.	Height: 8-10 inches (20-25cm) Spread: 5-6 inches (13-15cm) **Hardy bulb:** Well-drained, light and slightly alkaline soil.

WATER GARDENS

Of all the features in a garden, a pond is often the most captivating and interesting, especially if it provides a setting for scented plants. There are fragrant plants such as water lilies that are true aquatics and grow in water, as well as a wide range of primroses and other plants that find an ideal home in the wet and boggy areas around a pond.

The movement, reflective nature and music of splashing fountains are all elements of a water garden scene that can be further enriched by scents. The Sweet-scented Rush, *Acorus calamus*, has many names that indicate its perfume – Sweet Flag, Sweet Root, Sweet Rush, Sweet Myrtle and Cinnamon Sedge. It is this last name that gives the important clue to the pleasing scent of the long stems, which is sweetly cinnamon-like.

Confusingly, the common name Sweet Flag may indicate that it is a member of the iris family, but this is not so. It belongs to the arum family and bears rather insignificant but sweetly scented, yellowish flowers. It is the agreeable, sweet and persistent aroma of the stems and leaves through which the plant gains acclaim. The stone floors of medieval castles, halls and churches were strewn with the plant as a way of combating the winter weather and to cloak the smells of damp and decay which were so prevalent at the time.

One of the charges levied against Cardinal Wolsey by Henry VIII, and which led to his prosecution in 1529, was one of extravagence – that he was in the habit of too frequently strewing his floors with fresh flags that had to be brought from distances up to 100 miles (160 km) away from the counties of Suffolk and Norfolk.

The variegated form *Acorus calamus* 'Variegatus' is visually more exciting and better suited to small gardens. The broad, stiff and erect sword-like leaves are striped with a cream color.

For a blending of sweet cinnamon leaves and vanilla-scented flowers, plant the aquatic Water Hawthorn, *Aponogeton distachyos*, along with the Sweet Flag. Its narrowly oval, light green leaves rest on the water's surface, while clusters of vanilla-scented, deeply-lobed white flowers with

For added interest, water gardens can be combined with other, complimentary features such as trees, shrubs and a variety of moisture-loving plants.

distinctive black anthers hold their faces a few inches above the surface. It looks best when the leaves can spread on the surface, unimpeded by other plants. The Water Hawthorn comes from South Africa, where it gained the name Cape Asparagus because the flower heads were picked, cooked and eaten.

If the tangy redolence of mint appeals, then the Water Mint, *Mentha aquatica*, will not disappoint you. Its leaves and stems, with their strong, minty aroma, have been used to strew the floors of churches and kitchens to create a fresh ambience. The aroma of mint lingers for a long time on the hands if you crush the stems and leaves. The scent can be overpowering, so take care not to plant it close to plants whose fragrance is attractive but slight.

The Yellow Water Lily, *Nuphar lutea*, is eye-catching, with its bright yellow flowers. These have a faint aroma of brandy, giving rise to another of its common names, Brandy Bottle. When planted in a bold group close to the edge of a pond it never fails to draw attention, attracting the nose as well as the eye.

Other water lilies bear scented flowers, usually not as strongly aromatic but enough to create a further dimension to their beautiful flowers. The pond that does not have at least one water lily growing in it is a rarity, and the range of colors within this group of scented aquatic plants is wide enough to suit most tastes. These include *Nymphaea odorata* 'Sulphurea' with primrose-yellow flowers, the Cape Cod Lily *N. o.* 'Rosea' with pale pink flowers, *N. o.* 'Minor', star-shaped and white, and *N. o.* 'Alba', which displays white flowers with yellow centers. There are many others, some of which are described on pages 66 to 67. The original form of this water lily is native to sluggish streams, ponds and marshes in North America, and invariably grows near the coast. Its several common names indicate its sweet fragrance – Sweet Water Lily, Sweet-scented Water Lily, Fragrant Water Lily and Water Nymph.

The Swamp Lizard, *Saururus cernuus*, is another North American water plant with scented flowers. It grows best in shallow water at the side of a pool, where its white, sweetly scented flowers are borne amid bright green, heart-shaped leaves. Its roots,

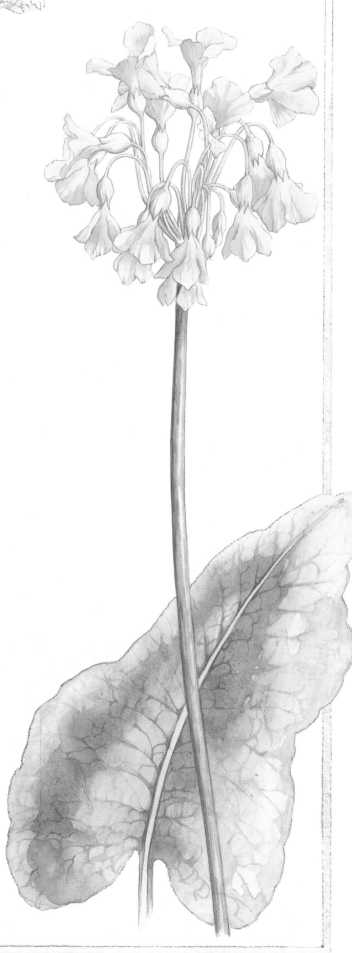

The water lily, above, is the most evocative of all water plants. The Giant Cowslip (Primula florindae), right, has richly sweet yellow flowers. Primroses, far right, enliven the edges of streams and ponds.

like those of the water lily, can be used medicinally, both as a poultice in the treatment of wounds and as a sedative.

Adding a pleasing scent to a garden pond is only part of the skill of water gardening. The surrounding area, often boggy and particular about the nature of plants introduced to it, can be given a rich redolence with plants that will reappear year after year with little trouble. Primroses head this list, and foremost must be the Giant Cowslip or Bog Primula, *Primula florindae*, which has lusciously sweet flowers. As if the heady bouquet were not enough, the pale yellow flowers are borne in large, dominant, drooping clusters that last for several months. Few sights in the garden can be quite as eye-catching as a large drift of this Tibetan giant. The Himalayan Cowslip, *P. sikkimensis*, is not so showy, but when planted in a large drift creates a superb display of sweetly scented, pale yellow, funnel-shaped pendant flowers. *P. vialii* is rather unusual, with spire-like heads densely packed with lavender-blue flowers. Plant it in large groupings to get the full benefit of its scent. If the soil starts to become drier, with slight shade, at the outer edges of the moist area around the pool, then this is the spot in which to plant small clusters of the English Primrose, *P. vulgaris*. Plant it to bring to your garden the fragrance of the countryside in spring, even though you may live in a town or city – all that you need is fertile, moisture-retentive soil.

The sweetly scented Cape Cod Lily
(Nymphaea odorata 'Rosea').

WATER GARDENS				
PLANT	SCENT	COLOR	SITUATION	CULTIVATION
BRANDY				
Nuphar lutea Yellow Water Lily/ Brandy Bottle	Faint brandy scent.	Bright yellow flowers, 2-3 inches (5-7.5cm) wide, protruding several inches out of the water amid oval leaves up to 15 inches (38cm) wide. Flowering period is mid- to late summer.	Only suitable for planting in a large pool.	Height: Leaves float on surface Spread: 4-6ft (1.2-1.8m) or more **Hardy perennial water plant:** Plant in water 1½-3ft (45-90cm) deep.
CINNAMON				
Acorus calamus Sweet Flag/Sweet Scented Rush	Sweet and persistent, slightly resembling cinnamon. All parts of the plant, including the roots, have an agreeable aroma.	Yellowish-green, upright, sword-like leaves and yellowish flowers on long stems during midsummer.	At the edge of a pond, in 3-5 inches (7.5-13cm) of water.	Height: 2-3ft (60-90cm) Spread: 18 inches (45cm) **Hardy herbaceous perennial:** Plant the rhizomes just below the surface of the compost.
Acorus calamus 'Variegatus' Variegated Sweet Flag	Sweet and persistent, slightly resembling cinnamon. All parts of the plant, including the roots, have an agreeable aroma.	Broad, stiffly erect, sword-like leaves striped with white.	At the edge of a pond, in 3-5 inches (7.5-13cm) of water. Position as a backdrop for small plants or as a feature on its own.	Height: 2-2½ft (60-75cm) Spread: 18 inches (45cm) **Hardy herbaceous perennial:** Plant the rhizomes just below the surface of the soil.
MINT				
Mentha aquatica Water Mint/Marsh Mint/Wild Mint	Strongly mint-like.	Aromatic purple stems and small, lance-like leaves. Lilac to purple flowers in heads up to 1 inch (2.5cm) wide during summer.	At the edge of a pond or in a marshy position.	Height: 1½-2½ft (45-75cm) Spread: 18 inches (45cm) **Hardy perennial:** Plant in fertile soil in 1-2 inches (2.5-5cm) of water. It is reputed to keep water clear.
TANGY				
Houttuynia cordata 'Plena'	Tangy aroma.	White, clustered flower heads borne on short stems during summer amid metallic, blue-green, heart-shaped leaves.	In wet soil or 1-2 inches (2.5-5cm) of water at the edge of a pond. Once established it may become invasive.	Height: 12-18 inches (30-45cm) Spread: 9-12 inches (23-30cm) **Hardy herbaceous perennial:** Fertile soil in light, dappled shade. Plant dormant runners horizontally, 3 inches (7.5cm) deep, in spring or autumn. Cut back invasive plants in autumn.
VANILLA				
Aponogeton distachyos Water Hawthorn/ Cape Pondweed	Vanilla-scented flowers.	White, deeply-lobed flowers with black anthers rising in forked clusters up to 4 inches (10cm) wide. Flowers protrude a few inches above the water's surface from midsummer to early autumn. The narrowly oval, light green leaves with maroon-brown markings rest on the water's surface.	Position several feet from the edge of the pond so that the leaves can spread freely.	Height: Water surface Surface spread: 15-24 inches (38-60cm) **Hardy herbaceous perennial:** Plant in fertile soil in water 8-18 inches (20-45cm) deep, in full sun or slight shade; it flowers best when in full sun.

WATER GARDENS				
PLANT	**SCENT**	**COLOR**	**SITUATION**	**CULTIVATION**
SWEET				
Nymphaea 'Brackleyi Rosea' Water Lily	Sweet.	Rose-pink flowers, freely borne from mid- to late summer.	Treat as for *N. odorata* 'Alba' (see below).	Height: Leaves float on surface Spread: 2½-3½ft (0.75-1m) **Hardy perennial water plant:** Treat as for *N. odorata* 'Alba' but plant in water 1-2½ft (30-75cm) deep.
Nymphaea 'Caroliniana Perfecta' Water Lily	Sweet.	Pale cerise flowers from mid- to late summer.	Treat as for *N. odorata* 'Alba' (see below).	Height: Leaves float on surface Spread: 1½-2ft (45-60cm) **Hardy perennial water plant:** Treat as for *N. odorata* 'Alba', but plant in water 9-12 inches (23-30cm) deep.
Nymphaea 'Gloire du Temple-sur-Lot' Water Lily	Sweet.	Double, salmon-pink flowers, becoming deep cream with age, from mid- to late summer.	Treat as for *N. odorata* 'Alba' (see below).	Height: Leaves float on surface Spread: 2-3ft (60-90cm) **Hardy perennial water plant:** Treat as for *N. odorata* 'Alba' but plant in water 15-18 inches (38-45cm) deep.
Nymphaea odorata 'Alba' Water Lily	Sweet but slight.	White, yellow-centered flowers from mid- to late summer.	Position each basket of water lilies at a distance away from the edge of the pond that equals the indicated spread of the plant. If the pond is large, position the lilies towards the outside. Take care that the plants do not totally cover the pond's surface.	Height: Leaves float on surface Spread: 1½-2ft (45-60cm) **Hardy perennial water plant:** Fertile soil and a sunny position. Plant the roots during late spring and early summer in a plastic-mesh basket and position in water 12-15 inches (30-38cm) deep. It may initially be necessary to stand the basket on a brick so that young leaves are not totally submerged. As they grow, remove the brick and stand the basket on the base of the pond. Remove dead flowers and leaves and cut back and replant rampant plants in spring.
Nymphaea odorata 'Minor' Water Lily	Sweet but faint.	White, star-shaped flowers, 2-3 inches (5-7.5cm) wide, from mid- to late summer.	Treat as for *N. odorata* 'Alba' (see above).	Height: Leaves float on surface Spread: 12-15 inches (30-38cm) **Hardy perennial water plant:** Treat as for *N. odorata* 'Alba', but plant in water 9-12 inches (23-30cm) deep.
Nymphaea odorata 'Rosea' Cape Cod Lily	Sweet but slight.	Pale pink flowers from mid- to late summer.	Treat as for *N. odorata* 'Alba' (see above).	Height: Leaves float on surface Spread: 2-3ft (60-90cm) **Hardy perennial water plant:** Treat as for *N. odorata* 'Alba', but plant in water 1-2ft (30-60cm) deep.
Nymphaea odorata 'Sulphurea' Water Lily	Sweet but faint.	Primrose-yellow flowers, 3 inches (7.5cm) wide, from mid- to late summer.	Treat as for *N. odorata* 'Alba' (see above).	Height: Leaves float on surface Spread: 2½-3ft (75-90cm) **Hardy perennial water plant:** Treat as for *N. odorata* 'Alba', but plant in water 15-18 inches (38-45cm) deep.
Nymphaea odorata 'Sulphurea Grandiflora' Sweet Water Lily	Sweet.	Primrose-yellow flowers, 4-6 inches (10-15cm) wide, from mid- to late summer.	Treat as for *N. odorata* 'Alba' (see above).	Height: Leaves float on surface Spread: 2-2½ft (60-75cm) **Hardy perennial water plant:** Treat as for *N. odorata* 'Alba' but plant in water 12-15 inches (30-38cm) deep.

WATER GARDENS

PLANT	SCENT	COLOR	SITUATION	CULTIVATION
SWEET				
Nymphaea odorata 'Turicensis' Water Lily	Sweet.	Pale pink flowers, 3-4 inches (7.5-10cm) wide, from mid- to late summer.	Treat as for *N. odorata* 'Alba' (see opposite).	Height: Leaves float on surface Spread: 2-3ft (60-90cm) **Hardy perennial water plant:** Treat as for *N. odorata* 'Alba' but plant in water 12-15 inches (30-38cm) deep.
Nymphaea odorata 'W. B. Shaw' Water Lily	Sweet.	Soft oyster-pink, star-shaped flowers from mid- to late summer.	Treat as for *N. odorata* 'Alba' (see opposite).	Height: Leaves float on surface Spread: 2-3ft (60-90cm) **Hardy perennial water plant:** Treat as for *N. odorata* 'Alba' but plant in water 12-18 inches (30-45cm) deep.
Nymphaea tuberosa 'Rosea' Water Lily	Strongly sweet.	Shell-pink flowers, 4-6 inches (10-15cm) wide, from mid- to late summer.	Treat as for *N. odorata* 'Alba' (see opposite).	Height: Leaves float on surface Spread: 2-3ft (60-90cm) **Hardy perennial water plant:** Treat as for *N. odorata* 'Alba' but plant in water 12-18 inches (30-45cm) deep.
Primula alpicola (syn. *P. microdonta alpicola*)	Delicately sweet.	Pale yellow flowers in drooping clusters during midsummer.	In moist soil around a pond. Position the plants in small groups, so that the scent is accentuated and there is a bold color display.	Height: 15-20 inches (38-50cm) Spread: 6-9 inches (15-23cm) **Hardy perennial:** Plant in fertile, moisture-retentive soil in full sun or light shade. Keep the soil moist during dry summers and mulch with damp peat in spring.
Primula florindae Giant Cowslip	Richly sweet.	Pale yellow, bell-shaped flowers in drooping clusters during midsummer. Light orange to blood-red forms are available.	In a moist area around a pond. Position the plants in small groups, so that the scent is accentuated and there is a bold display of color.	Height: 2-2½ft (60-75cm) Spread: 12-15 inches (30-38cm) **Hardy perennial:** Plant in fertile, moisture-retentive soil in full sun or light shade. Keep the soil moist during dry summers and mulch with damp peat in spring.
Primula sikkimensis Himalayan Cowslip	Delicately sweet.	Pale yellow, funnel-shaped, pendant flowers in clusters during midsummer.	In a moist area around a pond. Position the plants in small groups, so that the scent is accentuated and there is a bold display of color.	Height: 15-18 inches (38-45cm) Spread: 9-12 inches (23-30cm) **Hardy perennial:** Plant in fertile, moisture-retentive soil in full sun or light shade. Keep the soil moist during dry summers and mulch with damp peat in spring.
Primula vialii	Delicately sweet.	Lavender-blue flowers in dense spikes 3-5 inches (7.5-13cm) long during midsummer.	In a moist area around a pond. Position the plants in small groups, so that the scent is accentuated and there is a bold display of color.	Height: 9-12 inches (23-30cm) Spread: 6-8 inches (15-20cm) **Hardy perennial:** Plant in fertile, moisture-retentive soil in full sun or slight shade. Keep the soil moist during dry summers and mulch with damp peat in spring.
Primula vulgaris (syn. *P. acaulis*) English Primrose	Delicately sweet.	Yellow flowers with deeper yellow centers during spring.	Plant towards the outer edges of the moist areas around a pond. Position the plants in small groups, so that the scent is accentuated and there is a bold display of color.	Height: 6 inches (15cm) Spread: 9 inches (23cm) **Hardy perennial:** Plant in fertile, moisture-retentive soil, although it will survive drier conditions than the other primroses in this chapter.
Saururus cernuus Swamp Lily/Lizard's Tail	Sweet.	White flowers amid bright green, heart-shaped leaves during midsummer.	At the edge of a pond.	Height: 12 inches (30cm) Spread: 12 inches (30cm) **Hardy herbaceous perennial:** Plant in moist soil or in water up to 2 inches (5cm) deep, in full sun or light shade.

CHAPTER FIVE

Scents at the Window

*The captivating scent and bright
colors of plants grown in window
boxes will enliven a house both
inside and out.*

CENTLESS window boxes and tubs are rather like strawberries without cream. Flowers that are only colorful certainly feast the eyes and enrich the exterior of the house, but they do not have the near-magical quality that scented flowers possess of making heads turn suddenly, of stopping visitors in mid-sentence or of creating a feeling of being in total harmony with the garden.

Patio plants are ambassadors for the rest of the garden. They act like a preface for a book, but unlike most forewords, which pass into posterity unread, they are immediately noticeable.

There are many ways of displaying plants on patios and around windows. Tubs, troughs, ornamental wheelbarrows, urns and large clay pots all compete to create a setting for patio scent and color, but window boxes are the real vanguards of a perfumed window garden. Evening and night-scented plants are a special delight on patios and under windows, and are described in Chapter 2. Colorful plants brighten the day, but if they are also richly aromatic their value is increased tenfold.

WINDOW BOXES

The range of plants that can be used in window boxes is wide. Early in the year flowering bulbs or biennial plants that were planted at the end of the previous season will be in bloom, while during summer there is a large variety of colors and shapes available from summer-flowering bedding plants.

As well as seasonal plants for spring and summer displays, permanent types like aromatic miniature conifers and small, evergreen, sweetly flowered shrubs can be planted in window boxes. Colorful and transient plants, such as stocks, crocuses, some irises, hyacinths, violets and primroses can be set between these larger plants to add variety and further scent and color.

The skill of gardening is not just one of sowing, growing and harvesting, but of selecting plants for special or difficult places, of choosing types that will grow happily together, creating a pleasing picture which will harmonize with their backgrounds. Blending window box plants into their locations is an essential ingredient for success on patios.

The sweetly scented Polyanthus Primrose (Primula polyantha), *with its sparkling range of colors, is perfect for creating a bright, perfume-packed patio in spring.*

WHITE WALLS IN SPRING

White walls are superb for showing off yellow, blue, gold and scarlet flowers. In spring the stiff, upright and soldier-like spires of blue hyacinths (*Hyacinthus orientalis*) create a superb picture. For added scent and an attractive color combination try the deep blue 'Ostara' or 'King of the Blues' with primroses set between them. The yellow primrose flowers, with deeper-colored centers, combine with their green, corrugated, spoon-shaped leaves to present a startling combination with the hyacinths. Blue hyacinths also harmonize with the double white flowers of *Arabis caucasica* 'Flore-plena', descriptively known as Snow in Summer. Perversely, as if to contradict its common name, it flowers in early spring.

Violets, the symbol of humility, also blend with hyacinths: yellow or white forms are best with blue hyacinths. They cover the ground with green leaves, creating a feeling of vitality early in the year.

The double-flowered form of the ubiquitous daisy, so often removed with chemicals from the immaculate but characterless lawns of many houses, forms a happy companionship with red Wallflowers (*Cheiranthus cheiri*). The bright white faces of the daisies create a background for the powerfully scented Wallflowers; choose low-growing forms of the latter so that the height of the flowers is not out of balance with the size of the window box. The pleasure created by this highly fragrant plant is revealed in the early name of Chevisaunce or Cherisaunce, an old word for comfort. Its long and frequent planting in gardens has certainly created a sense of comfort and reassurance with most gardeners. Apart from its superb scent, it is easy to grow and is available in a wide range of colors, including white, orange, crimson and purple.

Another superb spring-flowering combination for planting in window boxes against a white wall is golden Wallflowers and blue Forget-me-nots (*Myosotis*). The distinctive name Forget-me-not preserves the memory of an enchanting old legend that after all plants had been named a small, dreamy, pale blue flower forgot hers. She was so distressed that the bestower of names visited her; he did not tell her the name she had forgotten, but answered *Forget-me-not*.

For a honey-like fragrance *Crocus chrysanthus* has few peers. When planting bulbs against a white background choose gold and yellow forms, setting them close together so that the box becomes a sea of color.

WHITE WALLS IN SUMMER

With summer comes a wealth of scented flowers and foliage and few enrich the air better than geraniums. There are flowering types to suit all window boxes but the ones with aromatic leaves are best in tubs or positioned at the back of wide window boxes.

The fragrance of scented geranium leaves is captivating. The Lemon-scented Geranium (*Pelargonium crispum*) is cloaked in a balm-like aroma reminiscent of lemon. The bouquet is more apparent when the leaves are crushed. Do not use the variegated form, which has creamy-white-edged leaves, against a white wall, as their color impact is lost.

The Peppermint Geranium (*Pelargonium tomentosum*) has peppermint-scented leaves when crushed. Its mound-forming habit demands a large container, allowing the spread of the softly hairy, shallow-lobed, pale green leaves.

The leaves of the Rose-scented Geranium (*Pelargonium graveolens*) are, as its name implies, rose-scented when crushed. The rose-pink flowers are a bonus from mid- to late summer. For a feast of apple scents, try *Pelargonium odoratissimum*, with its light green, round leaves. All of these pelargoniums are quickly damaged by frost, so do not plant them out until all risk of cold weather has passed. For further information on pelargoniums see Chapter 10.

One of the marigolds, *Tagetes lucida*, has fragrant, golden or orange-yellow flowers that seem to reach out when grown against a white background. The African Marigold (*Tagetes erecta*), however, has received contrasting opinions about its scent. An early botanist talked of the flowers as having the aroma of new wax or a honeycomb, but nearly a century and a half later another referred to them as stinking flowers!

Botanists from a century or so ago would have been just as scathing about nasturtiums, those sprawling, round-leaved summer beauties that are frequently planted to soften the outlines of window boxes, tubs and troughs. The scented, semi-double Gleam strains did not originate until the 1930s, and were raised from plants growing in a cottage garden in California. The yellow, orange and scarlet shades of these plants are superb against a white background.

RED BRICK WALLS IN SPRING

To many eyes, a large area of red brick wall is too dominant and needs to be tastefully subdued with plants. Flower colors that blend best with red walls are white, soft blue, silver and lemon. For a spring display, the ever reliant Forget-me-not creates a soft-edged outline and a slightly cottage-garden appearance. It is a bushy, hardy perennial, but best grown

as a biennial, creating a wealth of azure-blue flowers with distinctive yellow eyes on plants 3-8 inches (7.5-20cm) high. Many varieties are available, some white, but for a red background use the blue ones.

The English Daisy *(Bellis perennis)* in combination with bronze and cream Wallflowers *(Cheiranthus cheiri)* creates a superbly scented and colored picture; the Wallflowers stand above a carpet of white daisies. The daisy has a colorful history and is rich in folklore. In Welsh it is known as Llygad y Dydd, meaning Eye of the Day, and Chaucer referred to it as the Day's Eye in the 14th century. In Scotland it was known as Bairnwort, in reference to the millions of flowers picked annually by children to make daisy chains. The flowers were also of interest to lovers who pulled off the individual petals to the count of 'he loves me, he loves me not', the daisy also being known as Measure of a Lover. In medieval times the daisy was used by ladies to impart a message to knights in tournaments, meaning 'I return your affection'.

The positioning of a daisy influenced its meaning: when a lady granted a knight permission to emblazon his shield with a double daisy this was to make it widely known that she returned his affection. How-

Spring-flowering bulbs such as the honey-scented Crocus chrysanthus *(left) are superb under windows and in containers. Below is the sweetly scented Swan River Daisy* (Brachycome iberidifolia).

The Grape Hyacinth (Muscari
armeniacum) enhances a handsome
stone urn.

ever, if a lady was unsure of her sentiments towards the knight she wore a wreath of white daisies on her brow. This implied that she wished for time in which to think about her position.

This daisy is also considered to have medicinal and culinary qualities. In the 15th century it was said to be an herb for salads, but the taste of the leaves is acrid and neither cattle nor insects are apparently willing to eat them. Medicinally, an ointment prepared from daisies has been used externally to cure wounds and, indeed, the daisy derives its Latin name from its ability to staunch the wounds of battle.

RED BRICK WALLS IN SUMMER

An exciting color combination for placing against red brick walls is the dwarf form of Stock (*Matthiola incana*) and the silvery-white foliage of *Senecio bicolor* 'Diamond'. The richly clove-scented flowers of Brompton Stock – its colors include red, pink, yellow, white and purple, but choose soft pink for this combination – blend well against a red background with the deeply lobed and divided silvery-white leaves of senecio. This senecio is perhaps better known by its former botanical name *Cineraria maritima* 'Diamond'.

Sweet Alyssum (*Lobularia maritima*, often better known as *Alyssum maritimum*), has the bouquet of new-mown grass and creates a mass of white, lilac or purple flowers from mid- to late summer, completely smothering its container. For this display, select a white form that will contrast with the red wall.

GRAY STONE WALLS IN SPRING

Soft gray walls have a gentle and harmonious nature that blends well with deep blue, deep purple, pink and red flowers. Mixed Wallflowers (*Cheiranthus cheiri*) create a scented and colorful display that is a delight in window boxes. Hyacinths (*Hyacinthus orientalis*) in pink or blue produce a rather formal result on their own, but can be softened in cottage garden settings by interplanting white varieties with Forget-me-nots.

GRAY STONE WALLS IN SUMMER

Once again, Brompton Stocks (*Matthiola incana*), with their clove-like bouquet, are a superb choice, but this time in red, pink or purple. Scented geraniums are also well worth planting for a memorable display.

SCENTS AND WINDOWS

The type of window influences the ease with which scents enter homes. Sash windows enable boxes to be positioned with the plants showing above the windowledge, allowing fragrances to enter a room unhindered, whereas casement windows that open outwards dictate that the flowers must be below their base. Much of the scent is then lost to the room.

The penetratingly sweet and soldier-like heads of the Common Hyacinth (Hyacinthus orientalis) *are superb beneath windows, in containers or in raised beds.*

HANGING BASKETS, TUBS AND TROUGHS

While window boxes are the chief glorifiers of windows, hanging baskets, troughs and tubs can also be used. Troughs are best placed in a position out of the normal walking area but where they can be easily seen and the scented flowers most appreciated.

Hanging baskets need careful positioning, from both an aesthetic and a practical viewpoint. A couple of colorful hanging baskets secured on brackets on either side of a window, so that they leave a small area of wall between the edge of the basket and the window, are superb. Fix the brackets securely to the wall at a height at which the basket bases will be about 6ft (1.8m) above the ground. Take care to position the baskets so that the soil cannot be seen, as they never look good when viewed from above. They need daily watering during summer, so ensure easy access.

Half-baskets, resembling hanging baskets cut in half, are ideal for decorating the wall around a window. However, they are likely to drip excess water down the wall. Avoid this by lining the basket with black plastic and piercing holes in it as far to the front as possible. Do not position half-baskets as high as hanging baskets – about 3ft (90cm) from the ground is ideal. They look best with a combination of upright, branching plants and cascading types.

The midsummer flowers of Brompton Stocks (Matthiola incana) emit a richly clove-like perfume. As an added bonus, they are available in a range of vivid colors.

Large tubs on either side of a patio window – or outside a front door – look distinguished when planted with clipped Sweet Bay trees, *Laurus nobilis*, also known as Bay Laurel. The strongly aromatic, evergreen, bright green leaves (used for flavoring stews, soups and sauces) look superb throughout the year, especially when highlighted against a white background. Unfortunately, the leaves are soon damaged by severe frosts, so care must be taken.

MINIATURE ROSES FOR WINDOW BOXES

Rosarians wishing to extend the range of roses they grow can have miniature types flowering in containers such as window boxes, stone troughs and tubs. They are also ideal in very small gardens as a path edging and in raised beds. Most of them grow between 6-15 inches (15-38cm) high, forming bushy plants with almost thornless branches bearing mid-green leaves. The flowers are semi-double or double, ¾-1½ inches (18-40mm) wide and borne in small clusters during midsummer.

These small roses are best grown on their own roots rather than being grafted or budded, when they tend to lose their miniature nature.

When planting these roses, do not mix ones of contrasting size in the same container. Use the smallest varieties in window boxes, retaining the slightly higher-growing ones for tubs and larger containers. Scented varieties to plant in window boxes include:

'BABY FAURAX' Height: 12-15 inches (30-38cm)
Fragrant, semi-double, lavender-purple flowers.

'BABY GOLDSTAR' Height: 15 inches (38cm)
Slightly fragrant, cream to buttercup-yellow flowers.

'DARLING FLAME' Height: 12-15 inches (30-38cm)
Slightly fruity-scented, bright orange-red, double flowers with a gold reverse.

'LITTLE FLIRT' Height: 12 inches (30cm)
Slightly fragrant, orange-red, double flowers with gold at the base as well as on the reverse of the petals.

'SILVER TIPS' Height: 12 inches (30cm)
Slightly fragrant, pink flowers with a silver reverse, becoming soft lavender-colored.

'YELLOW DOLL' Height: 12 inches (30cm)
Slightly fragrant, soft yellow, small double flowers.

CONIFERS FOR WINDOW BOXES

The scent qualities of conifers are described in Chapters 4 and 9. As well as being grown in gardens and, occasionally, being used as part of a flower arrangement, they also create scent and color in window boxes and tubs. Obviously, not all of them are suited to the confined space and limited amount of soil in window boxes, but those that are small enough will create interest throughout the year.

PLANT	SCENT	COLOR	SITUATION	CULTIVATION
CLOVES				
Matthiola incana Brompton Stocks	Clove-like and rich.	Wide range, including red, pink, yellow, purple and white, during midsummer.	They are best planted under windows rather than in window boxes or other containers.	Height: 18 inches (45cm) Spread: 12 inches (30cm) **Hardy biennial:** Sow seeds ¼ inch (6mm) deep in a well-prepared seedbed in early summer. When the seedlings are large enough to handle, thin them to 4-6 inches (10-15cm) apart. During early autumn, transplant the young plants to their flowering position, setting them 12 inches (30cm) apart.
Matthiola incana East Lothian Stocks	Clove-like and rich.	Range includes red, pink, yellow, purple and white, from midsummer to autumn.	Plant them in window boxes or flower beds beneath windows.	Height: 15 inches (38cm) Spread: 12 inches (30cm) **Hardy biennial:** During late winter and early spring, sow seeds ¼ inch (6mm) deep in flats and keep at 61°F (16°C). When the seedlings are large enough to handle, transplant into flats of loam-based soil mix and slowly harden off. Plant into the garden in late spring.
Matthiola incana Perpetual Flowering Stocks	Clove-like and rich.	White, during midsummer.	Plant them in window boxes or flower beds beneath windows.	Height: 15 inches (38cm) Spread: 12 inches (30cm) **Hardy annual:** Treat in the same way as for Ten Week Stocks (see below).
Matthiola incana Ten Week Stocks	Clove-like and rich.	Wide range, from mid- to late summer.	These stocks are best for sowing under windows rather than for growing in window boxes or other containers. They are sub-divided into several strains, including Dwarf Large Flowering (12 inches/30cm high); Excelsior, or Column (2½ft/75cm high); Mammoth, or Beauty (1½ft/45cm high); Giant Imperial (2ft/60cm high) and Giant Perfection (2½ft/75cm high).	Height: (see left). Spread: 6-8 inches (15-20cm) **Hardy annual:** Sow seeds where the plants are to flower. When large enough to handle, thin out the seedlings to 12 inches (30cm) apart.
HONEY				
Crocus chrysanthus Crocus	Honey-like and very sweet.	Originally bright yellow but now in a wide color range, flowering during late winter and early spring.	Ideal for window boxes and other containers.	Height: 3 inches (7.5cm) Spread: 1-1½ inches (2.5-4cm) **Bulb:** Buy corms in late summer or early autumn as soon as they are available, and plant them with their bases 2-3 inches (5-7.5cm) deep and spaced 3 inches (7.5cm) apart.
Iris danfordiae Bulbous Iris	Honey-like and sweet.	Vivid lemon-yellow flowers during early spring.	Ideal for window boxes and other containers.	Height: 4 inches (10cm) Spread: 3 inches (7.5cm) **Bulb:** Plant bulbs during autumn with their bases 2-3 inches (5-7.5cm) deep and spaced 3-4 inches (7.5-10cm) apart.
NEW-MOWN HAY				
Lobularia maritima (syn. *Alyssum maritimum*) Sweet Alyssum	New-mown hay, attractive to bees.	White, lilac or purple, from early to late summer.	Ideal in all containers and as an edging for borders under windows.	Height: 3-6 inches (7.5-15cm) Spread: 8-10 inches (20-25cm) **Hardy annual:** Sow seeds ¼ inch (6mm) deep in flats during early spring in temperatures of 50-60°F (10-15°C). Transplant the seedlings into flats and slowly harden off for planting out during May.

PLANT	SCENT	COLOR	SITUATION	CULTIVATION
VIOLET				
Iris reticulata Bulbous Iris	Violet-like perfume.	Deep blue-purple, with orange blazes on the falls, during early spring.	Superb in window boxes and other containers.	Height: 6 inches (15cm) Spread: 2½-3 inches (6.5-7.5cm) **Bulb:** Plant bulbs during autumn with their bases 2-3 inches (5-7.5cm) deep and spaced 3-4 inches (7.5-10cm) apart.
SWEET				
Brachycome iberidifolia Swan River Daisy	Sweet.	Wide color range, in lilac, pink, white or blue-purple, from mid- to late summer.	Plant as an edging for borders under windows or in window boxes and tubs.	Height: 15-18 inches (38-45cm) Spread: 12-15 inches (30-38cm) **Hardy annual:** When grown for planting in window boxes and other containers, sow seeds in seed trays in spring with bottom heat. When large enough to handle, prick out the seedlings and plant out when all risk of frost has passed. For a border under a window, sow seeds during mid-spring where they are to flower.
Cheiranthus cheiri Wallflower	Sweet.	Wide color range, including white, yellow, orange, scarlet, crimson and purple, during spring and early summer.	Choose dwarf varieties for window boxes, taller ones for planting under windows.	Height: 8-24 inches (20-60cm) Spread: 3-6 inches (8-15cm) **Hardy perennial grown as a hardy biennial:** Sow seeds outdoors in a seedbed during early summer, ¼ inch (6mm) deep. Seeds take 10-14 days to germinate; when large enough to handle, transplant into a nursery bed. Plant out young plants into containers or beds during late summer or early autumn. Neutral or slightly limy soil is essential.
Dianthus barbatus Sweet William	Sweet.	Single and double-flowered varieties, in a color range that includes crimson, pink, salmon-pink and scarlet, during early to midsummer.	Ideal for planting in containers or borders beneath windows. When planting them in window boxes or a trough, choose dwarf varieties. Plants grow 1-2ft (30-60cm) high and 10-12 inches (25-30cm) wide, depending on the variety.	Height: (see left). Spread: (see left). **Tender perennial grown as a hardy biennial:** Sow seeds outdoors, ¼ inch (6mm) deep, in a seedbed during early to mid-summer. Germination takes 10-21 days; when the seedlings are large enough to handle, transplant to their flowering positions, 10-12 inches (25-30cm) apart.
Erysimum hieraciifolium (syn. *Cheiranthus* x *allionii*) Siberian Wallflower	Sweet.	Wide range, including orange, deep orange and orange-gold.	In window boxes or tubs or for planting under windows.	Height: 15 inches (38cm) Spread: 10-12 inches (25-30cm) **Hardy perennial grown as a hardy biennial:** Treat in the same way as *Cheiranthus cheiri* (see above).
Erysimum alpinum Alpine Wallflower/ Fairy Wallflower	Sweet.	Sulphur-yellow flowers during early summer.	In window boxes.	Height: 6 inches (15cm) Spread: 4-6 inches (10-15cm) **Hardy biennial:** Sow seeds during late winter with bottom heat. Germination takes up to 14 days; when large enough to handle prick off the seedlings into flats. Put the plants into their flowering positions in autumn.
Hyacinthus orientalis Dutch Hyacinth/ Common Garden Hyacinth	Sweet and penetrating.	Wide range, including white, yellow, pink, red, blue, purple and mauve. Single or double flowers during spring.	Ideal for window boxes and other containers as well as for planting in borders under windows. They are ideal for narrow borders, as they do not straggle over paths.	Height: 6-9 inches (15-23cm) Spread: 3-5 inches (7.5-13cm) **Bulb:** Plant bulbs in autumn after summer-flowering plants have been removed. Set the bases of the bulbs 5-6 inches (13-15cm) deep and about the same distance apart.

PLANT	SCENT	COLOR	SITUATION	CULTIVATION
SWEET				
Iberis amara Rocket Candytuft	Sweet.	White.	It is best for sowing under windows rather than in window boxes or troughs.	Height: 12-15 inches (30-38cm) Spread: 6-8 inches (15-20cm) **Hardy annual:** Sow seeds ¼ inch (6mm) deep in their flowering position from late spring to early summer. Germination takes 10-14 days; thin the seedlings to 8 inches (20cm) apart when they are large enough to handle.
Matthiola bicornis Night-scented Stock	Heavy, sweet and penetrating.	Lilac flowers during mid- to late summer.	It is best sown under windows rather than in window boxes or troughs.	Height: 12-15 inches (30-38cm) Spread: 7-9 inches (18-23cm) **Hardy annual:** Sow seeds ¼ inch (6mm) deep from spring onwards where the plants are to flower. Germination takes 10-14 days. Thin the seedlings to 9 inches (23cm) apart when large enough to handle.
Muscari armeniacum Grape Hyacinth	Sweet.	Deep blue flowers with white rims during spring and early summer. 	Best left to form large clumps along the edges of borders under windows.	Height: 8-10 inches (20-25cm) Spread: Forms large clumps **Bulb:** During late summer and into autumn, plant the bulbs with their bases 2½-3 inches (6-7.5cm) deep and 2½ inches (6cm) apart. Full sun is essential, otherwise the bulbs produce more leaves than flowers.
Nicotiana x sanderae Sweet-scented Flowering Tobacco	Sweet and heady.	Pale yellow flowers tinged with carmine-rose from early to late summer.	Select low-growing varieties such as 'Top Arts Mixed' for window boxes, taller varieties for planting under windows.	Height: 9-24 inches (23-60cm) Spread: 8-15 inches (20-38cm) **Tender annual:** Sow seeds with bottom heat in early spring. When seedlings are large enough to handle, transplant into flats and plant in containers or the garden after all risk of frost has passed. passed.
Primula polyantha Polyanthus Primrose	Sweet.	Wide range of brilliant colors, including cream, yellow, pink, crimson, blue and scarlet – all with yellow centers – during spring.	Ideal for window boxes and tubs, as well as along path edges under windows.	Height: 8-10 inches (20-25cm) Spread: 9-12 inches (23-30cm) **Hardy perennial:** Sow seeds ⅛ inch (3mm) deep in flats in late winter or early spring in a heated greenhouse. When the seedlings are large enough to handle, transplant into pots and plant into flowering positions during late summer.
Primula veris Cowslip	Sweet.	The cultivated form of this wildflower is available in a range of colors, including yellow, red and crimson, and flowers in spring.	In window boxes and tubs as well as in beds under windows. 	Height: 6 inches (15cm) Spread: 5-8 inches (13-20cm) **Hardy perennial:** Sow seeds ⅛ inch (3mm) deep with bottom heat from mid-spring to early summer. Germination takes a long time, up to six or seven weeks; when the seedlings are large enough to handle, transplant into flats. Plant into their flowering positions in late summer or autumn.
Viola odorata Sweet Violet	Sweet and cool.	Shades of purple and white from late winter to mid-spring.	They are superb in window boxes and other containers, as an edging for borders, or mixed with tulips.	Height: 4-6 inches (10-15cm) Spread: 8-10 inches (20-25cm) **Hardy perennial best grown as a biennial:** Sow seeds ¼ inch (6mm) deep in flats during late summer and early autumn and place in a cold frame. In spring, transplant the seedlings into flats and place outdoors in a slightly shaded position. Plant out in autumn.

CHAPTER SIX

Scented Patios

*A wide range of scented plants can be used to
create fragrant oases of tranquility on even
the smallest of patios.*

ROWING plants in containers can bring an exciting dimension to gardening, with scent and color cloaking even the smallest of paved areas outside a house. Quick-change planting schemes from spring to summer create variety and, even during winter, many of the conifers that can be planted in tubs and placed on a patio emit a delightful fragrance when their foliage is bruised or crushed. Many also have colorful foliage.

The term 'patio' has entered our language mainly because of its misuse by estate agents who seek to glamorize everything they sell. We owe the term 'patio' to the Spaniards, who used it to describe an inner court open to the sky and surrounded by the house. These courts were designed as an integral part of the house, with the walls of the dwelling providing shelter from the sun for the rooms on the opposite side. Pools and fountains were often incorporated into them to provide the coolness needed in a warm climate as well as aesthetic appeal. In Spain and the southern states of North America, where generous periods of sunshine are normal, patios are therefore ideal. Few real patios exist in regions where the weather is unpredictable and a week of uninterrupted sunshine is taken to be the height of summer! However, such is the natural development of language that the term 'patio' is now generously applied to any paved area in a yard.

The prettiest patios do not, of course, rely on plants solely grown in containers. Vines and climbing shrubs (see also Chapter 3) that cover walls or twine around trellises, arbors and rustic poles can also be integrated into the patio. In addition, window boxes play an important role in brightening vertical areas, and suitable plants for these uses are suggested in Chapter 5. The plants described in this chapter are those that can be successfully grown in tubs or large pots and placed on a patio. A large selection of plants falls into this category: they range from lilies, conifers and shrubs to a wide variety of herbaceous plants.

Most of these plants are hardy and can be left outside throughout the year, but others need the protection of a frost-proof sunroom or greenhouse during the coldest and wettest months. The sweetly almond-scented Oleander, *Nerium oleander*, which has clusters of white flowers from mid- to late summer, needs the winter comfort of a sunroom, while some lilies and the Common Myrtle, *Myrtus communis*, grow better in a cool greenhouse or a sunroom, if a warm and sheltered spot on the patio cannot be found.

CONTAINER MATERIALS

Plants can be grown in almost any container as long as it is strong enough to support the weight of the soil mix needed to ensure good growth. It must, of course, have holes in its base through which excess water can drain.

As well as being functional and able to survive the rigors of frost, snow, rain and hot sunshine – not to mention the boisterous activities of children and large dogs – the container should also be attractive. Those available range from traditional wooden tubs to ones made of fiberglass, real and faux, terracotta, concrete, metal, real and bonded stone: each has its merits and uses.

Stone: Containers made from natural stone are invariably very expensive and extremely heavy. If you have inherited one from an old garden, be thankful and treasure it. Natural stone, especially when weathered, blends with plants and creates an impression of a long-established garden. Usually, however, such containers are not at their best in an ultramodern setting, which tends to have a clinical air about it. Stone containers are invariably difficult to move, especially when planted, so do not use them for tender plants that may need to be transported to a sunroom or greenhouse for the winter.

Bonded stone: This material is used to construct stone-type pots and urns that are much cheaper than those formed of real stone. The material is a form of reconstructed limestone, and has a texture resembling natural Portland stone. It mellows quicker than natural stone and soon blends in with plants and the garden. Containers formed of this material are available in a range of finishes and colors. They have a long life and the surface resists the effects of weathering. Clean them with soapy water, but bear in mind that vigorous scrubbing will damage them in time. Unlike stone containers, they have little structural strength and cannot be

Salvia officinalis 'Icterina' is a form of sage that creates extra interest through its brightly colored leaves. Here it nestles against a clematis.

Scented plants in pots, tubs and urns form a wonderland of aroma and color on patios, and are useful for bringing scent to small gardens.

The edges of patios and other paved areas can be merged into the rest of the garden with plantings of scented bulbous and shrubby plants.

used as a load-bearing surface. Urns and vases can be secured to pedestals with a mortar mixture of eight parts sand and one of cement powder. This will hold the container securely to its support, yet enable the joint to be broken at a later date if movement is necessary.

Fiberglass: This is a relatively modern material which has many excellent qualities. It can be cast into a wide range of shapes, enabling it to act as a substitute for stone, wood or lead containers. It is a light material in comparison with bonded or real stone, and a small container planted with a large shrub is likely to be blown over when buffeted by high winds. The lightness, however, is an advantage when it is used for window boxes, where the qualities of strength and lightness are paramount.

Plastic: This also is a relatively recent material, increasingly used for plant containers both indoors and out. Plastic containers have the advantage of being relatively cheap and capable of being molded into many different sizes and shapes. They are also available in a wide color range. Their main disadvantages are that they tend not to harmonize with cottage-like settings, they lack rigidity and durability, and soil mix in them becomes very hot during summer and excessively cold in winter. They are therefore best reserved for annual plants, when they can be inspected at the end of each season, and, if necessary, replaced. However, for all their disadvantages, they

are sold each year in their millions as plant pots, window boxes, troughs, planters, urns and tubs.

Glazed pottery: The sheer variety of glazed containers is staggering. From solid colors to rustic flower-painted pots to sophisticated abstracts, and from standard geometric shapes to flowing lines, these planters cover the spectrum. To avoid breakage, bring glazed pots in for the winter. If the pots have no drainage holes, use them to hold well-drained plastic or clay pots.

Metal: Traditional lead jardinières are good examples of metal containers. They are highly ornate and very expensive and, of course, do not rust. Aluminum jardinières are available in ornamental castings; they are long-lived, but tend to heat up rapidly during summer and are therefore best positioned in slight shade.

Timber: Wood has traditionally been the material used to construct window boxes and tubs for shrubs, small trees and conifers. It is easily worked by do-it-yourself enthusiasts, and it keeps the roots of plants cool in summer and relatively warm in winter. Wooden tubs are ideal for patios as they harmonize with all settings and, because they are quite heavy, especially when filled with compost, they will not blow over during winter storms.

Clay pots: This is the traditional material used to construct plant pots of all sizes. Those suitable for use on a patio are 8 inches (20cm) or more across. They are

*The sweetly almond-scented flowers
of the tender Mediterranean shrub,
Oleander (Nerium oleander), emit
an enticing scent in summer.*

usually left unglazed so that moisture can readily evaporate from the surface, keeping the compost cool during summer. Clay is also used for strawberry pots, herb pots, vases and urns. These specialised containers are pleasing to look at in their own right but are even more attractive when full of scented and colorful plants.

CONTAINER TYPES

The choice of containers for a patio is wide, ranging from traditional window boxes to tubs, modified wooden wheelbarrows and painted tires stacked into tub-like shapes.

Window boxes: These are usually constructed from either wood, plastic or fiberglass, and are used to create homes for spring and summer bedding plants as well as bulbs, miniature conifers, roses and small trailing plants that soften the container's outline.

Troughs: These resemble window boxes positioned on short legs, usually 1–1½ft (30–45cm) high. The same range of plants used for window boxes can be planted in them. They are, however, vulnerable to being accidentally knocked over and are therefore best positioned at the side or in a corner of the patio.

Tubs: These are frequently custom-made, although they may be recycled beer barrels or wine casks. They can be used for permanent plants such as shrubs, small trees, conifers and herbaceous perennials, or for seasonal types such as bulbs and spring and summer bedding plants.

Wheelbarrows: Old-fashioned wooden wheelbarrows – perhaps unobtrusively reinforced with metal angle-brackets – create a superb feature when planted with spring or summer bedding plants. They are not suited to permanent plants such as shrubs. Metal wheelbarrows should not be used for this type of display.

Hanging baskets: These are ideal for displaying summer bedding plants, especially trailing types. They create superb splashes of scent and color when hung from porches, balconies, verandas, against walls, in courtyards and on terraces and patios. They are indispensable if you are trying to create a look of vertical color, and as they are usually positioned at head-height, their scents are easily accessible.

Wall baskets: These resemble hanging baskets cut in half and can be filled with the same type of plants. They are fixed to a wall, usually about 3-3½ft (0.9-1m) above the ground. Because they have a tendency to drip excess water over the wall, they are best not used against one that is color-washed.

An assortment of hanging baskets and free-standing pots (top) creates a stunning display on a patio. The Common Rosemary (Rosmarinus officinalis) looks attractive in a pot or at the edge of a patio (above).

The Sweet Bay (Laurus nobilis) brings a sweet bouquet to gardens. It is superb when planted in large tubs and clipped to a uniform shape.

Stone sinks: These are superb for growing small alpine plants, small bulbs and dwarf conifers. The ideal is to use an old, unglazed stone sink. These traditional sinks are shallow, with sides about 6 inches (15cm) high. The next generation of sinks were glazed and much deeper but they can be made presentable for the garden if their sides are painted with a bonding glue and then coated with a thin layer of mortar; they never have the old-world charm of stone sinks, however. Attractive sinks are also available made from bonded stone. Stone sinks can be planted with many of the alpine plants, bulbs and dwarf conifers described in Chapter 4.

Urns: These large, often ornate vases are best seen at head-height, supported on pillars or on piers in walls. Their eye-catching appearance is enhanced when they are full of scented plants. These are usually annual types which can be planted in late spring or early summer to create a wonderful display until autumn.

PLANTS FOR THE SCENTED PATIO

A patio seems to bring the garden right into the home, and when scented plants are grown in containers next to a patio or kitchen door, their presence is even more appreciated – particularly by infirm and elderly people who are perhaps unable to reach the garden. The Oleander, *Nerium oleander*, is a well-known Mediterranean shrub that succeeds outdoors only in warm areas or, in slightly less hospitable climes, against a south- or west-facing wall. In a tub in temperate regions, it is best placed in a frost-proof sunroom or greenhouse during winter. Its beautiful almond-scented flowers belie its poisonous nature; while it was suggested in ancient Greece that the addition of a root of Oleander to wine would modify the temper, all parts of the plant are in fact extremely poisonous – even the flowers. About 2,000 years ago the Greek physician Dioscorides said that while the tree was poisonous it also yielded an effective medicine. It was said to 'have a bad effect on dogs, asses, mules and most quadrupeds; but, when taken with wine, it is wholesome for men against the bites of animals, especially if mixed with Rue; but when the smaller animals, like goats and sheep, drink of this, they die'. Whatever the truth of this, it is certainly not a shrub to experiment with. It is recorded that during the Peninsular War (1808-1814) some French soldiers stationed near Madrid used Oleander wood as skewers for meat. Of the twelve soldiers who ate the meat seven died and the rest were seriously ill. The plant can have its uses, however. An ancient way of dealing with mice was to block up their holes with Oleander leaves!

The Sweet Bay or Bay Laurel, *Laurus nobilis*, is another Mediterranean shrub, well-known for its use in the culinary arts – the bay leaf is an essential part of any *bouquet garni*. Although reputed to have a wide range of medicinal virtues, its modern use medicinally is small; however, herbalists sometimes apply the oil externally in the treatment of rheumatism. It is a shrub that has become woven into history and steeped in superstitions. The Roman Emperor Tiberius believed it afforded protection against thunder and lightning, and during bad storms he would cover his head with laurel branches and retire under his bed.

Many scented lilies are superb when grown in large clay pots on a patio. There are many to choose from, including the well-known Gold-banded Lily (*Lilium auratum*), the Easter Lily (*Lilium longiflorum*), and the Madonna Lily (*Lilium candidum*). All of the lilies described in this chapter are scented and all of them have an exotic and colorful appearance that brings further interest to a patio.

The Common Myrtle, *Myrtus communis*, with its sweetly scented white flowers and highly aromatic, balsam-like leaves, is another shrub steeped in legend. One of the most amusing anecdotes about it is that a girl will not succeed in rooting cuttings of myrtle if her destiny is to be an old maid. To ensure successful rooting, and thus to ward off the risk of being unwed, it was necessary to spread the tail of one's dress when inserting the cuttings. Myrtle was also used in bridal bouquets, but it was thought to be unwise for the bride to plant the sprigs.

Many dwarf and slow-growing conifers happily grow in tubs on a patio. The dwarf ones are, as the name suggests, small and can be left in a tub for many years – some even do well in window boxes. Slow-growing types are only really suitable when small, as eventually they will outgrow the container. They can then be moved without harm into the garden.

*The sweetly scented flowers of
Adam's Needle (*Yucca filamentosa*)
create a distinctive focal point either in
a border, or in a large tub on a patio.*

*Few people can fail to be captivated by
the strongly sweet bowl-shaped
flowers of the Gold-banded Lily
(Lilium auratum).*

PLANT	SCENT	COLOR	SITUATION	CULTIVATION
ALMOND				
Nerium oleander Oleander	Sweet and almond-scented.	Clusters of single white flowers from mid- to late summer. Single and double varieties are available in white, cream, pink and red.	Grow in a large tub, placing it outside during summer and in a sunroom or greenhouse in winter.	Height: 4-8ft (1.2-2.4m) Spread: 3-5ft (0.9-1.5m) **Tender evergreen shrub:** Grow in good potting soil and a sheltered, sunny position.
APPLE				
Juniperus communis 'Compressa' Common Juniper	Apple-like scent when foliage is crushed.	Prickly, light gray-green leaves with a bluish tinge.	In small tubs, window boxes and rock gardens.	Height: 1½-2ft (45-60cm) Spread: 6 inches (15cm) **Evergreen conifer:** Well-drained soil in full sun or light shade.
Juniperus communis 'Hibernica' (syn. *Juniperus communis* 'Stricta') Irish Juniper	Apple-like scent when foliage is crushed.	Dense, narrow, columnar form with gray-blue foliage.	When small, it is ideal for planting in large tubs.	Height: 4-10ft (1.2-3m) Spread: 12-18 inches (30-45cm) **Evergreen conifer:** Well-drained soil in full sun or light shade.
Juniperis communis 'Repandum'	Apple-like aroma when foliage is crushed.	Dwarf, prostrate habit with stems densely packed with gray-blue foliage that becomes slightly bronze during winter.	In a large tub on a patio, or for creating ground cover in a heather or conifer garden.	Height: 12-15 inches (30-38cm) Spread: 3-4ft (0.9-1.2m) **Evergreen conifer:** Well-drained soil in full sun.
Thuja occidentalis 'Danica' American Arborvitae/ Eastern White Cedar	Foliage emits a fruity, apple-like aroma when crushed.	Slow-growing and bun-shaped, with bright green foliage that turns bronze during winter.	In a tub on a patio.	Height: 1½-2½ft (45-75cm) Spread: 1½-3ft (45-90cm) **Evergreen conifer:** Well-drained but moisture-retentive soil and a sheltered position in full sun.
Thuja occidentalis 'Holmstrupii'	Foliage emits a fruity, apple-like aroma when crushed.	Slow-growing and forming a narrow cone, with bright yellow-green foliage in fans of scale-like leaves.	When young it is ideal for growing in a tub on a patio.	Height: 6-10ft (1.8-3m) Spread: 3-4ft (0.9-1.2m) **Evergreen conifer:** Well-drained but moisture-retentive soil and a sheltered position in full sun.
Thuja occidentalis 'Rheingold'	Foliage emits a fruity, apple-like aroma when crushed.	Dwarf, slow-growing with a rounded outline and old-gold foliage in summer, turning to a rich copper in winter.	In a tub on a patio.	Height: 3-4ft (0.9-1.2m) Spread: 3-3½ft (0.9-1m) **Evergreen conifer:** Well-drained but moisture-retentive soil and a sheltered position in full sun.
CHAMOMILE				
Santolina chamaecyparissus (syn. *Santolina incana*) Lavender Cotton	Resembles that of chamomile.	Bright lemon-yellow flowers during midsummer. Woolly, thread-like aromatic leaves.	Ideal in a low tub, where it forms a mound.	Height: 1½-2ft (45-60cm) Spread: 1½-2ft (45-60cm) **Somewhat hardy evergreen shrub:** Well-drained soil in full sun.
HONEY				
Buxus sempervirens 'Elegantissima' Dwarf Box	Honey-scented flowers.	Nearly inconspicuous pale green flowers with yellow anthers during spring. Gray-green leaves edged with silver.	As a specimen in a large tub. The variety 'Suffruticosa', the Edging Box, is smaller and is ideal in small tubs or large pots.	Height: 3-4ft (0.9-1.2m) Spread: 1½ft (45cm) **Somewhat hardy evergreen shrub:** Well-drained soil and a position in full sun or light shade.
Lilium candidum Madonna Lily/White Madonna Lily/ Bourbon Lily/White Lily	Honey-like and sweet.	Widely bell-shaped, pure white flowers with golden anthers during mid- to late summer.	In pots on a warm, sheltered patio.	Height: 4-5ft (1.2-1.5m) Spread: 15-18 inches (38-45cm) **Basal-rooting bulb:** Well-drained, moisture-retentive soil and a position in light shade.

PLANT	SCENT	COLOR	SITUATION	CULTIVATION
JASMINE				
Lilium longiflorum Easter Lily/Bermuda Lily	Heavily sweet and reminiscent of jasmine.	Trumpet-shaped, glistening white flowers with golden pollen during late summer.	In pots on a warm, sheltered patio.	Height: 2-3ft (60-90cm) Spread: 10-12 inches (25-30cm) **Tender, stem-rooting bulb:** Well-drained and moisture-retentive soil. It is tolerant of lime in the soil. Position in light shade.
MINT JELLY				
Nepeta x faassenii (syn. *Nepeta mussinii*) Catmint	Leaves emit a fragrance of slightly bitter mint jelly when crushed. Flowers are sweeter, with a gentle mint-jelly aroma.	Spikes of lavender-blue flowers from early to late summer.	Ideal in large square tubs on either side of a door.	Height: 12-18 inches (30-45cm) Spread: 12-15 inches (30-38cm) **Hardy herbaceous perennial:** Well-drained soil in full sun or light shade.
LAVENDER				
Lavandula angustifolia (often listed as *L. spica* or *L. officinalis*) Old English Lavender	Air-drenching lavender aroma.	Grayish-blue flowers from midsummer to autumn. Narrow silvery-gray leaves. Many excellent varieties, in colors including white, lavender blue and pale pink.	In a large tub.	Height: 3-4ft (0.9-1.2m) Spread: 3-4ft (0.9-1.2m) **Hardy, evergreen shrub:** Well-drained soil and a sunny position.
LILY-OF-THE-VALLEY				
Skimmia japonica 'Fragrans' Japanese Skimmia	Sweet, Lily-of-the-Valley fragrance.	Dense clusters of small, star-like, white flowers at the ends of shoots during late spring. This is a male form and does not bear berries.	In a large tub.	Height: 3-4ft (0.9-1.2m) Spread: 4-5ft (1..2-1.5m) **Evergreen shrub:** Well-drained soil in light shade. In the open soil, this shrub grows slightly larger.
PINEAPPLE				
Thuja plicata 'Rogersii' Giant Arborvitae	Fruity, with the fragrance of pineapples.	Globular outline, with golden bronze and green foliage.	In a tub on a patio.	Height: 12-18 inches (30-45cm) Spread: 15 inches (38cm) **Evergreen conifer:** Well-drained but moisture-retentive soil and a sheltered position in full sun.
Thuja plicata 'Stoneham Gold'	Fruity, with the fragrance of pineapples.	Closely-packed, rich golden-yellow foliage.	In a tub on a patio.	Height: 2-3ft (60-90cm) Spread: 15-18 inches (38-45cm) **Evergreen conifer:** Well-drained but moisture-retentive soil and a sheltered position in full sun.
RESIN				
Chamaecyparis pisifera 'Filifera Aurea' Sawara Cypress	Resinous fragrance.	Domed bush (occasionally as a slender tree) with golden-yellow foliage.	In the domed variety, planted in a large tub.	Height: 2½-3ft (75-90cm) Spread: 3-5ft (0.9-1.5m) **Evergreen conifer:** Well-drained soil in full sun or light shade.
Chamaecyparis pisifera 'Plumosa Pygmaea'	Resinous fragrance.	Conical bush with golden foliage.	In a tub on a patio.	Height: 2½-3ft (75-90cm) Spread: 2ft (60cm) **Evergreen conifer:** Well-drained soil in full sun or light shade.

PLANT	SCENT	COLOR	SITUATION	CULTIVATION
RESIN AND PARSLEY				
Chamaecyparis lawsoniana 'Ellwoodii' Lawson Cypress	Crushed foliage emits a fragrance reminiscent of resin and parsley.	Slow-growing, columnar outline with feathery sprays of gray-green foliage that becomes steel blue during winter.	When young it can be grown in a tub on a patio, but it will eventually outgrow this situation.	Height: 6-10ft (1.8-3m) Spread: 15-24 inches (38-60cm) **Evergreen conifer:** Well-drained soil in full sun or light shade.
Chamaecyparis lawsoniana 'Ellwood's Gold'	Crushed foliage emits a fragrance reminiscent of resin and parsley.	Slow-growing, compact, columnar form with yellow-tinged foliage that becomes light green with growth.	When young it can be grown in a tub on a patio, but it will eventually outgrow this situation.	Height: 5-6ft (1.5-1.8m) Spread: 15-18 inches (38-45cm) **Evergreen conifer:** Well-drained soil in full sun or light shade.
Chamaecyparis lawsoniana 'Minima'	Crushed foliage emits a fragrance reminiscent of resin and parsley.	Globular outline, with neat sprays of green foliage.	In a tub on a patio.	Height: 2½-3ft (75-90cm) Spread: 2½-3ft (75-90cm) **Evergreen conifer:** Well-drained soil in full sun or light shade.
Chamaecyparis lawsoniana 'Minima Aurea'	Crushed foliage emits a fragrance reminiscent of resin and parsley.	Conical shape, with sprays of golden-yellow foliage.	In a tub on a patio.	Height: 2½-3ft (75-90cm) Spread: 2½-3ft (75-90cm) **Evergreen conifer:** Well-drained soil in full sun or light shade.
Chamaecyparis lawsoniana 'Minima Glauca'	Crushed foliage emits a fragrance reminiscent of resin and parsley.	Globular bush, with densely-packed sprays of sea-green foliage.	In a tub on a patio.	Height: 2½-3ft (75-90cm) Spread: 2½-3ft (75-90cm) **Evergreen conifer:** Well-drained soil in full sun or light shade.
ROSEMARY				
Rosmarinus officinalis Common Rosemary	Rosemary.	Mauve flowers during early summer amid narrow green or grayish-green leaves with white undersides. Flowering sometimes continues sporadically until late summer.	Large tub on a patio; it grows slightly larger when planted in a border.	Height: 4-6ft (1.2-1.8m) Spread: 3-5ft (0.9-1.5m) **Tender evergreen shrub:** Well-drained soil and a sunny position.
SAGE				
Perovskia atriplicifolia Russian Sage	Sage-like.	Lavender-blue flowers from mid- to late summer, amid gray-green leaves. The form 'Blue Spire' has larger flowers and deeply-cut foliage.	In a large tub.	Height: 3-5ft (0.9-1.5m) Spread: 1½-2½ft (45-75cm) **Hardy, shrubby, herbaceous perennial:** Well-drained soil and a sunny position. Cut down the stems in spring to encourage the development of fresh shoots.
Salvia officinalis Sage	Sage fragrance; the leaves are slightly bitter-tasting.	Gray-green, wrinkled and woolly leaves clasp stiff, four-sided stems. Violet-purple, tubular flowers in midsummer. There are also varieties with highly attractive leaves: 'Icterina' (green and gold), Purpurascens' (stems and leaves suffused with purple) and 'Tricolor' (gray-green leaves splashed with creamy-white and suffused pink and purple).	In a large tub.	Height: 1½-2ft (45-60cm) Spread: 15-18 inches (38-45cm) **Hardy, evergreen sub-shrub:** Well-drained soil and a bright, sunny position.
SOAP OR PAINT				
Juniperus virginiana 'Globosa' Red Cedar	Soap or paint-like aroma when foliage is crushed.	Close, rounded and dense habit with scaly, bright green leaves.	In a low tub on a patio or in a rock garden.	Height: 2½-3ft (75-90cm) Spread: 2½-3ft (75-90cm) **Evergreen conifer:** Well-drained soil in full sun or light shade.

PLANT	SCENT	COLOR	SITUATION	CULTIVATION
SOAP OR PAINT				
Juniperus virginiana 'Skyrocket' Pencil Cedar	Soap or paint-like aroma when foliage is crushed.	Narrow, columnar habit with blue-gray foliage.	In a tub on a patio.	Height: 6-8ft (1.8-2.4m) Spread: 6-9 inches (15-23cm) **Evergreen conifer:** Well-drained soil in full sun or light shade.
WARM AND SWEET				
Chamaecyparis obtusa 'Kosteri' Hinoki Cypress	When crushed, the foliage emits a warm and sweet aroma.	Dwarf, conical outline, with flattened and moss-like sprays of bright green foliage that becomes bronze during winter.	In a tub or a rock garden.	Height: 2½-3ft (75-90cm) Spread: 2ft (60cm) **Evergreen conifer:** Well-drained soil in full sun or light shade.
Chamaecyparis obtusa 'Nana'	When crushed, the foliage emits a warm and sweet aroma.	Dwarf, flat-topped dome with flattened sprays of dark green foliage.	In a tub or a rock garden.	Height: 1½-2ft (45-60cm) Spread: 1½-2ft (45-60cm) **Evergreen conifer:** Well-drained soil in full sun or light shade.
Chamaecyparis obtusa 'Nana Aurea'	When crushed, the foliage emits a warm and sweet aroma.	Dwarf, flat-topped dome with flattened sprays of golden-tinged foliage.	In a tub or in a rock garden.	Height: 1½-2ft (45-60cm) Spread: 1½-2ft (45-60cm) **Evergreen conifer:** Well-drained soil in full sun or light shade.
Chamaecyparis obtusa 'Pygmaea'	When crushed, the folage emits a warm and sweet aroma.	Flat-topped outline, with fan-like sprays of bronze-green foliage, tinged reddish-bronze in winter.	In a tub or a rock garden.	Height: 9-12 inches (23-30cm) Spread: 2-3ft (60-90cm) **Evergreen conifer:** Well-drained soil in full sun or light shade.
SWEET				
Bergenia cordifolia Heartleaf Bergenia/ Elephant's Ear	Sweet.	Drooping heads of bell-shaped, lilac-rose flowers during spring.	In a large tub.	Height: 10-12 inches (25-30cm) Spread: 12-18 inches (30-45cm) **Hardy herbaceous perennial:** Treat as *B. crassifolia* (see below).
Bergenia crassifolia Siberian Tea/ Elephant's Ear	Sweet.	Bell-shaped, pale pink flowers from midwinter to late spring.	In a large tub.	Height: 12 inches (30cm) Spread: 12 inches (30cm) **Hardy herbaceous perennial:** Any soil, as long as it is not waterlogged. Position in light shade.
Laurus nobilis Sweet Bay/Laurel Bay	Sweet.	Glossy, medium-green, evergreen leaves.	Ideal for large tubs.	Height: 4-6ft (1.2-1.8m) – in a tub Spread: 3-4ft (0.9-1.2m) – in a tub **Tender, evergreen shrub:** When in a tub, usually grown as a standard or half-standard. If planted in a border in zones 9 and 10, expect a height and spread of 10-18ft (3-5.4m). Well-drained soil and a sunny position are needed.
Lilium auratum Gold-banded Lily/ Golden-rayed Lily of Japan	Sweet and strong.	Bowl-shaped, brilliant white flowers, up to 12 inches (30cm) wide and with golden yellow rays or bands, during late summer.	In pots on a warm, sheltered patio.	Height: 5-7ft (1.5-2.1m) Spread: 18 inches (45cm) **Stem-rooting bulb:** Well-drained, lime-free and moisture-retentive soil, in full sun or light shade.
Lilium brownii	Slight, but very sweet.	Trumpet-shaped flowers, pure creamy-white within and dull rose-purple, sometimes tinged green, outside, during midsummer.	In pots on a warm, sheltered patio.	Height: 3-4ft (0.9-1.2m) Spread: 18 inches (45cm) **Stem-rooting bulb:** Well-drained, moisture-retentive soil and a position in light shade.

PLANT	SCENT	COLOR	SITUATION	CULTIVATION
SWEET				
Lilium 'Empress of China'	Sweet.	Bowl-shaped, chalk-white flowers, up to 9 inches (23cm) wide, during mid- to late summer.	In pots on a warm, sheltered patio. In cool areas it is best grown in a cool greenhouse.	Height: 3-5ft (0.9-1.5m) Spread: 12-15 inches (30-38cm) **Tender stem-rooting bulb:** Well-drained, moisture-retentive soil and full sun.
Lilium 'Empress of Japan'	Sweet.	Bowl-shaped, pure white flowers covered with deep maroon spots and golden bands.	In pots on a warm, sheltered patio. In cool areas it is best grown in a cool greenhouse.	Height: 3-5ft (0.9-1.5m) Spread: 12-15 inches (30-38cm) **Tender stem-rooting bulb:** Well-drained, moisture-retentive soil and full sun. .
Lilium 'First Love'	Sweet but slight.	Golden-yellow flowers, 6-8 inches (15-20cm) wide with pink edges, during late summer.	Ideal in pots on a warm patio.	Height: 4-5ft (1.2-1.5m) Spread: 12-15 inches (30-38cm) **Stem-rooting bulb:** Well-drained, loamy soil and a position in light shade.
Lilium 'Golden Splendour Strain'	Sweet.	Deep orange-yellow flowers, the reverse of the petals showing contrasting maroon strips, during mid- to late summer.	In pots on a warm, sheltered patio.	Height: 5-6ft (1.5-1.8m) Spread: 15-18 inches (30-45cm) **Stem-rooting bulb:** Well-drained soil in partial shade.
Lilium hansonii Japanese Turk's-cap Lily	Sweet.	Nodding, waxy, pale orange-yellow flowers with brown spots, during midsummer.	In pots on a warm, sheltered patio.	Height: 5ft (1.5m) Spread: 15-18 inches (38-45cm) **Stem-rooting bulb:** Well-drained, lime-free and leafmold-rich soil and a position in dappled shade.
Lilium japonicum Japanese Lily	Sweet.	Trumpet-shaped white flowers, pink when in bud, during midsummer.	In pots on a warm and sheltered patio or in a cool greenhouse.	Height: 2½-3ft (75-90cm) Spread: 10-15 inches (25-38cm) **Stem-rooting bulb:** Well-drained, sandy and lime-free soil and a position in partial shade.
Lilium 'Parkmannii'	Sweet.	Bowl-shaped, rose-crimson flowers up to 8 inches (20cm) wide, with pure white wavy edges to the petals, during mid- to late summer.	In pots on a warm and sheltered patio or in a cool greenhouse.	Height: 3-5ft (0.9-1.5m) Spread: 12-15 inches (25-38cm) **Tender stem-rooting bulb:** Well-drained, moisture-retentive soil and full sun.
Lilium rubellum	Sweet.	Bell-shaped, rose-pink flowers, 3 inches (7.5cm) wide and with golden-yellow stamens, during early and midsummer. It is one of the earliest lilies to flower.	Ideal on a warm patio or in a cool greenhouse.	Height: 15-30 inches (38-75cm) Spread: 9-12 inches (23-30cm) **Stem-rooting bulb:** Well-drained, lime-free soil in partial shade.
Lilium speciosum Showy Lily/ Japanese Lily	Sweet.	Bowl-shaped, 3-5 inches (7.5-13cm) wide, white flowers, heavily shaded with crimson, during late summer.	In pots in a warm, sheltered position on a patio.	Height: 4-6ft (1.2-1.8m) Spread: 12-15 inches (30-38cm) **Stem-rooting bulb:** Well-drained, lime-free, moisture-retentive soil in light shade or sun.
Myrtus communis Common Myrtle	Sweet.	Saucer-shaped, 1-inch- (2.5cm) wide, fragrant white flowers during midsummer and highly aromatic, deep green leaves.	In a pot or tub on a patio or greenhouse. Can also be grown in zones 9 and 10 outdoors against a warm wall, where it reaches a height of 7-9ft (2.1-2.7m).	Height: 2½-3ft (75-90cm) Spread: 2½-3ft (75-90cm) **Tender, evergreen shrub:** Well-drained soil and a sunny, sheltered position.
Yucca filamentosa Adam's Needle	Sweet.	Creamy-white, bell-shaped flowers during mid- to late summer, on stems up to 5ft (1.5m) high.	In a large tub on a formal patio.	Height: 2-2½ft (60-75cm) Spread: 3-3½ft (0.9-1m) **Hardy evergreen shrub:** Well-drained, sandy soil and a position in full sun.
Yucca flaccida 'Ivory'	Sweet.	Creamy-white, green-stained, bell-shaped flowers during mid- and late summer, on stems 5-6ft (1.5-1.8m) high.	In a large tub on a formal patio.	Height: 2½ft (75cm) Spread: 2½-3ft (75-90cm) **Hardy evergreen shrub:** Well-drained, sandy soil and a position in full sun.

CHAPTER SEVEN

The Herb Garden

Herb gardens are traditionally rich in
fragrant plants, and herbs are an essential
feature of the scented garden, where their
appeal combines with practical use.

BY THEIR very nature herb gardens are rich in scents of all kinds, creating an abundance of aromas that, as well as being of practical use in the preparation of food, are also a pleasure in themselves.

Traditional herb gardens are formal, with small beds divided by paths or low box hedges. Many are also formed in the shape of a large wheel, with small, clipped hedges radiating out from the center and creating neat sections. Small gravel paths or paving stones can be used to achieve the same effect. For most people, however, large herb gardens packed with many different plants are an impossibility, and a cluster of pots on a patio or balcony is all that can be arranged. Fortunately, many herbs are quite content in small containers, and pots with planting holes in the side can be used to accommodate several different types at the same time.

The range of plants now grown as herbs is much smaller than it was several hundred years ago. For many centuries there was a harmonious marriage between botany and medicine that created the need for medicinal and culinary plants in every garden. Folk medicine, which had been practiced since prehistoric times, began by the 17th century to gain a scientific identity. Indeed, Carolus Linnaeus, who is considered to be the father of modern botany, was a professor both of medicine and botany.

The term 'herb' then indicated a plant used in medicine or as a seasoning to cloak the incipient decay in foods, but since the parting of the two sciences herbs have been generally associated with culinary skills.

Growing herbs is like digging into the past, and even the term 'herb garden' evokes the time when these plants took pride of place. Many of the plants that once were grown only with other herbs are now planted throughout the garden – lavender, for instance, is now used as an ornamental as well as for color beside paths and in narrow borders by the side of walls. Its clean, crisp bouquet is superb for bringing freshness to sheets or for the manufacture of soaps and perfumes, but in the 17th century lavender was also added to sugar, both to extend its life and to cloak signs of decay.

Bergamot, a beautiful herbaceous plant with densely whorled heads of bright scarlet flowers, was highly prized in medicinal herb gardens. In the American colonies during the 18th century, an herbal tea was made from an infusion of young leaves and named after Oswego, a city on the shore of Lake Ontario, New York State. Bergamot gained its name from the similarity of its scent to that of the Bergamot Orange, *Citrus bergamia*, from which bergamot oil is extracted for use in perfumery, hair preparations and eau de cologne. It is also known as Bee Balm, because it is extremely attractive to bees.

Artemisias were also standard plants in early herb gardens. Mugwort, *Artemisia vulgaris*, a native of many parts of the northern hemisphere, was highly prized in England during Saxon times as a protection against evil spirits, while the hair-like leaves of Southernwood, *Artemisia abrotanum*, were thought to be good in the treatment of fevers and wounds. It was also said to ward off infection, and up to the beginning of the 19th century a bunch of Southernwood and Rue, *Ruta graveolens*, would be placed at the side of a prisoner as he stood in the dock to reduce the risk of court officials catching jail fever. Moths, as well as diseases, are said to be repelled by this plant. The French name for Southernwood is Garde-robes, reflecting its use when strewn in cupboards and drawers to repel these pests.

Mints, although commonplace, have such a wonderful range of scents that they never pall. The Apple Mint, *Mentha rotundifolia* (often known as the Woolly Mint), has leaves with a strong bouquet of apples, while the Peppermint, *M.* x *piperita*, produces the essential oil used to flavor chewing gum and other confections as well as the liqueur crème de menthe. It is also a source of menthol. Common Mint or Spearmint, *M. spicata*, is known for its culinary use – mint jelly and lamb are a traditional combination.

*T*he sweet, balsam-like leaves of the Common Marjoram (Origanum vulgare) are welcome in any garden. Here is 'Aureum', a golden-leaved form.

Sage (Salvia officinalis) *has many forms. Here is a narrow-leaved type that creates an ideal shape for filling the corner of a path with scent.*

Few garden scents are as pleasing and distinctive as those of the thymes, and the name of this herb constantly recurs in folk songs and in literature. In *A Midsummer Night's Dream*, Shakespeare wrote, '*I know a bank whereon the wild thyme blows*'; he was referring to *Thymus serpyllum*, sometimes called the Creeping Thyme, which is a spreading plant best suited to growing between paving stones and at the sides of paths rather than for use in the kitchen. Its correct botanical name is now *Thymus drucei*.

The Common Thyme, *Thymus vulgaris*, bushy and full of vitality, has leaves with a slightly sweet and spicy bouquet, and is a valuable ingredient in a wide range of dishes. The Lemon-scented Thyme, *T.* x *citriodorus*, has leaves that emit a strongly lemony and somewhat verbena-like fragrance. The Caraway-scented Thyme, *T. herba-barona*, has a wonderful aroma of caraway, and with its low, spreading habit is, like the Lemon-scented Thyme and Creeping Thyme, best reserved for growing between paving stones rather than for use in kitchens.

As well as their invaluable role in the kitchen, thymes were also used for strewing on floors to create a fresh atmosphere. In the symbolism of flowers thyme was the sign of courage, and ladies frequently embroidered a bee hovering over a sprig of thyme on the scarves they gave as favors to their knights.

A collection of herbs is not complete without Sage, widely used in the flavoring of food. In addition to the common type there are several forms, narrow or broad-leaved, as well as the Red Sage, of which the

The fresh, cucumber-like bouquet of Borage (Borage officinalis), *below, is supplemented by attractive blue flowers from mid- to late summer. Clary* (Salvia sclarea), *right, has leaves with a sage-like freshness.*

young leaves are tinged violet. Although the latter is now mainly grown for its decorative value, in earlier times it was more esteemed than the green form for use in the kitchen.

Clary – also known as Old Clary and Clary Sage – was invariably present in the herb gardens of centuries past. When picked and placed in a vase it brings a sage-like freshness to rooms, and is even better when displayed with foxgloves or catmint. Oil of clary, derived from the leaves, is widely used in perfumery and for flavoring wines such as Muscatel and Vermouth. The powdered leaves have also been taken as snuff.

Sage flowers, with their fragrant resin, were used to make a cordial that in the 17th century was believed to make men immortal and to retard the rapid progress of decay.

Parsley, *Petroselinum crispum*, with its delicate and distinctive bouquet, is invaluable both as a garnish and as a cooking ingredient. It is usually grown as an annual, often in small pots near a kitchen door. Positioned around the edge of a cluster of other herbs on a patio, it softens the outline of the group.

Balm, *Melissa officinalis*, has superbly lemon-scented, pale green leaves. If you want to plant it in a herbaceous border, choose the variegated form with golden-green leaves, which have a fragrance just as exciting as the green form. Bees are attracted to the sweet flowers, and the leaves, when rubbed on bee hives, are said to keep the bees together as well as enabling those in flight to find the hive.

Sweet Cicely, *Myrrhis odorata*, is another herb said to attract bees, and the seeds of this herbaceous perennial have been used in polishes for scenting oak floors and furniture.

The charm of herbs lies not only in their varying scents and the flavor they bring to food, but also in the nostalgia they arouse for the past. Their names recall songs, poetry and street cries many hundreds of years old, and they thus bring a sense of history into the garden.

Angelica (Archangelica angelica), *left, creates a dominant display in both herb gardens and herbaceous borders. The variegated form of Balm* (Melissa officinalis), *right, has a distinctive lemon scent.*

PLANT	SCENT	COLOR	SITUATION	CULTIVATION
AMBERGRIS				
Salvia sclarea Clary/Clary Sage	Emits an oil resembling ambergris.	Large, hairy leaves and high, loose heads of tubular, bluish-white flowers during late summer.	In an herb garden or perennial border.	Height: 2½ft (75cm) Spread: 15-18 inches (38-45cm) **Hardy biennial usually grown as an annual:** Sow seeds ¼ inch (6mm) deep in mid-spring in their flowering positions. Germination takes two to three weeks; when the seedlings are large enough to handle, thin them to 12-15 inches (30-38cm) apart.
ANISE				
Anthriscus cerefolium Chervil	Aniseed.	Bright green, finely-divided fern-like leaves on ridged, hollow stems. White flowers in umbrella-like heads, 3 inches (7.5cm) wide, from mid- to late summer.	In an herb garden or at the edge of a perennial border.	Height: 12-18 inches (30-45cm) Spread: 15 inches (38cm) **Hardy biennial:** Sow seeds in shallow drills from spring to late summer. When large enough to handle, thin seedlings first to 6 inches (15cm) apart, then 12 inches (30cm). To produce a succession of young leaves for cutting, sow seeds at 14-day intervals. Plants do not flower until mid- to late summer of their second year, but the leaves can be harvested during the first season.
Foeniculum vulgare Fennel	Strongly anise-like.	Bluish-green, thread-like leaves on upright stems. Golden-yellow flowers borne in umbrella-like heads up to 4 inches (10cm) wide during late summer.	In a large herb garden or a perennial border.	Height: 5-6ft (1.5-1.8m) Spread: 2-2½ft (60-75cm) **Hardy herbaceous perennial:** Divide and replant congested plants in spring, setting them 1½-2ft (45-60cm) apart. Alternatively, sow seeds ¼-½ inch (6-12mm) deep in mid-spring. Thin out the seedlings to 15-18 inches (38-45cm) apart when they are large enough to handle.
Anethum graveolens (syn: *Peucedanum graveolens*) Dill	Anise-like.	Bluish-green, thread-like, feathery leaves on upright, ridged and hollow stems. Small, starry, yellow flowers in umbrella-like heads up to 3 inches (7.5cm) wide from mid- to late summer.	In an herb garden or perennial border.	Height: 2½-3ft (75-90cm) Spread: 12-15 inches (30-38cm) **Hardy annual:** Sow seeds ½ inch (12mm) deep in seed drills from late spring to early summer. Germination takes about two weeks; when the seedlings are large enough to handle, thin them first to 6 inches (15cm) apart, later to 12 inches (30cm).
Pimpinella anisum Aniseed/Anise/Green Anise	Sweet and anise-like.	Brilliant green, feathery, fern-like leaves. Umbrella-like heads of dainty white flowers in midsummer.	In an herb garden or in large containers.	Height: 18 inches (45cm) Spread: 12-15 inches (30-38cm) **Hardy annual:** Sow seeds ¼ inch (6mm) deep in a nursery bed in mid-spring. Germination takes up to three weeks. When the seedlings are large enough to handle, transplant them to 12 inches (30cm) apart.
APPLE				
Mentha rotundifolia Apple Mint/Round-leaved Mint/Egyptian Mint/Woolly Mint	Resembles that of apple.	Pale green, oval leaves covered with whitish hairs. Purple flowers in dense whorls from mid- to late summer.	In an herb garden or in bottomless buckets to restrict the invasive roots.	Height: 2-2½ft (60-75cm) Spread: 2-4ft (0.75-1.2m) **Herbaceous perennial:** Plant 12 inches (30cm) apart in spring. Divide congested plants in spring, replanting the young parts.
BALSAM				
Origanum vulgare Wild Marjoram/Oregano/Common Marjoram	Sweet, balsam-like leaves with a warm, bitter taste.	Medium-green, rounded, and oval leaves. Rose-purple, tubular flowers borne in terminal clusters during midsummer.	In an herb garden or in pots.	Height: 12-18 inches (30-45cm) Spread: 15-18 inches (38-45cm) **Hardy perennial:** Set out young plants 12 inches (30cm) apart in spring. Sow seeds ¼ inch (6mm) deep *in situ* during late spring. When the seedlings are large enough to handle, thin them to 8-12 inches (20-30cm) apart.

PLANT	SCENT	COLOR	SITUATION	CULTIVATION
BAY				
Laurus nobilis Sweet Bay	Bay.	Medium to dark green, lance-shaped leaves with wavy edges.	In an herb garden or in large tubs. Position on either side of an entrance or small flight of steps. When grown with a white wall in the background, the plant's attractive appearance is further enhanced.	Height: 6-8ft (1.8-2.4m) in a large tub; 15-18ft (4.5-5.4m) in an herb garden Spread: 3-4ft (0.9-1.2m) in a large tub **Tender, evergreen tree:** Plant in well-drained soil in a sunny position. Clip in the summer with a sharp pair of pruners to encourage bushiness. Bring in for the winter in all but the warmest areas.
BITTER AND SPICY				
Salvia officinalis Sage	Sage.	Gray-green, wrinkled and woolly leaves clasp stiff, four-sided stems. Violet-purple, tubular flowers in midsummer.	In an herb garden or in large pots.	Height: 1½-2ft (45-60cm) Spread: 15-18 inches (38-45cm) **Hardy, evergreen sub-shrub:** Plant in well-drained soil in a bright, sunny position. Plants become leggy after three or four years and are best replaced with fresh specimens. Nip out the tops of young plants to encourage bushiness.
Satureja hortensis Summer Savory	Bitter, spicy, pungent and strong.	Dark green, lance-shaped leaves clasp square, hairy stems. Small, lilac-colored, tubular flowers from leaf joints from mid- to late summer.	In an herb garden or in containers.	Height: 10-12 inches (25-30cm) Spread: 6-9 inches (15-23cm) **Bushy, hardy annual:** Sow seeds in spring, ¼ inch (6mm) deep, where they are to grow. Germination takes two to three weeks; when the seedlings are large enough to handle, thin them to 6-9 inches (15-23cm) apart.
Satureja montana Winter Savory	Strong, coarsely bitter, pungent and peppery.	Gray-green, lance-shaped leaves borne on erect, woody, square stems. Rosy-purple, tubular flowers from mid- to late summer.	In an herb garden.	Height: 12 inches (30cm) Spread: 9-12 inches (23-30cm) **Hardy perennial:** Sow seeds ¼ inch (6mm) deep during mid-spring where the plants are to grow. Germination takes two to three weeks; when the seedlings are large enough to handle, thin them to 9-12 inches (23-30cm) apart.
CARAWAY				
Carum carvi Caraway	Caraway.	Medium-green, fern-like leaves. Small, green flowers borne in umbrella-like heads during midsummer.	In an herb garden or perennial border.	Height: 15-18 inches (38-45cm) Spread: 12-15 inches (30-38cm) **Hardy biennial:** Sow seeds in late summer where they are to flower. Thin the seedlings first to 6 inches (15cm) apart, later to 12 inches (30cm). Flowers are produced during the following season.
CLOVES				
Ocimum basilicum Basil	Strongly clove-like.	Bright green, oval leaves, grayish-green and purple below. White, tubular flowers in whorls during late summer.	In an herb garden or in large pots.	Height: 2-3ft (60-90cm) Spread: 15-18 inches (38-45cm) **Tender annual:** Sow seeds ¼ inch (6mm) deep in seed drills *in situ* during late spring. Germination takes two to three weeks. When large enough to handle, thin the seedlings first to 4 inches (10cm) apart, later to 12 inches (30cm).
CUCUMBER				
Borago officinalis Borage	Resembles cucumber.	Light green, oval, corrugated leaves covered with rough, silvery hairs. Upright, hollow stems. Blue, star-like flowers from mid- to late summer.	In an herb garden.	Height: 1½-2½ft (45-75cm) Spread: 12-15 inches (30-38cm) **Hardy annual:** Sow seeds in shallow drills during mid-spring. Seeds germinate in two to three weeks; when large enough to handle, thin to 12 inches (30cm) apart.

PLANT	SCENT	COLOR	SITUATION	CULTIVATION
GARLIC				
Allium sativum Garlic	Garlic.	Gray-green leaves. Rounded heads up to 1½ inches (4cm) wide bearing white, red-tinged flowers. It is the bulbs at the plant's base that are used in cooking.	In an herb garden.	Height: 1-2½ft (30-75cm) Spread: 10-15 inches (25-38cm) **Hardy perennial bulbous herb:** Plant garlic cloves in drills 3 inches (7.5cm) deep in fall, with their noses just below soil level. Pinch off flowering heads and lift bulbs in late summer.
GINGER				
Mentha x gentilis Ginger Mint/Scotch Mint	Spicy, gingerish scent with the tang of spearmint.	Medium-green, oval to lance-shaped leaves which clasp purple stems. Pale purple, tubular flowers from mid to late summer.	In an herb garden or in large containers to restrict the invasive roots.	Height: 9-18 inches (23-45cm) Spread: 2-3ft (60-90cm) **Herbaceous perennial:** Treat as for *Mentha rotundifolia* (see p.98).
LEMON				
Melissa officinalis Lemon Balm	Lemon-scented leaves.	Pale green, wrinkled and toothed, nettle-like leaves clasping hairy stems. White, tubular flowers appear during midsummer.	In an herb garden or perennial border.	Height: 2-4ft (0.60-1.2m) Spread: 15-18 inches (38-45cm) **Herbaceous perennial:** Set out new plants 15 inches (38cm) apart in spring in well-drained soil, in full sun. In autumn, cut back all shoots to just above soil level. Divide congested plants in spring, replanting young parts.
Thymus x citriodorus Lemon Thyme/ Lemon-scented Thyme	Lemon-like.	Medium-green, long, narrow leaves, broader than *T. vulgaris* (see opposite). Pale pink flowers in terminal clusters from mid- to late summer.	In an herb garden or in pots.	Height: 10-12 inches (25-30cm) Spread: 9-12 inches (23-30cm) **Hardy, evergreen, dwarf shrub:** Treat as for *Thymus vulgaris*.
LICORICE				
Myrrhis odorata Sweet Cicely	Sweet and licorice-like, with a tang of anise.	Bright green, fern-like leaves, delicately lacy and downy and flecked with creamy-white. Small white flowers during early summer, followed by large, green seeds that slowly turn black.	In an herb garden or perennial border.	Height: 3-4ft (0.9-1.2m) Spread: 2½-3ft (75-90cm) **Herbaceous perennial:** Sow seeds in shallow drills in a nursery bed during late spring and early summer. When the seedlings are large enough to handle, plant them 2ft (60cm) apart in their growing positions.
MINT				
Artemisia dracunculus Tarragon/French Tarragon	Sweet and slightly mint-like.	Gray-green, narrow leaves clustered around stiff stems, creating a bushy plant. In warm regions, small, greenish-white flowers are sometimes produced.	In an herb garden or in pots.	Height: 1½-2ft (45-60cm) Spread: 15-18 inches (38-45cm) **Hardy herbaceous perennial, evergreen in mild areas:** Divide plants in spring, planting them 2-3 inches (5-7.5cm) deep and 12-15 inches (30-38cm) apart.
Hyssopus officinalis Hyssop	Bitter and mint-like.	Medium-green, narrow, lance-like leaves crowded along upright stems. Purple-blue, lipped and tubular flowers from mid- to late summer.	In an herb garden or in pots.	Height: 15-24 inches (38-60cm) Spread: 12-15 inches (30-38cm) **Hardy herbaceous perennial:** Sow seeds ¼ inch (6mm) deep during mid-spring. Seeds germinate in two to three weeks. When the seedlings are large enough to handle, thin them first to 6 inches (15cm) apart, later to 12 inches (30cm).
Mentha spicata Spearmint/Garden Mint/Common Mint	Strongly mint-scented.	Medium-green, shiny-surfaced oval to lance-shaped leaves. Pale purple flowers in spikes from mid- to late summer.	In herb gardens or bottomless buckets to restrict the invasive roots.	Height: 1½-2ft (45-60cm) Spread: 15-18 inches (38-45cm) **Herbaceous perennial:** Treat as for *Mentha rotundifolia* (see p.98).
Mentha x villosa Bowles's Mint/French Mint	Fruity, strongly mint-scented.	Soft, downy, broad leaves. Pale purple flowers in spikes from mid- to late summer.	In an herb garden or in large buckets to restrict the invasive roots.	Height: 3-5ft (0.9-1.5m) Spread: 2½-3½ft (0.75-1m) **Herbaceous perennial:** Treat as for *Mentha rotundifolia* (see p.98).

PLANT	SCENT	COLOR	SITUATION	CULTIVATION
MUSK AND JUNIPER				
Angelica archangelica Angelica	Fusion of musk and juniper.	Light green, finely-toothed leaves, deeply dissected and divided. Stems ridged and hollow. Rounded, umbrella-like heads of yellow-green flowers during late summer.	In a large herb garden or perennial border.	Height: 5-8ft (1.5-2.4m) Spread: 3-4ft (0.9-1.2m) **Hardy biennial:** Sow seeds in a seedbed in spring. Germination takes two to three weeks; when the seedlings are established thin them to 12 inches (30cm) apart. Keep seedbed free from weeds and in spring of the following year transplant young plants to 3ft (90cm) apart.
ONION				
Allium schoenoprasum Chives	Mild and onion-like.	Medium-green, tubular, grass-like leaves. Starry, globular heads of rose-pink flowers during midsummer.	In an herb garden or in pots.	Height: 6-10 inches (15-25cm) Spread: 10-15 inches (25-38cm) **Hardy herbaceous perennial:** Set new plants 12 inches (30cm) apart in well-drained, fertile soil in full sun. Keep the soil moist during dry periods, and nip off flower stems. Lift and divide congested clumps in autumn, replanting young pieces from around the outside.
PARSLEY				
Petroselinum crispum (syn. *P. sativum*) Parsley	Spicy.	Medium-green, densely curled leaves borne on hollow, branching stems during summer. Young leaves have the best fragrance and the finest flavor.	In pots or in an herb garden.	Height: 8-15 inches (20-38cm) Spread: 8-10 inches (20-25cm) **Hardy biennial usually grown as an annual:** Sow seeds ¼ inch (6mm) deep in fertile soil from mid-spring to midsummer, in full sun or light shade. Germination is slow. Thin the seedlings, when large enough to handle, first to 3 inches (7.5cm) apart, later to 9 inches (23cm).
PEPPERMINT				
Mentha x piperita Peppermint/Brandy Mint	Strongly peppermint-scented leaves.	Spear to heart-shaped leaves. Reddish flowers in clusters on the upper leaf joints.	In an herb garden or a bottomless bucket to restrict the invasive roots.	Height: 1½-2ft (45-60cm) Spread: 15-18 inches (38-45cm) **Herbaceous perennial:** Treat as for *Mentha rotundifolia* (see p.98).
Mentha requienii Corsican Mint/ Spanish Mint/Crème de Menthe Mint	Peppermint-scented leaves.	Bright, pale green leaves. Tubular, pale purple flowers during summer.	In an herb garden or in pots.	Height: 1-3 inches (2.5-7.5cm) Spread: 12 inches (30cm) **Prostrate herbaceous perennial:** Treat as for *Mentha rotundifolia* (see p.98).
SWEET AND SPICY				
Thymus vulgaris Common Thyme/ Garden Thyme	Slightly sweet and spicy.	Dark green, long and narrow leaves. Midsummer clusters of tubular, mauve flowers from leaf joints.	In an herb garden or in pots.	Height: 4-8 inches (10-20cm) Spread: 9-12 inches (23-30cm) **Hardy, evergreen, dwarf shrub:** Divide congested plants in spring and replant young parts 9 inches (23cm) apart. Alternatively, take 2-3-inch-(5-7.5cm) long cuttings in early summer.
THYME				
Origanum majorana (syn. *Majorana hortensis*) Sweet Marjoram/ Knotted Marjoram/ Garden Marjoram	Sweet and thyme-like.	Gray, oval leaves borne in twos on four-sided red stems. White, mauve or pink tubular flowers from mid- to late summer.	In an herb garden.	Height: 2ft (60cm) Spread: 15-18 inches (38-45cm) **Bushy, perennial sub-shrub usually grown as an annual:** Treat as for *Origanum vulgare* (see p.98).
Origanum onites Pot Marjoram/French Marjoram	Slightly bitter and thyme-like.	Bright green, oval leaves on a sprawling, mound-forming plant. White to mauve tubular flowers from mid- to late summer.	In an herb garden or in pots.	Height: 12 inches (30cm) Spread: 15 inches (38cm) **Hardy perennial:** Treat as for *Origanum vulgare* (see p.98).

CHAPTER EIGHT

The Scented Flower Border

*A brilliantly eye-catching display of plants
billowing balmy scents all summer long can
be built up with a diverse selection of
annuals and perennials.*

ALL GARDENS, whether town or country, formal or informal, large or small, can be packed with rich and interesting perfumes. The flowers described in this chapter, as well as trees, shrubs, herbs and scented vines can all be used to create a picturesque scene that has nose-appeal as well as being pleasant to the eye.

Rich kaleidoscopes of color make an instant impact on visitors, but it is often the hidden depths of a garden – the scent of a certain flower or a heavily fragrant corner – that create the most lasting memory. It may be the nearly indefinable dual aroma of cloves and carnations that pervades *Babiana plicata*, the lingering and honey-like redolence of the Peruvian Daffodil, the honey-like Madonna Lily, or the sweet and plumlike bouquet of *Iris graminea*. All enrich the garden and create an enchanted world of fragrances.

Many plants have fascinating histories and names that confirm their fragrance. The Sweet Sultan, *Centaurea moschata*, has also been known as the Honey Flower, Blackamore's Beauty and Sultan's Flower by virtue of its introduction to Europe through Constantinople (now Istanbul) and of its patronage by the Sultan, who wore it himself.

St. Bernard's Lily, *Anthericum lilago*, and St. Bruno's Lily, *Paradisea liliastrum* (although frequently known as *Anthericum liliastrum*), have sweetly fragrant starry white flowers borne on slender stems. At one time they were considered to be an antidote to the bite of a venomous spider known as Phalangium, and so for many years were named after the spider. Their common name was also corrupted into Spiderwort, although this was usually interpreted as referring to the creeping nature of these attractive herbaceous plants rather than their claimed efficacy against spider bites.

The Sweet Scabious, *Scabiosa atropurpurea*, has a warm, honeyed fragrance. Its long flowering period over much of the summer and dark crimson flowers packed in pincushion-like heads up to 2 inches (5cm) wide make it a flower arranger's dream. Another common name for it is the Pincushion Flower. In the symbolism of flowers it is said to infer 'I have lost all', and small bouquets of it were once worn by widows mourning their dead husbands. This led to it being called Mournful Widow, although in North America it is known as Mourning Bride. On a more practical note, the botanical name *Scabiosa* is derived from the reputed power of some of the plants in this genus to cure scabies and other skin complaints which, during the 15th century, earned them the name of Skabiose or Scabyas.

The lilies are a glorious group of plants with wonderfully eye-catching flowers, many of which are renowned for their scent. They are especially useful in woodland settings with light shade. Few of these scented beauties are as well known as the Madonna Lily, *Lilium candidum*, with its rich, honey-like scent. It can probably lay claim to being the oldest lily in cultivation, and was grown by the Ancient Egyptians, who regarded it as a sacred and medicinal plant. It was known for a long time as the White Lily, until the Renaissance, when it became associated in paintings with the Virgin Mary and took on the name Madonna Lily and the symbolism of purity. It delights in a warm, lightly shaded position, sheltered from wind, where the beautiful perfume is not rapidly dispersed. Besides a lightly shaded woodland setting, it grows in a partially shaded herbaceous border where it can nestle among leafy plants. In mixed borders it mingles well with low shrubs and annuals. Few gardens, therefore, are unable to offer a home for it.

Just as well-known is the Gold-banded Lily, *Lilium auratum*, with its sweetly and strongly perfumed, bowl-shaped, brilliant white flowers that bear characteristic golden-yellow rays or bands. For late summer fragrance the profuse flowers, which are up to 12 inches (30cm) wide, have few peers. Indeed, it is often considered to be the most floriferous of all lilies, both enriching the air and pleasing the eye with its beauty.

Lilium cernuum has sweetly fragrant, pale pink flowers with red-purple spots borne on stems only 18 inches (45cm) high, allowing it to be grown in even the smallest of gardens. Another lily with a sweet bouquet is the Scarlet Turk's-cap Lily, *Lilium chalcedonicum*. It gains part of its name from the Chalcedon district (now Kadi-Keui) opposite Constantinople, although the plant is a native of Greece. The combination of the sweet aroma and the brilliant, intense scarlet

The familiar, sweetly scented flowers of Nasturtiums (Tropaeolum majus) *are welcome in any garden, whether as climbers or as fillers for border edges.*

flowers earn it a place in any garden, where it will grow in superb combination with other aromatic plants such as the Russian Sage *(Perovskia atriplicifolia)* and the Tree Poppy *(Romneya x coulteri)*. Indeed, such is the impact of this lily that in some places it was known as "Turn Again Gentlemen". Few plants can lay claim to such a delightful and descriptive name!

The Regal Lily, *Lilium regale*, very much assumes the superior role indicated in its name, having sweet, strongly scented white flowers with sulphur-yellow centers and rose-purple shaded backs. As many as 30 scented flowers are carried on a single stem. The Nankeen Lily, *Lilium x testaceum*, is a cross between two other lilies that resulted in a sweetly scented hybrid, an aristocrat among lilies that grows well in city gardens. For a heavily sweet scent, reminiscent of jasmine, choose the Easter Lily, *Lilium longiflorum*. It is often a central part of spring wedding bouquets after being forced into bloom at a time far earlier than its normal late-summer period – hence its rather confusing common name. Equally confusing is its other name, Bermuda Lily, which does not refer to its place of origin – which is in fact the south of Japan – but to where a great amount of development occurred to improve and develop it.

The Giant Lily of the Himalayas, *Cardiocrinum giganteum*, was earlier classified as *Lilium giganteum* and is still frequently listed in this way. It actually differs from lilies in having large, heart-shaped leaves. The sweetly fragrant flowers are cream or greenish-white and narrowly trumpet-like, and hang their heads from a stiff and upright stem that sometimes reaches 10ft (3m) high. Light shade and compost-rich, moisture-retentive soil are essential for the development of the mid- to late-summer flowers.

The charming *Muscari racemosum* bears deep blue flowers with white mouths and a sweet, plummy scent. This bulbous plant is superb for a small garden, bringing an unusual fragrance to path edges and fronts of borders as well as to rock gardens. The Musk Hyacinth, *Muscarimia moschatum*, which is frequently known as *Muscari moschatum*, can be planted in the same sites as its plum-scented relative. Another delightful muscari is the unfortunately named *Muscari neglectum*, which paints an attractive picture at the edges of borders. Its sweetly scented, densely packed heads have dark blue flowers with white mouths during mid- to late spring. It is one of the easiest muscaris to grow, and it would be nice to think that it gained its name for this reason rather than from its often excessively leafy habit which seems too much for a plant of its size.

The Grape Hyacinth, *Muscari botryoides*, is a favorite in spring, with a sweet, honey-like fragrance that makes it delightful for window boxes and the edges of borders near the house. If it has a fault, it is that it soon covers the ground and suffocates less boisterous plants, but if you'd enjoy a sea of scented blue flowers packed like beads on stems some 4-6 inches (10-15cm) high, then plant the bulbs in late summer and autumn and forget its foibles. There is also a white form of Grape Hyacinth, whose appearance has been wonderfully captured in an earlier name, "Pearls of Spain" – a beautiful and apt description that must surely deserve more use.

For many gardeners, spring is not worthwhile without carpets of yellow and white daffodils warming the ground, and when they are scented this adds to their charm. (All daffodils are known as Narcissi, and are the types with large trumpets.)

The Old Pheasant's Eye, *Narcissus poeticus recurvus*, is popular for its fragrant flowers, and at one time was known as Sweet Nancy. The pretty flowers have snow-white petals and yellow eyes edged in tangerine.

The sweet and penetrating fragrance of the Jonquil or Wild Jonquil, *Narcissus jonquilla*, is well known, and the flowers are superb when cut for decoration indoors. The perfume is so strong that sometimes it is

For many gardeners, herbaceous borders massed with scented and colorful plants epitomise the beauty of a traditional garden.

*The sweetly scented flowers,
reminiscent of orange blossom, of the
Bearded Iris (Iris x germanica)
are distinctively shaped and colored.*

Walled gardens are ideal for scented plants, since the walls contain and concentrate fragrance, and they accentuate scents on hot summer days.

was kept in vessels of silver and gold. This sweetly scented lotion was used to ease the pain of gout, to remedy sprains and as part of a love potion. Site this hardy plant in wild gardens or in a lightly shaded corner. A word of warning is due about both the red berries, which have a bitter flavor and have caused fatalities, and the roots, which are invasive and are best kept away from brick terraces and patios.

As well as a general citron-like aroma, balsam-scented leaves and sweetly scented, spider-like flowers, the Gas Plant, *Dictamnus albus*, has an amazing quality – in hot, dry weather resinous glands in the leaves emit a vapor which is inflammable and can be set alight without harming the plant. For this reason it was also named Burning Bush and Candle Plant.

The Meadowsweet, *Filipendula ulmaria*, does, as its name reveals, fill meadows with a rich almond-like fragrance. This hardy herbaceous perennial opens its feathery plumes of scented, creamy-white flowers from early to late summer. The Manchurian *Filipendula kamtschatica* also has sweet flowers, fleecy white and in large, loose plumes on large plants.

The irises are rich in scent, and perhaps none is so well known as the Bearded Iris or German Iris, *Iris x germanica*. Its reliability and hardiness have made it a part of many gardens, creating a wealth of sweetly scented flowers with a hint of orange-blossom fragrance during early summer. When given a wind-sheltered border they soon reward the gardener with heady aromas and a wide range of flower colors. The Florentine Iris, now considered to be a form of the Bearded but better known as *Iris florentina*, has for many centuries provided the scent for many classic toiletries. The flowers have a wonderful fragrance, full of violet-like sweetness, that make it a wonderful plant for any scented garden.

There are many other scented irises, especially *Iris graminea*, with a sweet scent resembling ripe plums, and *Iris pallida*, with flowers that combine the rich aroma of orange blossom and elder. The Algerian or Winter Iris, *Iris unguicularis* (often better known as *Iris stylosa*), is demurely sweet with flowers that bloom from late autumn to early spring when the garden is lacking in color.

Catmint has such a magnetic attraction for cats that they can soon ruin a clump, but few gardeners would deny their own cat such enjoyment; a neighbor's cat would probably not be as welcome! The British native *Nepeta cataria* is widely grown in North America as Catnip. Nowadays the leaves are used as a tea, but in earlier times, Catmint was credited with the ability to make meek men fierce. A story is told of a gentle hangman who could not perform his role until he had first chewed the root of Catmint. 'Citriodora', a form of this plant, has lemon-scented leaves.

Nepeta x *faassenii*, also known as *Nepeta mussinii*, is the Catmint most widely grown, and has spikes of

nearly overpowering, but nonetheless welcome during spring. The Bunch-flowered Narcissus or Polyanthus Narcissus, *Narcissus tazetta*, needs a warm climate to assure its success outdoors. It tends to be a very variable species, but is distinguished by the many flowers that develop on each stem. There are many forms of it, mainly grown in greenhouses and for forcing into early flower indoors. In its warm native lands – from southern Europe eastwards to China and Japan – it has been known as the New Year Lily, Good-luck Flower and Sacred Chinese Lily. The Paper White Narcissus, *Narcissus tazetta papyraceus*, is an all-white form that can be forced into early flower.

The nodding, bell-shaped flowers and broad leaves of the Lily-of-the-Valley, *Convallaria majalis*, are familiar to everyone. The deliciously sweet and strong fragrance from the late spring flowers is a joy to every gardener, as well as to flower arrangers, who often create richly scented displays with them. During the 15th century the plant was used to create lily-of-the-valley water, which was so treasured in Europe that it

*Massed herbaceous perennials are
superb when planted to create a dense
wall of aroma and color alongside
well-manicured lawns.*

The sweetly scented, trumpet-shaped flowers of the Giant Lily (Cardiocrinum giganteum) create a dominant display in a lightly shaded woodland garden.

The leaves of Catmint (Nepeta x *faassenii*), *with a mint-jelly fragrance, are an attractive feature of gardens, particularly when set alongside paths.*

lavender-blue flowers from early to late summer. When crushed, the leaves emit a pungent mint-jelly fragrance, while the flowers are sweeter, with a gentle mint-jelly aroma. Its somewhat wispy habit makes it a good edging to paths with a cottage-garden appearance. *Nepeta nervosa* is superb in herbaceous or mixed beds, bearing leaves which emit a slightly pungent mint aroma when crushed.

The phloxes are North American plants; some are rock-garden plants, others annuals and a few perennials. It is the latter that are known for their sweetly scented flowers. The Wild Sweet William, *Phlox maculata*, bears very sweet heads of purple flowers from mid- to late summer; some people even find the sweetness overwhelming. The Garden Phlox, *Phlox paniculata*, has dense heads of very sweet-smelling purple flowers from mid- to late summer. However, it is its many attractive varieties, available in a wide color range, that are usually grown.

The Common Mignonette, *Reseda odorata*, offers a richness not to be missed by any gardener – nor by any lover, if the tradition that success and good fortune will attend a lover who rolls in a bed of mignonette three times holds true!

When Common Mignonette was introduced into Britain during the early 1700s, it was known as the Yellow-flowered Aegyptian Bastard Rocket. By the early 1800s it was widely used in London window boxes to drench the air with perfume. While some people found the scent overpowering, others welcomed a plant that could mask the unbearable smells often present in the streets. Roast coffee beans performed the same role in Paris, where the air was similarly fetid. Sweet Mignonette became a very fashionable plant in France when the Empress Josephine cultivated it; apparently Napoleon brought back its seed after his abortive attempt to conquer Egypt in the late 1790s.

The North American smilacinas are sweely scented hardy herbaceous perennials for a lightly shaded border. The beautiful and descriptively named Star-flowered Lily-of-the-Valley, *Smilacina stellata*, is strongly fragrant, with arching sprays of white, star-shaped flowers during early summer. The False Spikenard or False Solomon's Seal, *Smilacina racemosa*, has arching, terminal sprays of sweetly scented, creamy-white flowers. The real Solomon's Seal, *Polygonatum* x *hybridum* (also sold as *Polygonatum multiflorum*) is indigenous to Britain, where it is also known as David's Harp and Ladder to Heaven. The arching stems bear slightly waisted, sweetly scented white flowers in clusters of two to five during midsummer. Bumblebees are very attracted by its sweet flowers.

The Lemon-scented Verbena, *Aloysia triphylla*, has leaves which, when bruised, emit a strong, lemon-like odor. It is only hardy outside in the warmest of areas; elsewhere a frost-proof greenhouse is needed for this tender deciduous shrub. The small, tubular, pale mauve flowers are borne at the ends of shoots during late summer.

The Sand Verbena, *Abronia latifolia*, is another half-hardy plant, with a sweet, honey-like fragrance. It brightens midsummer with lemon-yellow flowers borne in dense clusters. A related species, *Abronia fragrans*, opens its very sweet, pure-white flowers during afternoons and into evenings.

Calamintha grandiflora holds in its name the promise of the strong minty aroma in its soft and hairy leaves. Rose-purple flowers appear during summer on this woody perennial.

The Rocket Candytuft, *Iberis amara*, is a hardy annual with sweetly scented heads of white flowers during summer. It can be grown either in annual borders or in pots in a cool sunroom or greenhouse, where it creates a pleasing aroma.

If you favor a vanilla-like fragrance with undertones of cloves, then the Tree Lupin, *Lupinus arboreus*, is an essential part of your scented garden. It is a short-lived, shrubby perennial native to California, and is a delight in a mixed border with its scented, lemon-yellow, clustered flower heads.

PLANT	SCENT	COLOR	SITUATION	CULTIVATION
ALMOND				
Filipendula ulmaria (syn. *Spiraea ulmaria*) Meadowsweet/ Queen-of-the-Meadow	Almond, but rather heavy.	Branching, flattened heads up to 6 inches (15cm) wide formed of creamy-white flowers from early to late summer.	In a perennial or mixed border.	Height: 2½-3ft (75-90cm) Spread: 1½ft (45cm) **Hardy herbaceous perennial:** Well-drained but moisture-retentive, slightly limy soil in full sun or slight shade.
CITRON				
Dictamnus albus (syn. *Dictamnus fraxinella*) Gas Plant/Burning Bush	Whole plant emits a heavy and rather citron-like aroma, while the leaves, when bruised, smell of balsam. The flowers are sweetly fragrant.	Spider-like white flowers during early and midsummer.	In a perennial or mixed border.	Height: 2ft (60cm) Spread: 18 inches (45cm) **Hardy herbaceous perennial:** Well-drained, slightly limy soil and a sunny position.
CLOVES				
Babiana plicata	Carnation and clove-like.	Pale lilac-mauve flowers, with darker basal markings, during early to midsummer.	In a small, warm and sheltered border or a cool greenhouse.	Height: 6-8 inches (15-20cm) Spread: 4-6 inches (10-15cm) **Tender cormous plant:** Well-drained soil and plenty of sun. Lift corms in late summer, replanting in pots in spring.
FRUITY				
Iris pumila Dwarf Bearded Iris	Sweet, attaining a fruity aroma with age.	Shades of purple, white, yellow, and yellow with brown tints. Hybrids are taller and in a wider color range. It flowers early, during mid- to late spring.	In a rock garden or a narrow and sheltered border.	Height: 4-5 inches (10-13cm) Spread: 3 inches (7.5cm) **Dwarf Bearded Iris:** Fertile, well-drained soil in a sunny positon.
HONEY				
Abronia latifolia Yellow Sand Verbena	Honey-like and sweet.	Lemon-yellow flowers in dense clusters during midsummer.	Plant at the base of south- or west-facing walls.	Height: 9-18 inches (23-45cm) Spread: 12-18 inches (30-45cm) **West Coast perennial:** Well-drained, sandy soil and a warm, sheltered position.
Hymenocallis narcissiflora (syn. *H. calathina/Pancratium narcissiflorum*) Peruvian Daffodil/ Spider Lily	Honey-like, lingering and sweet.	White, spider-like, funnel-shaped flowers up to 6 inches (15cm) wide during midsummer.	In a warm and sheltered border or a cool greenhouse.	Height: 1½-2ft (45-60cm) Spread: 12-15 inches (30-38cm) **Tender bulbous plant:** Well-drained soil and plenty of sun. Plant bulbs in spring.
Lilium candidum Madonna Lily/White Madonna Lily/ Bourbon Lily/White Lily	Honey-like scent.	Widely bell-shaped, pure white flowers with golden anthers during mid- to late summer.	In a warm, sheltered position in light shade.	Height: 4-5ft (1.2-1.5m) Spread: 15-18 inches (38-45cm) **Hardy basal-rooting bulb:** Well-drained and moisture-retentive soil.
Scabiosa atropurpurea Sweet Scabious/ Mournful Widow	Honey-like and warm.	Petal-packed heads, 2 inches (5cm) wide, of dark crimson flowers from mid- to late summer. Many varieties in a range of colors.	In mixed and perennial borders.	Height: 2-2½ft (60-75cm) Spread: 9-12 inches (23-30cm) **Hardy annual:** Well-drained, fertile soil and a sunny position.
HYACINTH				
Babiana disticha Hyacinth-scented Babiana	Hyacinth-scented.	Pale blue flowers in small clusters amid sword-like leaves during early summer.	In a small, warm and sheltered border or a cool greenhouse.	Height: 9-12 inches (23-30cm) Spread: 6-8 inches (15-20cm) **Tender cormous plant:·** Well-drained soil and plenty of sun. Lift corms in late summer, replanting in pots in spring.

PLANT	SCENT	COLOR	SITUATION	CULTIVATION
JASMINE				
Lilium longiflorum Easter Lily/Bermuda Lily	Heavily sweet, reminiscent of jasmine.	Trumpet-shaped, glistening white flowers with golden pollen during late summer.	In a warm, sheltered position in light shade. Also suitable for planting in pots.	Height: 2-3ft (60-90cm) Spread: 10-12 inches (25-30cm) **Tender stem-rooting bulb:** Well-drained and moisture-retentive soil. It is tolerant of lime in the soil.
LEMON				
Aloysia triphylla (syn. *Lippia citriodora*) Lemon Verbena/ Sweet-scented Verbena	Strongly lemon-scented leaves, especially when bruised.	Small, tubular, pale mauve flowers borne at the ends of shoots during late summer.	Only suitable outside in very warm areas, otherwise it needs a frost-proof greenhouse.	Height: 4-5ft (1.2-1.5m) Spread: 3½-4ft (1-1.2m) **Tender deciduous shrub:** Well-drained soil and a sheltered, sunny position, preferably against a wall.
MINT				
Calamintha grandiflora Calamint	Soft, hairy leaves have a minty and pungent aroma.	Rose-purple flowers during summer.	In a sheltered border.	Height: 9-18 inches (23-45cm) Spread: 1½-2ft (45-60cm) **Woody perennial:** Ordinary soil, as long as it is not continually moist, and a sunny or partially shaded position.
MINT JELLY				
Nepeta nervosa	Leaves emit a fragrance of slightly bitter mint jelly when crushed. Flowers are sweeter, with a gentle mint jelly aroma.	Spikes of tightly-packed, clear blue flowers from mid- to late summer.	In a perennial or mixed border.	Height: 18 inches (45cm) Spread: 12-15 inches (30-38cm) **Hardy herbaceous perennial:** Well-drained soil in full sun or light shade.
Nepeta x faassenii (syn. *Nepeta mussinii*) Catmint	Leaves emit a fragrance of slightly bitter mint jelly when crushed. Flowers are sweeter, with a gentle mint jelly aroma.	Spikes of lavender-blue flowers from early to late summer.	In a perennial or mixed border, or as an edging for a firm-surfaced path.	Height: 12-18 inches (30-45cm) Spread: 12-15 inches (30-38cm) **Hardy herbaceous perennial:** Well-drained soil in full sun or light shade.
MUSK				
Centaurea moschata Sweet Sultan	Musk-like and rich.	Cornflower-like heads, 3 inches (7.5cm) wide, in white, pink, yellow or purple from early summer to autumn.	In annual and mixed borders.	Height: 2ft (60cm) Spread: 9-12 inches (23-30cm) **Hardy annual:** Sow seeds ¼ inch (6mm) deep in spring where they are to flower.
Muscarimia moschatum (syn. *Muscari moschatum*) Musk Hyacinth	Musk-like and sweet.	Flowers first appear tinged purple, changing to a greenish-yellow and bright yellow. They have brown mouths and are borne in dense clusters at the tops of stems during spring and early summer.	As an edging for a bed, at the front of a border and in a rock garden.	Height: 6-9 inches (15-23cm) Spread: 4-5 inches (10-13cm) **Hardy bulb:** Well-drained soil and full sun.
NEW-MOWN HAY				
Lobularia maritima (syn. *Alyssum maritimum*) Sweet Alyssum	Sweet and like new-mown hay.	White, or various shades ot purple, from midsummer to autumn.	Along the edges of borders or paths. It often seeds itself throughout the garden, including in gravel drives.	Height: 3-6 inches (7.5-15cm) Spread: 4-8 inches (10-20cm) **Hardy annual:** Sow seeds in boxes in late winter and early spring in a greenhouse, or outside during late spring.

PLANT	SCENT	COLOR	SITUATION	CULTIVATION
ORANGE BLOSSOM				
Iris x germanica Bearded Iris/ German Iris	Sweet and reminiscent of orange blossom.	Bluish-purple falls and light purple standards, with white beards. Large variety of hybrids in a wide color range.	A narrow border against a wall, sheltered from strong winds.	Height: 2-3ft (60-90cm) Spread: 15-18 inches (38-45cm) **Intermediate Bearded Iris:** Fertile, well-drained soil in a sunny position.
Iris pallida Orris	Orange blossom and elderflowers.	Lavender-blue flowers, 4-5 inches (10-13cm) wide, during early summer.	Perennial borders or a narrow, sheltered border.	Height: 2-3ft (60-90cm) Spread: 15 inches (38cm) **Tall Bearded Iris:** Fertile, well-drained soil in a sunny position.
PLUM				
Iris graminea	Sweet, resembling ripe plums.	Reddish-purple; falls have blue-purple veins on a white background. Flowers during early summer on stems 9 inches (23cm) high.	In a perennial border.	Height: 12-18 inches (30-45cm) Spread: 10-12 inches (25-30cm) **Beardless Iris:** Fertile, well-drained soil in a sunny position.
Muscari racemosum Musk Hyacinth/ Nutmeg Hyacinth	Plum-scented and sweet.	Deep blue flowers with white mouths during spring.	As an edging for a bed, at the front of a border and in a rock garden.	Height: 8 inches (20cm) Spread: 3-4 inches (7.5-10cm) **Hardy bulb:** Well-drained soil and full sun.
SAGE				
Artemisia ludoviciana White Sage	Sweet and sage-like.	Aromatic, somewhat woolly and deeply divided leaves. Silver-white flowers during late summer and into autumn.	In a perennial or mixed border.	Height: 2-4ft (0.6-1.2m) Spread: 15-18 inches (38-45cm) **Hardy herbaceous perennial:** Light, well-drained soil in full sun.
Artemisia stelleriana Dusty Miller/Old Woman/Beach Wormwood	Sweet and sage-like.	Aromatic, deeply lobed white leaves and yellow flowers during late summer and into autumn.	In a perennial or mixed border.	Height: 1½-2ft (45-60cm) Spread: 15 inches (38cm) **Hardy herbaceous perennial:** Light, well-drained soil in full sun.
VANILLA				
Lupinus arboreus Tree Lupin	Vanilla, with undertones of cloves.	Lemon-yellow flowers in clustered heads from early to late summer.	In a mixed border.	Height: 2-4ft (0.6-1.2m) Spread: 2-3ft (0.6-1.2m) **Short-lived shrubby perennial:** Light, well-drained soil in full sun or light shade.
VIOLET				
Inula hookeri	Slightly sweet, resembling violets.	Pale yellow flowers with finely dissected petals, 2½-3½ inches (6-8cm) wide, during late summer and early autumn.	In a perennial border.	Height: 1½-2ft (45-60cm) Spread: 1½-2ft (45-60cm) **Hardy herbaceous perennial:** Moisture-retentive soil and a sunny position.
Iris x germanica var. *florentina* Florentine Iris/Orris Root/Flower de Luce	Flowers and dried root emit a sweet violet fragrance.	Pale bluish-white flowers, 3-5 inches (7.5-13cm) wide, during early summer.	A narrow border against a wall, sheltered from strong winds.	Height: 2-3ft (60-90cm) Spread: 15-18 inches (38-45cm) **Intermediate Bearded Iris:** Fertile, well-drained soil in a sunny position.

PLANT	SCENT	COLOR	SITUATION	CULTIVATION
SWEET				
Acidanthera bicolor var. *murielae* (syn. *Acidanthera murielae*)	Sweet and penetrating.	Star-shaped, 2-inch-(5cm) wide flowers with purple centers during late summer and early autumn.	In a sheltered border, alongside a path. Ideal as a cut flower for room decoration.	Height: 2½-3ft (75-90cm) Spread: 8-10 inches (20-25cm) **Tender bulbous plant:** Well-drained, sunny position. Lift bulbs after flowering and replant in groups in spring.
Allium moly Golden Garlic/ Lily Leek	Sweet and demure.	Golden-yellow, star-shaped flowers in loose, rounded heads during early and midsummer.	Towards the edge of a border.	Height: 9-12 inches (23-30cm) Spread: 6-8 inches (15-20cm) **Hardy bulbous plant:** Well-drained soil and plenty of sun. Can be left to form large clumps.
Allium neapolitanum Daffodil Garlic	Sweet and delicate.	Star-shaped white flowers in heads up to 2½ inches (6.5cm) wide during spring and early summer.	In a small, sheltered border.	Height: 8-12 inches (20-30cm) Spread: 6-8 inches (15-20cm) **Tender bulbous plant:** Well-drained soil and plenty of sun. Only suitable for mild areas.
Allium rosenbachianum	Sweet.	Star-shaped, purplish-violet or rosy-purple flowers in tightly-packed heads up to 6 inches (15cm) wide during early to midsummer.	In the middle of a border.	Height: 2ft (60cm) Spread: 8-10 inches (20-25cm) **Hardy bulbous plant:** Well-drained soil and plenty of sun.
Aquilegia fragrans Fragrant Columbine	Sweet and demure.	White or pale claret-purple flowers from early to midsummer.	In a warm, sheltered border.	Height: 1½-2ft (45-60cm) Spread: 15-18 inches (38-45cm) **Frost-tolerant annual:** Moist, sandy soil and plenty of sun.
Arabis caucasica (syn. *Arabis albida*) Wall Rock Cress/ Wall Cress	Demurely sweet.	White, cross-shaped flowers with rounded petals from late winter to midsummer.	On dry walls or banks. The plant is too invasive for small rock gardens.	Height: 6-9 inches (15-23cm) Spread: 15-24 inches (38-60cm) **Hardy perennial:** Well-drained soil in light shade.
Artemisia lactiflora White Mugwort	Sweet.	Fragrant plumes of creamy-white flowers during late summer and into autumn.	In a perennial or mixed border.	Height: 4-5ft (1.2-1.5m) Spread: 15-18 inches (38-45cm) **Hardy herbaceous perennial:** Light, well-drained soil in full sun.
Babiana stricta Baboon Root	Sweet and penetrating.	Flowers in wide color range, including pale blue, lilac, mauve and crimson, in early summer.	In a small, warm and sheltered border or a cool greenhouse.	Height: 10-12 inches (25-30cm) Spread: 6-8 inches (15-20cm) **Tender cormous plant:** Well-drained soil and plenty of sun. Lift corms in late summer, replanting in pots in spring.
Bergenia cordifolia Heartleaf Bergenia/ Elephant's Ears	Sweet.	Drooping, somewhat dome-shaped heads of bell-shaped lilac-rose flowers during early and mid-spring.	Towards the edge or corner of a narrow border.	Height: 10-12 inches (25-30cm) Spread: 15-18 inches (38-45cm) **Hardy herbaceous perennial:** Light, well-drained soil in light shade.
Bergenia crassifolia Siberian Tea/ Elephant's Ears	Sweet.	Domed heads of bell-shaped pink flowers from midwinter to mid-spring.	Towards the edge or corner of a narrow border.	Height: 10-12 inches (25-30cm) Spread: 12 inches (30cm) **Hardy herbaceous perennial:** Light, well-drained soil in light shade.
Calendula officinalis Pot Marigold/ Calendula	Pungent aroma from leaves and stems; flowers are slightly sweet.	Daisy-like orange or yellow flowers from late spring to autumn.	In a border or in pots in a sunroom or greenhouse.	Height: 1½-2ft (45-60cm) Spread: 12-15 inches (30-38cm) **Hardy annual:** Thrives in most soils, but prefers those that are well-drained and moderately fertile.

PLANT	SCENT	COLOR	SITUATION	CULTIVATION
SWEET				
Cardiocrinum giganteum (syn. *Lilium giganteum*)	Sweet.	Elongated and trumpet-shaped cream or greenish-white flowers during late summer.	In a woodland setting with light shade.	Height: 6-10ft (1.8-3m) Spread: 3-4ft (0.9-1.2m) **Hardy bulbous perennial:** Moisture-retentive and compost-rich soil.
Convallaria majalis Lily-of-the-Valley	Very sweet and strong.	White, waxy, bell-shaped flowers borne on slightly arching stems during late spring.	Naturalized in a wild garden or in clumps in a corner.	Height: 6-8 inches (15-20cm) Spread: 1-2ft (30-60cm) – clump forming **Hardy rhizomatous-rooted plant:** Well-drained but moisture-retentive soil in light shade. Roots can be invasive close to a building.
Cyclamen purpurascens (syn. *Cyclamen europeaum*)	Strongly sweet.	Rich carmine, shuttlecock-shaped flowers, borne amid silvery-marked kidney-shaped leaves, from midsummer to early autumn.	Naturalized on banks, in woodland and around trees and shrubs.	Height: 4 inches (10cm) Spread: 4-6 inches (10-15cm) **Hardy cormous plant:** Well-drained, leafmold-rich soil in light shade.
Cyclamen repandum	Sweet.	Pink, 1-inch-(2.5cm) long shuttlecock-shaped flowers with twisted petals from spring to midsummer.	Naturalized on banks, in woodland and around trees and shrubs.	Height: 4-6 inches (10-15cm) Spread: 6-8 inches (15-20cm) **Hardy cormous plant:** Well-drained, leafmold-rich soil in light shade.
Filipendula camtschatica (syn. *Spiraea camtschatica/ Spiraea gigantea*)	Sweet.	Large loose plumes, 6-8 inches (15-20cm) wide, full of fleecy white flowers during mid- to late summer.	In perennial or mixed borders.	Height: 5-7ft (1.2-2.1m) Spread: 1½-2ft (45-60cm) **Hardy herbaceous perennial:** Well-drained but moisture-retentive, slightly limy soil in full sun or slight shade.
Galtonia candicans Giant Summer Hyacinth	Light and sweet.	Glistening white, pendant, bell-shaped flowers in loose spires from mid- to late summer.	In a warm and sheltered border.	Height: 3-3½ft (0.9-1m) Spread: 8-10 inches (20-25cm) **Hardy bulbous plant:** Well-drained soil and plenty of sun. Plant in clumps in spring and leave undisturbed to form a large group.
Hosta plantaginea Fragrant Plantain Lily	Gently sweet.	Tubular white flowers that slowly open wider during late summer.	In woodland borders and at the edge of water or in narrow and more formal borders.	Height: 1½-2ft (45-60cm) Spread: 2-2½ft (60-75cm) **Hardy herbaceous perennial:** Well-drained but moisture-retentive soil containing plenty of leafmold.
Iberis amara Rocket Candytuft	Sweet.	White flowers borne in 2-inch-(5cm) long heads during summer.	In an annual border or as a pot plant in a cool greenhouse.	Height: 12-15 inches (30-38cm) Spread: 6-10 inches (15-25cm) **Hardy annual:** Sow in spring where the plants are to flower.
Iris bucharica	Sweet.	Creamy-white and bright yellow flowers, 2½ inches (6cm) wide, during late spring.	In a border overhung with shrubs or trees that keep the soil dry during summer.	Height: 18 inches (45cm) Spread: 6-9 inches (15-23cm) **Bulbous Iris:** Light, well-drained, slightly limy soil.
Iris unguicularis (syn. *Iris stylosa*) Algerian Iris/Winter Iris	Demurely sweet.	Soft lavender or lilac flowers, 3 inches (7.5cm) wide, from late autumn to early spring.	In a narrow, sheltered border against a wall.	Height: 2ft (60cm) Spread: 15 inches (38cm) **Beardless Iris:** Fertile, slightly limy, well-drained soil and a warm, sheltered position.

PLANT	SCENT	COLOR	SITUATION	CULTIVATION
		SWEET		
Lilium auratum Gold-banded Lily/ Golded-rayed Lily of Japan	Sweet and strong.	Bowl-shaped, brilliant white flowers, up to 12 inches (30cm) wide and with golden-yellow rays or bands, during late summer.	In a warm, sheltered position in full sun or light shade. Also suitable for growing in pots.	Height: 5-8ft (1.5-2.4m) Spread: 18 inches (45cm) **Hardy stem-rooting bulb:** Well-drained, lime-free and moisture-retentive soil.
Lilium 'Aurelian Hybrids'	Sweet.	Pale yellow to orange flowers, all with a soft apricot tinge, during midsummer.	In a warm and sheltered position.	Height: 5ft (1.5m) Spread: 12-15 inches (30-38cm) **Hardy stem-rooting bulb:** Well-drained soil and a sunny position, but make sure there is some shade for the roots.
Lilium 'Bright Star'	Sweet.	White, 5-inch-(13cm) wide flowers, with a conspicuous orange star in the center of each flower during midsummer.	In a warm and sheltered position.	Height: 4-6ft (1.2-1.8m) Spread: 12-15 inches (30-38cm) **Hardy stem-rooting bulb:** Light, loamy soil and a partially shaded position.
Lilium brownii	Slight but very sweet.	Trumpet-shaped flowers, pure creamy-white within and dull rose-purple, sometimes tinged green, outside.	In a warm, sheltered position in light shade.	Height: 3-4ft (0.9-1.2m) Spread: 18 inches (45cm) **Hardy stem-rooting bulb:** Well-drained, moisture-retentive soil.
Lilium cernuum	Sweetly fragrant.	Nodding, pale pink flowers with red-purple spots during midsummer.	In a warm, sheltered position in light shade or full sun.	Height: 18 inches (45cm) Spread: 10-12 inches (25-30cm) **Hardy stem-rooting bulb:** Well-drained and moisture-retentive soil.
Lilium chalcedonicum Scarlet Turk's cap Lily/Old Scarlet Martagon	Sweet.	Pendulous, brilliant scarlet flowers during midsummer.	In a warm, sheltered position in light shade.	Height: 3-4ft (0.9-1.2m) Spread: 12-15 inches (30-38cm) **Hardy basal-rooting bulb:** Well-drained and moisture-retentive soil. Once established it dislikes root disturbance.
Lilium duchartrei Marbled Martagon	Sweet.	Nodding white flowers with deep purple spots during midsummer.	In a warm, sheltered position in dappled light.	Height: 2½-3½ft (0.75-1m) Spread: 12-15 inches (30-38cm) **Hardy stem-rooting bulb:** Well-drained and moisture-retentive soil. Stems need support.
Lilium 'Empress of China'	Sweet.	Bowl-shaped, chalk-white flowers, up to 9 inches (23cm) wide, during mid- to late summer.	In a warm, sheltered position in full sun. In cool areas it is best grown in pots in a cool greenhouse or sunroom.	Height: 3-5ft (0.9-1.5m) Spread: 12-15 inches (30-38cm) **Tender stem-rooting bulb:** Well-drained and moisture-retentive soil.
Lilium 'Empress of Japan'	Sweet.	Bowl-shaped, pure white flowers covered with deep maroon spots and golden bands.	In a warm, sheltered position in full sun. In cool areas it is best grown in pots in a cool greenhouse or sunroom.	Height: 3-5ft (0.9-1.5m) Spread: 12-15 inches (30-38cm) **Tender stem-rooting bulb:** Well-drained and moisture-retentive soil.
Lilium 'Golden Splendour Strain'	Sweet.	Deep orange-yellow flowers, with the reverses of the petals showing contrasting maroon strips, during mid- to late summer.	In a warm and sheltered position.	Height: 5-6ft (1.5-1.8m) Spread:15-18 inches (38-45cm) **Hardy stem-rooting bulb:** Well-drained soil and a position in partial shade.
Lilium hansonii Japanese Turk's cap Lily	Sweet.	Nodding, waxy pale orange-yellow flowers with brown spots during midsummer.	In a warm, sheltered position in dappled light.	Height: 5ft (1.5m) Spread: 15-18 inches (38-45cm) **Hardy stem-rooting bulb:** Well-drained, lime-free and leafmold-enriched soil.
Lilium henryi Orange Speciosum Lily	Sweet.	Nodding, recurved, pale apricot-yellow flowers with red spots during late summer.	In a warm, sheltered position in light shade.	Height: 5-8ft (1.5-2.4m) Spread: 18 inches (45cm) **Hardy stem-rooting bulb:** Well-drained and moisture-retentive soil.

PLANT	SCENT	COLOR	SITUATION	CULTIVATION
SWEET				
Lilium 'Imperial Crimson'	Sweet.	Flat, star-shaped, deep crimson flowers, up to 8 inches (20cm) wide and with white edges to the petals, during late summer.	In a warm, sheltered position in light shade.	Height: 5-7ft (1.5-2.1m) Spread: 12-18 inches (30-45cm) **Hardy stem-rooting bulb:** Well-drained and moisture-retentive soil.
Lilium 'Imperial Gold'	Sweet.	Flat, star-shaped, pure white flowers up to 10 inches (25cm) wide, dotted with crimson and with a golden band on each petal, during late summer.	In a warm, sheltered position in full sun.	Height: 5-7ft (1.5-2.1m) Spread: 12-18 inches (30-45cm) **Hardy stem-rooting bulb:** Well-drained and moisture-retentive soil.
Lilium 'Limelight'	Sweet.	Narrowly funnel-shaped and slightly pendant, lime-yellow flowers up to 8 inches (20cm) wide during mid- to late summer.	In a warm, sheltered position in light shade.	Height: 5-6ft (1.5-1.8m) Spread: 10-15 inches (25-38cm) **Hardy stem-rooting bulb:** Well-drained and moisture-retentive soil.
Lilium 'Olympic Hybrids'	Sweet.	Trumpet-shaped, waxy flowers, 6-8 inches (15-20cm) wide, with white outsides and variously colored inside, during mid- to late summer.	In a warm, sheltered position in light shade.	Height: 5-6ft (1.5-1.8m) Spread: 10-15 inches (25-38cm) **Hardy stem-rooting bulb:** Well-drained and moisture-retentive soil. Tolerates lime in the soil.
Lilium 'Parkmannii'	Sweet.	Bowl-shaped, rose-crimson flowers up to 8 inches (20cm) wide, with pure-white and wavy edges to the petals, during mid- to late summer.	In a warm, sheltered position in full sun. In cool areas it is best grown in pots in a cool greenhouse or sunroom.	Height: 3-5ft (0.9-1.5m) Spread: 12-15 inches (30-38cm) **Tender stem-rooting bulb:** Well-drained and moisture-retentive soil.
Lilium regale Regal Lily/Royal Lily	Sweet and strong.	Funnel-shaped white flowers, up to 5 inches (13cm) long, during midsummer. The centers of the flowers are sulphur-yellow, with backs shaded rose-purple.	In a warm, sheltered position in full sun.	Height: 4-6ft (1.2-1.8m) Spread: 12-15 inches (30-38cm) **Hardy stem-rooting bulb:** Well-drained and moisture-retentive soil.
Lilium sargentiae	Sweet.	Trumpet-shaped, 4-5 inch (10-13cm) wide white flowers, shaded brown on the back, in clusters during mid- to late summer.	In a warm, sheltered position in full sun.	Height: 4-5ft (1.2-1.5m) Spread: 12-15 inches (30-38cm) **Hardy stem-rooting bulb:** Well-drained, lime-free and moisture-retentive soil.
Lilium speciosum Showy Lily/Japanese Lily	Sweet.	Bowl-shaped, 3-5 inch (7.5-13cm) wide, white flowers, heavily shaded with crimson, during late summer.	In a warm, sheltered position in full sun.	Height: 4-6ft (1.2-1.8m) Spread: 12-15 inches (30-38cm) **Hardy stem-rooting bulb:** Well-drained, lime-free and moisture-retentive soil.
Lilium x testaceum (syn. *Lilium excelsum*) The Nankeen Lily	Sweet.	Pendant, 3 inch (7.5cm) long, apricot-yellow flowers during midsummer.	In a warm, sheltered position in full sun.	Height: 4-6ft (1.2-1.8m) Spread: 12-15 inches (30-38cm) **Hardy basal-rooting bulb:** Well-drained and moisture-retentive soil.
Lilium wardii	Pleasingly sweet.	Pink flowers with purple spotting during mid- to late summer.	In a warm, sheltered position in light shade.	Height: 3-5ft (0.9-1.5m) Spread: 12-15 inches (30-38cm) **Hardy stem-rooting bulb:** Well-drained, lime-free and moisture-retentive soil.
Monarda didyma Bee Balm/Bergamot/ Sweet Bergamot/ Oswego Tea	Sweet flowers, attractive to bees and butterflies; whole plant emits an attractive fragrance.	Dense whorls, 2½-3 inches (6-7.5cm) wide, of bright scarlet flowers from early to late summer. Range of varieties and colors.	In a perennial border.	Height: 2-3ft (60-90cm) Spread: 15-18 inches (38-45cm) **Hardy herbaceous perennial:** Moisture-retentive, compost-rich soil in full sun or light shade.

PLANT	SCENT	COLOR	SITUATION	CULTIVATION
SWEET				
Muscari neglectum	Sweet.	Densely packed heads of dark blue flowers during mid- to late spring.	As an edging for a bed, at the front of a border and in a rock garden.	Height: 8-9 inches (20-23cm) Spread: 4-5 inches (10-13cm) **Hardy bulb:** Well-drained soil and full sun.
Narcissus jonquilla Jonquil/Wild Jonquil	Sweet and penetrating.	Deep yellow flowers, 1½-2 inches (4-5cm) wide, during spring.	Naturalized in borders or meadows, in pots in a sunroom and also as cut flowers.	Height: 12 inches (30cm) Spread: 4-5 inches (10-13cm) **Hardy bulb:** Well-drained soil in full sun or light shade.
Narcissus x *odorus* Campernelle Jonquil	Sweet.	Pale yellow flowers, 2½ inches (6cm) wide, with bell-shaped cups in mid-spring. Many varieties of this species have scented flowers.	Naturalized in borders or meadows. Some varieties are grown in pots.	Height: 15-18 inches (38-45cm) Spread: 4-6 inches (10-15cm) **Hardy bulb:** Well-drained soil in full sun or light shade.
Nicotiana suaveolens Nicotiana/Flowering Tobacco	Sweet.	Trumpet-shaped white flowers, 2 inches (5cm) long and 1 inch (2.5cm) wide, in loose terminal heads from mid- to late summer.	In a mixed border.	Height: 1½-2ft (45-60cm) Spread: 12-15 inches (30-38cm) **Tender annual:** Well-drained, rich soil and a sunny position.
Nicotiana sylvestris Nicotiana/Flowering Tobacco	Very sweet and heavy.	Trumpet-shaped white flowers up to 3½ inches (8cm) long during late summer.	In a mixed border.	Height: 3-4ft (0.9-1.2m) Spread: 1½-2ft (45-60cm) **Tender plant grown as a biennial:** Well-drained, rich soil and a sunny position.
Pancratium maritimum Sea Daffodil/Sea Lily	Sweet and strong.	White, six-petalled flowers amid narrow, strap-like leaves during mid- and late summer.	In a narrow, warm border or a frost-free greenhouse.	Height: 12 inches (30cm) Spread: 9 inches (23cm) **Tender bulbous plant:** Well-drained soil and a sheltered position outdoors.
Phlox maculata Wild Sweet William	Very sweet.	Tapering heads, up to 6 inches (15cm) long, of purple flowers from mid- to late summer. Varieties in pure white and pink.	In a perennial or mixed border.	Height: 2-3ft (60-90cm) Spread: 15-18 inches (38-45cm) **Herbaceous perennial:** Well-drained but moisture-retentive soil, enriched with compost and in light shade or full sun.
Polygonum x *hybridum* Solomon's Seal/ David's Harp	Sweet.	White, narrow-waisted, pendulous flowers borne in clusters of two to five.	In a mixed border or a lightly shaded woodland setting.	Height: 2-4ft (0.6-1.2m) Spread: 12-18 inches (30-45cm) **Hardy herbaceous perennial:** Lightly shaded, peat- and compost-rich soil.
Smilacina racemosa False Solomon's Seal/ False Spikenard	Sweet.	Arching, terminal sprays of densely packed, creamy-white flowers during early summer.	In a shady, woodland border.	Height: 2½-3ft (75-90cm) Spread: 18 inches (45cm) **Hardy herbaceous perennial:** Moisture-retentive, rich soil in light shade.
Smilacina stellata Starflower/Star-flowered Lily-of-the-Valley	Strongly sweet.	Arching sprays of white, star-shaped flowers during early summer.	In a shady, woodland border.	Height: 1½-2ft (45-60cm) Spread: 12-15 inches (30-38cm) **Hardy herbaceous perennial:** Moisture-retentive, rich soil in light shade.
Tropaeolum majus Nasturtium	Sweet.	Orange or yellow, 2-inch-(5cm) wide flowers with long spurs from midsummer to autumn.	Some forms climb and trail, while others are dwarf and compact and suitable for growing in containers. Gleam strains are 15 inches (38cm) high, with sweet flowers.	Height: Climbing forms up to 8ft (2.4m) high; shorter forms 10 inches (25cm) high and 10–18 inches (25–45cm) wide **Hardy annual:** Well-drained but moisture-retentive soil in full sun. Avoid extremely wet sites, as they encourage lush growth at the expense of flowers.
Verbena x *hybrida* (syn. *Verbena hortensis*) Garden Verbena	Sweet.	White, pink, red, blue and lilac flowers, in tightly clustered heads, from midsummer to autumn.	In an annual or perennial border.	Height: 6-18 inches (15-45cm) Spread: 9-15 inches (23-38cm) **Tender perennial grown as a frost-tolerant annual:** Well-drained, fertile soil in a sunny position.
Verbena rigida (syn. *Verbena venosa*) Vervain	Sweet.	Branched stems bearing dense clusters of purple flowers from midsummer to autumn.	In a perennial border.	Height: 1-2ft (30-60cm) Spread: 15 inches (38cm) **Hardy herbaceous perennial:** Well-drained, fertile soil in a sunny position.

CHAPTER NINE

Scented Trees and Shrubs

*Indispensable and versatile scented trees and
shrubs form the framework of a garden,
enriching it year after year.*

EW OTHER plants conjure up such an expectation of gloriously rich scents as roses. To many flower enthusiasts, they are the aristocrats of the flower world and have a status unrivalled by most other shrubs. Roses have been grown for many centuries and, indeed, their cultivation can be traced back for more than 3,000 years.

SWEET ROSES

More prolonged attention has been given to the creation of new forms and varieties of roses than any other plant, and these have been developed from about 120 of the 250 or so wild species native solely to the Northern Hemisphere, mainly to temperate regions. The colors of these wild species range from white through pink, red and yellow. Not all of them are worthy of a great deal of attention; only about a third reveal the distinction needed for decorating gardens, although many have attractive scents.

The Dog Rose, *Rosa canina*, widespread and common in English hedgerows and in much of Europe (as well as being naturalized in North America) has fragrant pink or white flowers with numerous yellow stamens. It is now mainly used as a rootstock for other roses, although in the forms 'Andersonii' and 'Abbotswood' it has a great deal of charm. Both forms are scented, with 'Andersonii' having a raspberry-like fragrance.

If the name *Rosa rubiginosa* does not conjure up thoughts of a sweet, lingering and heavy fragrance, then its common names Eglantine and Sweet Brier or, more often, Sweet Briar, should. Somewhat similar to the Dog Rose, it excels in the delicious, sweet fragrance of its leaves. It is native to Britain and much of Europe, as well as being naturalized in North America. From this one rose many other forms with fragrant foliage have originated, including 'Janet's Pride', with white centers, rosy edges and yellow stamens; 'Julia (sometimes Julie) Mannering', semi-double, clear pale pink; and 'Lord Penzance', fawn yellow.

The Burnet Rose, Scotch Rose or Scots Brier, *Rosa pimpinellifolia* (earlier called *R. spinosissima*), has deliciously scented solitary, creamy-white flowers that appear amid fern-like foliage. Like the Eglantine, its superb progeny are widely grown, and include the lily-of-the-valley-scented 'Double White', with small, fully double, globular flowers; 'Double Yellow', with deep yellow, double flowers with a heavy scent; 'Harison's Yellow', with vivid, sulphur-yellow, double flowers with a strong fragrance; and 'Stanwell Perpetual', with a repeat-flowering habit, shell-like, blush-pink buds and a delicate fragrance.

Pruning these wild species is easy. During their early years, shape them to encourage strong growth and a well-proportioned shrub. Cut out old and twiggy growths. As the shrub ages, remove gnarled shoots during winter to encourage the development of strong shoots.

The Modern Shrub rose 'Golden Wings', which has attractive yellow flowers with mahogany-colored stamens, brings an appealing fragrance to gardens in summer.

Rose 'Vanity', a Hybrid Musk type, has a sweet pea fragrance and single, deep pink flowers borne in large, open and loose clusters.

Rosa rugosa 'Sarah Van Fleet' is richly scented, with long flower buds that open to semi-double, clear, true-pink flowers with eye-catching cream stamens.

The Floribunda rose 'Victoriana' pervades gardens with the sweet fragrance emitted by its full, rounded flowers borne on short, sturdy bushes.

OLD ROSES

It is from the wild species that "Old Roses" originated when they were hybridized, many becoming popular during the 18th and 19th centuries.

These "Old Roses" are famed for their sweetly scented flowers, which are mostly double with masses of petals that give them a petal-packed appearance. They are, in practical terms, fully hardy and have, unlike many modern roses such as Hybrid Teas and Floribundas, the ability to blend in with other shrubs in a border. If they lack a quality at all, it is that most have only one flowering period during the year. Nevertheless, anyone planting an "Old Rose" will never be disappointed by its rich scent.

These "Old Roses" need very little pruning. All that is needed is to cut out some of the old wood after the flowers fade. This will encourage the development of strong growths from the soil level. The long shoots that subsequently arise are best cut back by one-third during late autumn to prevent the plant, and its roots, from being damaged by wind whipping.

A wide range of rose types comprise this grouping. They are derived from many different species and classified accordingly.

Gallica Roses

These form the largest group and are, perhaps, the oldest of all garden roses. The original Gallica rose, widely known as the French Rose or Provins Rose, has single pink flowers, but its other name of Rose d'Amour suggests that it was originally more red than pink. Indeed, some authorities claim it was the only red rose native to Europe. Provins, some 60 miles (96 km) or so south-east of Paris, was famous from the 13th to the 19th century for the culture of medicinal roses, and it is from here that it gained one of its common names. There is no doubt that R. gallica has spawned many superb forms, including the nearly thornless 'Belle de Crécy', with arching stems and very fragrant, rich cerise-pink flowers, that turn a soft parma violet. 'Charles de Mills' is a sheer joy in a garden, with a glorious fragrance and rich crimson flowers. Its closely packed petals have a unique formation – flat and with the appearance of being sliced off. Indeed, so unusual is the arrangement that it has given rise to an alternative name of 'Bizarre Triomphant'. 'Jenny Duval' has delightfully fragrant flowers in a rich mixture of purple, violet, brown and gray, with the outer edges fading to lilac-white.

'Tuscany Superb' is richly scented, with sumptuous deep crimson flowers (fading to purple) that give it a rightful place in any garden.

Alba Roses

This is a very old group that dates back to the Middle Ages. Alba roses are vigorous, upright shrubs with only a few large thorns and pink, blush and white flowers. *Rosa alba* is thought to be descended from the Damask Rose, *Rosa damascena*, which has a wonderful fragrance, a quality which has been passed on to Alba roses. There are many superbly scented forms, including the Jacobite Rose or Great Double White, 'Alba Maxima'. This is an ancient rose, with ivory, fully double flowers that slowly turn a creamy color. 'Alba Semi-Plena', a close relative, is famed for its fragrance, the clusters of large, almost single milk-white flowers being grown for the distillation of attar of roses at Kazanlik in Bulgaria. 'Celestial' (often known as 'The Celestial') has sweetly scented semi-double, shell-pink flowers with golden-yellow stamens. 'Mme Plantier' is classified either as an Alba or as a Noisette, but for convenience, and because of its delicious scent, it is included here. The creamy-white, pompon-like blooms are borne profusely on arching growths, and the rose forms a superb climber as well as a large bush. 'Maiden's Blush' dates back to

The gloriously fragrant Rosa gallica *'Charles de Mills' has rich crimson, purple-tinted flowers that have a unique sliced-off appearance.*

before the 15th century and has fresh, blush-pink, semi-double flowers that give off a superb scent. In France it is known as 'Cuisse de Nymphe' (Nymph's Thigh), while in the 16th century it was called the Incarnation Rose at a time when "carnation" meant "flesh-colored". 'Queen of Denmark' (also known as 'Königin von Dänemark') has a very strong fragrance and is well worthy of a place in any garden. The soft pink flowers are an intense scarlet-pink when in bud and only half open.

Damask Roses

During the mid-16th century, Damask roses were known as *Damascenae* because they came from Damascus, a city in Syria famed for its roses. *Rosa damascena*, a native of Western Asia, has elegant growth and richly fragrant flowers, a characteristic carried through to many of the forms derived from it. 'Jacques Cartier', although not a true Damask type but so closely related that it is included here, is known for the strong fragrance of its large, rich pink flowers. A Damask hybrid, 'La Ville de Bruxelles' has highly fragrant, rich pink flowers that weigh down the branches. 'Mme Hardy' has the most beautiful white flowers, with a hint of lemon in their fragrance, and is a real joy to have in a shrub border. For a small garden the diminutive 'Petite Lisette' is an excellent choice, with fragrant, blush-pink flowers. 'Rose de Resht' is really a Portland type, repeat-flowering, with highly scented, dark crimson-pink flowers that later become lilac and mauve.

Centifolia Roses

These are descended from *Rosa centifolia*, the Provence or Cabbage Rose (not to be confused with the Provins Rose – see p.120). The flowers are usually globular, large and very fragrant, with an attractive drooping habit. 'Burgundy Rose', also known as 'Parvifolia', 'Pompon de Bourgogne', 'Pompon de St Francois' and 'Pompon de Rheims', is a delightfully scented rose with dark pink flowers suffused with claret; its small, compact shape makes it ideal even for small gardens. 'Centifolia', the Old Cabbage Rose or Provence Rose, bears a mass of richly scented, large and drooping, globular, clear pink flowers. 'Chapeau de Napoleon', also known as 'Centifolia Cristata' or 'Crested Moss', has wonderfully scented, pure pink flowers. An added attraction is the frill of greenery around each bud. 'Fantin Latour' is a charming rose that richly deserves a place in a shrub border, with delicately fragrant, blush-pink flowers that deepen to a shell-pink at their centers.

The range of superbly fragrant Centifolia roses is wide, and further varieties include 'Paul Ricault', with densely packed, rose-pink flowers; 'Petite de Hollande', with pale-pink, miniature flowers; and the magnificent 'Tour de Malakoff'. If you have the room to plant it in a shrub border, you will not be disappointed. Its large, fragrant, peony-like flowers are first bluish-pink, then a rich violet-blue, and finally lavender and gray.

Moss Roses

These are derived from *Rosa centifolia* and evolved mainly during the 19th century. *Rosa centifolia* is sterile and does not produce viable seed, but has instead created many bud-sports, the best-known being the Moss roses. They are distinguished by having a moss-like growth around the bud and flowers, which creates added interest and gives a pleasing effect. Many are well-known for their fragrance. 'Comtesse de Murinais', thought to be a Damask hybrid, has magnificent, full-petalled, blush-pink flowers that fade to white, while 'Little Gem' is ideal for a small garden where it displays small, light crimson flowers tinged with pink. 'Louis Gimard' is a beautiful rose, with fragrant, light crimson flowers with lilac tones as they open. 'Maréchal Davoust' is another splendid shrub for the garden, with intense carmine-pink flowers that turn lilac and purple. 'Soupert et Notting' has a strong fragrance and displays neatly formed, deep pink flowers, while 'William Lobb', also known as the 'Old Velvet Moss' or 'Duchesse d'Istrie', has dark crimson flowers that fade to an attractive violet-gray.

Bourbon and Hybrid Perpetual Roses

These two types are quite similar and are the predecessors of the modern Hybrid Tea roses. The Bourbon types are vigorous, with a perpetual-flowering habit. The Hybrid Perpetuals are of slightly later development and more like Hybrid Tea types. Many forms of these two groups have flowers heavy with scent. 'Adam Messerich' (Bourbon) is eye-catching, with raspberry-scented, semi-double, rich pink flowers. 'Honorine de Brabant' (Bourbon) has similarly aromatic pale pink flowers that are spotted and striped with mauve and crimson. 'Baroness Rothschild' (Hybrid Perpetual) is one of the most beautiful of its type, with richly scented, dark-rose flowers shading to shell-pink at the edges.

The pruning of Bourbon and Hybrid Perpetual types is best postponed until early spring. Cut out old and twiggy growth, and prune back excessively long canes by one-third on plants grown as bushes.

China Roses

These owe their descent to *Rosa chinensis*, the China Rose. They form twiggy bushes with flowers that

Rose 'Escapade', a Floribunda rose, emits a sweet fragrance from its single, rosy-violet flowers, which are similar to those of a wild rose.

appear earlier than Hybrid Tea roses and, after a short pause, continue to bloom for a few more months, often into autumn or even later during a mild season. They are not totally hardy and are unsuited for cold, frosty areas. Many, however, are ideal for bringing fragrance to a garden. Some of those listed here are not strictly China roses, but for convenience are included under this heading. 'Hermosa' is very fragrant, with small, globular, pink flowers; 'Cécile Brunner' displays sweetly scented, blush-pink flowers; while 'Perle d'Or' is delicately scented, with rich apricot buds that fade almost to cream when fully open.

The pruning of China roses involves cutting out twiggy, old or weak wood in early spring.

HYBRID MUSKS

These are related to the Musk roses, from which they are bred. They have a rich, intense fragrance and most owe their development to the Rev. J. Pemberton in the early part of this century. They have the habit of very vigorous Floribunda roses. There are several gloriously scented forms to choose from, including 'Cornelia', which has rosette-shaped flowers that change from a coppery-apricot to coppery-pink. 'Day Break' bears small, rich yellow buds that open to reveal semi-double, light yellow flowers with dark golden stamens, while 'Penelope' has large clusters of creamy-pink flowers, and 'Vanity' has pink blooms.

Pruning Hybrid Musk roses is easy – leave them alone. However, to improve the quality of the flowers and to prolong the flowering period, remove the flowering twigs when the flowers fade. Also, in early spring, shorten sideshoots to three buds. Any long, strong shoots that develop from the plant's base and produce flowers can be shortened by one-third.

RUGOSA ROSES

Rosa rugosa, from Eastern Asia, has produced many forms of itself, as well as hybridizing with other roses. Many have a superb fragrance, and these include 'Lady Curzon', with large, single, rose-pink flowers shading to white at their centers; 'Mrs. Anthony Waterer', with a rich fragrance and arching branches heavily laden with crimson flowers; and 'Sarah Van Fleet' with richly scented, semi-double, clear true-pink flowers with cream stamens.

The Rugosa roses require very little pruning, other than cutting back long shoots to encourage better quality blooms over a longer flowering period.

HYBRID TEA AND FLORIBUNDA ROSES

Many of these have fragrant flowers, and some are described in the tables within this chapter.

Scented climbing and rambling roses are included in Chapter 3, while miniature types are described in Chapter 5.

The strongly fragrant Rosa pimpinellifolia *'Harison's Yellow' has double, vivid sulphur-yellow flowers borne amid light green leaves.*

SHRUB ROSES

RASPBERRY

'Adam Masserich'
Bourbon Rose
Height: 6ft (1.8m)
Spread: 5ft (1.5m)
Large, rich pink, semi-double flowers.

'Cerise Bouquet'
Modern Shrub Type
Height: 9ft (2.7m)
Spread: 8ft (2.4m)
Cerise-pink, semi-double flowers borne in arching sprays.

'Honorine de Brabant'
Bourbon Rose
Height: 6ft (1.8m)
Spread: 6ft (1.8m)
Pale pink flowers, spotted and striped with mauve and crimson.

MUSK

'Day Break'
Hybrid Musk
Height: 4ft (1.2m)
Spread: 4ft (1.2m)
Rich yellow buds opening to semi-double, light yellow flowers with dark gold stamens.

'Penelope'
Hybrid Musk
Height: 6ft (1.8m)
Spread: 6ft (1.8m)
Creamy-pink flowers borne in large clusters.

SWEET, APPLE

'Nymphenburg'
Modern Shrub Type
Height: 8ft (2.4m)
Spread: 6ft (1.8m)
Fully double, warm salmon-pink flowers shaded with cerise and orange-yellow at the base of the petals.

CLOVER

'Fritz Nobis'
Modern Shrub Rose
Height: 6ft (1.8m)
Spread: 6ft (1.8m)
Fresh pink flowers with darker shading.

SWEET PEA

'Vanity'
Hybrid Musk
Height: 7ft (2.1m)
Spread: 6ft (1.8m)
Single, deep pink flowers borne in large, loose clusters.

SWEET, LEMONY

'Mme Hardy'
Damask Rose
Height: 6ft (1.8m)
Spread: 5ft (1.5m)
White flowers, cupped at first then becoming flat. The flowers are blush-tinted when in bud and have small green centers when fully open.

ATTRACTIVELY FRAGRANT

'Alba Maxima'
(The Jacobite Rose)
Alba Rose
Height: 6ft (1.8m)
Spread: 5ft (1.5m)
Creamy-white, double flowers, blush-tinted at first.

'Alba Semi-Plena'
Alba Rose
Height: 6ft (1.8m)
Spread: 5ft (1.5m)
Milky-white, almost single flowers with golden stamens, borne in large clusters.

'Aloha'
Modern Shrub Rose
Height: 5ft (1.5m)
Spread: 5ft (1.5m)
Clear pink, old-fashioned flowers borne intermittently during summer.

'Baroness Rothschild'
Hybrid Perpetual
Height: 5ft (1.5m)
Spread: 3ft (90cm)
Dark rose flowers, shading to shell-pink at their edges.

'Belle de Crécy'
Gallica Rose
Height: 4ft (1.2m)
Spread: 3ft (90cm)
Rich cerise-pink flowers, slowly becoming soft violet.

'Burgundy Rose'
Centifolia Rose
Height: 3ft (90cm)
Spread: 2ft (60cm)
Small flowers, dark pink and suffused with claret.

'Centifolia'
Centifolia Rose
Height: 5ft (1.5m)
Spread: 4ft (1.2m)
Large, deeply globular, clear pink flowers.

'Chapeau de Napoleon'
Centifolia Rose
Height: 5ft (1.5m)
Spread: 4ft (1.2m)
Pure pink, slightly drooping flowers.

'Charles de Mills'
Gallica Rose
Height: 5ft (1.5m)
Spread: 4ft (1.2m)
Rich crimson flowers with a tint of purple with maturity.

'Comtesse de Murinais'
Centifolia Muscosa Rose
Height: 6ft (1.8m)
Spread: 4ft (1.2m)
Full-petalled, blush-pink flowers fading to white.

'Cornelia'
Hybrid Musk
Height: 5ft (1.5m)
Spread: 5ft (1.5m)
Coppery-apricot, rosette-shaped blooms which fade to coppery-pink.

'Fantin Latour'
Centifolia Rose
Height: 6ft (1.8m)
Spread: 4ft (1.2m)
Blush-pink flowers deepening to shell-pink at their edges.

'Golden Wings'
Modern Shrub Rose
Height: 4ft (1.2m)
Spread: 4ft (1.2m)
Yellow flowers with mahogany-colored stamens.

'Hermosa'
China Rose
Height: 3ft (90cm)
Spread: 2ft (60cm)
Pink, small and globular flowers.

SHRUB ROSES

'Jacques Cartier'
Damask Rose
Height: 4ft (1.2m)
Spread: 3ft (90cm)
Large, rich pink flowers.

'Jenny Duval'
Gallica Rose
Height: 4ft (1.2m)
Spread: 3ft (90cm)
Flowers a mixture of rich purple, violet, brown and gray, with the outer edges fading to lilac.

'La Ville de Bruxelles'
Damask Rose
Height: 5ft (1.5m)
Spread: 4ft (1.2m)
Large, rich pink flowers.

'Lady Curzon'
Rugosa Rose
Height: 6ft (1.8m)
Spread: 8ft (2.4m)
Rose-pink, large, single flowers shading to white at their centers and with slightly crinkled petals. Attractive creamy stamens.

'Little Gem'
Centifolia Muscosa Rose
Height: 3ft (90cm)
Spread: 2ft (60cm)
Small, light crimson, pompon flowers.

'Louis Gimard'
Centifolia Muscosa Rose
Height: 5ft (1.5m)
Spread: 3ft (90cm)
Large, globular, light crimson flowers with lilac tones.

'Louise Odier'
Bourbon Rose
Height: 5ft (1.5m)
Spread: 4ft (1.2m)
Warm pink flowers, softly shaded with lilac.

'Mme Isaac Pereire'
Bourbon Rose
Height: 7ft (2.1m)
Spread: 5ft (1.5m)
Large crimson flowers.

'Mme Plantier'
Alba Rose
Height: 6ft (1.8m)
Spread: 6ft (1.8m)
Creamy-white, medium-sized pompon flowers borne in great profusion.

'Mrs. Anthony Waterer'
Rugosa Rose
Height: 5ft (1.5m)
Spread: 5ft (1.5m)
Crimson flowers borne on arching branches.

'Paul Ricault'
Centifolia Rose'
Height: 5ft (1.5m)
Spread: 3ft (90cm)
Rich rose-pink flowers.

'Petite de Hollande'
Centifolia Rose
Height: 4ft (1.2m)
Spread: 3ft (90cm)
Pale pink flowers, deepening in color at their edges.

'Petite Lisette'
Damask Rose
Height: 4ft (1.2m)
Spread: 3ft (90cm)
Blush-pink flowers.

'Queen of Denmark'
Alba Rose
Height: 5ft (1.5m)
Spread: 4ft (1.2m)
Soft, glowing pink, beautifully formed flowers.

'Rose de Resht'
Damask Rose
Height: 3ft (90cm)
Spread: 2½ft (75cm)
Dark crimson-pink flowers, later turning to lilac and mauve.

'Roseraie de l'Hay'
Rugosa Rose
Height: 7ft (2.1m)
Spread: 7ft (2.1m)
Rich wine-purple buds opening to reveal crimson-purple flowers.

'Sarah Van Fleet'
Rugosa Rose
Height: 8ft (2.4m)
Spread: 6ft (1.8m)
Clear pink, semi-double flowers with cream stamens.

'Soupert et Notting'
Centifolia Muscosa Rose
Height: 3ft (90cm)
Spread: 2ft (60cm)
Deep pink flowers.

'Souvenir de la Malmaison'
Bourbon Rose
Height: 5ft (1.5m)
Spread: 5ft (1.5m)
Large, soft-pink flowers that eventually fade at their edges.

'Tour de Malakoff'
Centifolia Rose
Height: 6ft (1.8m)
Spread: 5ft (1.5m)
Bluish-pink flowers turning later to lavender and gray.

'Tuscany Superb'
Gallica Rose
Height: 5ft (1.5m)
Spread: 3ft (90cm)
Deep crimson flowers fading to purple.

'William Lobb'
Centifolia Muscosa Rose
Height: 6ft (1.8m)
Spread: 6ft (1.8m)
Dark crimson flowers, fading to violet-gray.

HYBRID TEA AND FLORIBUNDA ROSES

ATTRACTIVELY FRAGRANT

'Alec's Red'
Hybrid Tea
Height: 3ft (90cm)
Spread: 2½-3ft (75-90cm)
Cherry-red, well-formed, full-petalled flowers.

'Arthur Bell'
Floribunda Type
Height: 3ft (90cm)
Spread: 2½-3ft (75-90cm)
Deep golden-yellow at first, fading to creamy-yellow with maturity.

'Blessings'
Hybrid Tea
Height: 3ft (90cm)
Spread: 2½-3ft (85-90cm)
Salmon-pink flowers.

'Blue Moon'
Hybrid Tea
Height: 3ft (90cm)
Spread: 2½-3ft (75-90cm)
Silvery-lilac flowers.

'Chrysler Imperial'
Hybrid Tea
Height: 3ft (90cm)
Spread: 2½-3ft (75-90cm)
Vivid crimson flowers with darker shading.

'Dusky Maiden'
Floribunda Type
Height: 2-2½ft (60-75cm)
Spread: 2-2½ft (60-75cm)
Large crimson blooms with deeper shading and golden anthers.

'Dutch Gold'
Hybrid Tea
Height: 3ft (90cm)
Spread: 2½-3ft (75-90cm)
Deep golden-yellow blooms.

'Escapade'
Floribunda Type
Height: 3½-4ft (1-1.2m)
Spread: 3½ft (1m)
Rosy-violet blooms, verging slightly towards pink.

'Fragrant Cloud'
Hybrid Tea
Height: 3ft (90cm)
Spread: 2½-3ft (75-90cm)
Coral-scarlet blooms with a smoky overtone.

'Geranium Red'
Floribunda Type
Height: 2½ft (75cm)
Spread: 2½ft (75cm)
Dusky red, large, full-petalled flowers tinged with purple.

'Iceberg'
Floribunda Type
Height: 4ft (1.2m)
Spread: 3-4ft (1-1.2m)
Pure white flowers, tinted pink when in bud.

'Margaret Merril'
Floribunda Type
Height: 2½ft (75cm)
Spread: 2½ft (75cm)
Dainty buds opening to white flowers overlaid with a satiny-pink sheen.

'Mojave'
Hybrid Tea
Height: 3ft (90cm)
Spread: 2½-3ft (75-90cm)
Rich, deep orange blooms.

'Mullard Jubilee'
Hybrid Tea
Height: 3ft (90cm)
Spread: 2½-3ft (75-90cm)
Rose-pink blooms.

'Orange Sensation'
Floribunda Type
Height: 2½ft (75cm)
Spread: 2½ft (75cm)
Large, semi-double, brilliant vermilion flowers.

'Papa Meilland'
Hybrid Tea
Height: 2½ft (75cm)
Spread: 2-2½ft (60-75cm)
Magnificent crimson blooms.

'Pink Parfait'
Floribunda Type
Height: 2½ft (75cm)
Spread: 2½ft (75cm)
Light pink flowers, shading to pale yellow at their bases.

'Prima Ballerina'
Hybrid Tea
Height: 3ft (90cm)
Spread: 2½-3ft (75-90cm)
Bright pink flowers slowly becoming rose pink.

'Sutter's Gold'
Hybrid Tea
Height: 3ft (90cm)
Spread: 2½-3ft (75-90cm)
Deep, rich gold blooms flushed with peach.

'Victoriana'
Floribunda Type
Height: 2½ft (75cm)
Spread: 2½ft (75cm)
Rounded blooms with vermilion on the inner side of each petal and a soft silvery shade on the reverse.

'Wendy Cussons'
Hybrid Tea
Height: 3ft (90cm)
Spread: 2½-3ft (75-90cm)
Light, rosy-red blooms.

'Whisky Mac'
Hybrid Tea
Height: 2½ft (75cm)
Spread: 2-2½ft (60-75cm)
Amber-yellow blooms.

SHRUBS WITH AROMATIC FOLIAGE

Many shrubs have leaves with an attractive fragrance that creates interest throughout the entire year, often as well as pleasantly scented flowers.

The Mexican Orange Blossom, *Choisya ternata*, has sweetly scented white flowers displayed in large, loose heads, as well as glossy, evergreen leaves that emit a pungent, orange-like aroma when crushed. Some people think that the smell of the leaves is rather unpleasant and reminiscent of furniture polish, but this is a matter of opinion. Mixed reactions to the leaves probably explain why the shrub was not particularly popular in its native Mexico. Although it originates in a warm country, it also grows in colder climates, especially when given the shelter of a south- or west-facing wall.

The Gum Cistus, *Cistus ladanifer*, has long been known for its richly sweet scent. The gum exuded by this evergreen shrub from Southern Europe and Mediterranean regions is collected and distilled to produce labdanum, a heavily fragrant oil used in the preparation of some perfumes. Other cistus shrubs produce labdanum, including *C. laurifolius*, *C. monspeliensis*, *C. salvifolius* and *C. incanus* subsp. *creticus*. Such is the redolence of many of these Mediterranean shrubs that Napoleon is reported to have said that he would know his native Corsica even with his eyes shut. In cooler countries, the perfume also carries on light breezes during warm weather. The leaves of *Cistus salvifolius* have been used with the fruit coat of the Pomegranate in tanning, and a decoction of the roots was an Arab remedy for stopping bleeding and curing bronchitis. *Cistus ladanifer* is not such a useful plant, but its eye-catching white flowers create a superb display during midsummer, especially as each petal has a chocolate-maroon blotch at its base.

'Where Rosemary rules, so does the Mistress' is a common saying from early times – perhaps because it was freely grown in kitchen gardens which came under the influence of the lady of the house. Whatever its reputation, the Common Rosemary, *Rosmarinus officinalis*, is highly aromatic and imparts a rich bouquet to gardens. To some people it is reminiscent of nutmeg and to others slightly camphoric. Indeed, it has been burnt, together with juniper berries, in French hospitals to purify the air and to prevent infection. Today, it is used mainly for culinary purposes, flavoring meat dishes and sausages, and for the delightful fragrance it gives to rooms.

Rosemary also has the curious common names Compass-weed, Compass Plant and Polar Plant, which infer that it was possible to gain a compass bearing from its growth.

The Herb of Grace, *Ruta graveolens*, also known as Countryman's Treacle, Herb of Repentance and Ave Grace, emits a fetid, bitter odor from its leaves; some people immediately find this disagreeable, while

others say that under the acrid smell they detect an attractive aroma. The leaves can be finely chopped and used sparingly in salads to impart a bitter flavor. However, the leaves harbor a powerful irritant which often causes blisters on the skin, although it has also been credited with the ability to act as an antidote to pestilence. Indeed, it is part of the composition of the French perfume known as "Vinegar of the Four Thieves," a concoction originated several centuries ago. It was said to be so potent that the thieves of Marseilles who created it could, with impunity, enter and rob homes stricken with the plague.

The Lavender Cotton, *Santolina chamaecyparissus*, has thread-like, silver foliage with a chamomile-like fragrance, which some people find disagreeable. It is enhanced by bright lemon-yellow flowers during midsummer. An oil is extracted from the leaves and occasionally used in perfumery. *Santolina neapolitana*, another Lavender Cotton, has similarly scented, feathery gray leaves.

SCENTED FLOWERING TREES AND SHRUBS

Trees covered with scented blossom gently waving in light spring breezes create an idyllic picture that we would all like to see in our yards. Fragrant flowering shrubs and trees, however, are not just to be enjoyed during spring: each of the seasons brings scent and color, perhaps never more welcome than during winter.

Winter

Few winter-fragrant shrubs are as well known as the viburnums, with a strongly sweet fragrance that makes the onset of the dark and cold months more bearable. The richly sweet *Viburnum* x *bodnantense* 'Dawn' scents the air from autumn to early spring, decking its bare branches with shell-pink buds that open to waxy white. It is a welcome shrub in any yard, and especially so if it is positioned near a firm-surfaced path so that the scent can be readily appreciated. (When designing a fragrant winter landscape, always plan for a good path near shrubs, as having to wade across a waterlogged lawn in order to get near the scent will eventually spoil the enjoyment you will get from the plants.)

Viburnum farreri has, as its earlier name *Viburnum fragrans* suggests, a rich scent. With its richly sweet flowers from early to late winter, it is an essential

The Mexican Orange Blossom (Choisya ternata), bottom left, is a scented gem, with leaves that emit an orange-like fragrance when crushed. The flowers are also sweetly scented.

element of a scented winter landscape. If it has a failing, it is its eventual large size. However, it has a rather upright stance, so in a big yard its size is not a problem, and for filling a large area with scent it is a shrub that has few peers. *Viburnum grandiflorum* also has a stiff, upright habit, although it is slightly smaller. Its deep pink flowers create an exquisitely scented atmosphere that refreshes any landscape from midwinter to spring.

The Winter Sweet fills the garden with a rich fragrance, heavy and spicy. Formerly *Chimonanthus fragrans*, now *Chimonanthus praecox*, its midwinter flowers were cut during the early 19th century to add a rich perfume to drawing rooms and boudoirs. Chinese women used the scented flowers to decorate their hair, while the aromatic stems were tied in bundles and placed in linen cupboards and wardrobes. Indeed, so strong is the rich fragrance of the flowers that when a specimen was introduced into England from China in 1766, and planted in a conservatory at Croome in Worcestershire, its fragrance could be detected more than 50 yards (45m) away. When planted outside, it is hardy through USDA hardiness zone 7. However, it is best planted against a south- or west-facing wall.

The Winter Sweet's flowers have a distinctive shape as well as an appealing fragrance. Their cup-shaped structure, with ivory-colored petals and purple centers, creates an attractive picture along bare, leafless shoots.

The mahonias present their fragrant flowers amid evergreen foliage that creates an attractive setting for the mainly yellow flowers. *Mahonia* 'Charity' presents cascading spires of sweetly scented, deep yellow flowers from early to late winter. If your predilection is towards the glorious fragrance of lily-of-the-valley, then the winter-flowering *Mahonia japonica* is a must for your landscape. Its lemon-yellow flowers are borne in drooping clusters amid shiny, deep green leaves. Its evergreen nature makes it ideal for covering an unsightly corner, yet at the same time filling the yard with a delicious scent. The sweet and penetrating scent of the flowers of *Mahonia lomariifolia* is matched by their beauty – this mahonia carries spire-like heads up to 10 inches (25cm) long, packed with up to 250 small, deep yellow flowers. The leaves are also attractive and unusual, with 15-19 pairs of rigid leaflets borne along them.

Also yellow-flowered, but with an entirely different appearance, is the Chinese Witch Hazel, *Hamamelis*

Ceanothus *'Gloire de Versailles'*,
left, has sweetly scented flowers.
The Chinese Witch Hazel
(Hamamelis mollis), *right, bears its*
scented flowers during winter.

mollis. The fragrance is sweet and the slightly twisted, ribbon-like petals form small clusters along the bare branches during midwinter. During autumn, the deciduous foliage takes on glorious yellow shades before falling. The flowers of the Japanese Witch Hazel are somewhat similar, but narrower and unevenly wavy, like a piece of ribbon that has become damp and has shrunk. Although they are sweetly scented, their fragrance is faint.

The winter-blooming Vernal Witch Hazel, *Hamamelis vernalis*, is also scented, but the aroma is heavy and pungent and not to everyone's taste though not totally unpleasant. Another species is *Hamamelis virginiana*, with a faint but sweet scent. It is the source of witch hazel, and is grown commercially in Tennessee, Virginia and South Carolina. However, the name Witch Hazel refers to the use of twigs of shrubs in this genus to divine water, in the same manner as hazel sticks; witch is also thought to be a derivative of the Anglo-Saxon *wice* or *wic*, meaning springy or pliant.

Just after the turn of the last century, Pond's Extract, a mixture originally attributed to the Oneida Indians and well known for its medically soothing qualities, was made from a distillation of the bark and twigs.

Two shrubby members of the honeysuckle family, the semi-evergreen *Lonicera fragrantissima* and the deciduous *Lonicera standishii*, both from China, create a wealth of sweet, penetratingly rich scent during winter. Both display fragrant, creamy-white flowers, those of the latter being slightly earlier and more prolific than those of the former. The stance of *Lonicera standishii* is also stiffer and more upright. A hybrid between these two, *Lonicera* x *purpusii*, also has fragrant, creamy-white flowers and is often considered to be superior to both of them.

Late winter

With midwinter coming to an end, many more fragrant shrubs and trees bear flowers. The February Daphne, *Daphne mezereum*, is a small shrub that bears a wealth of highly fragrant, warm and spicy flowers for a couple of months. The normal type has purple-red flowers clustered along leafless twigs, but there is

also a white-flowered form, 'Alba'. With a height of up to 5ft (1.5m) it can be nestled into most corners, but it does have two drawbacks; a fungus often infests the plant and causes leaves to drop off, and the berries contain the poisonous irritant mezerein.

The problem of the fungus can be overcome by giving the plants room and maintaining scrupulous garden sanitation, but the poisonous berries can be a problem as they are attractive and this might encourage children – and adults – to eat them. Indeed, a couple of centuries ago Linnaeus said that six berries would kill a wolf and that he had seen a girl die after eating twelve of them 'to check an ague'. However, it would be a great pity if all gardeners were deterred from planting this shrub, which has a delicious fragrance.

The daphnes are a wonderful genus for creating sweet aromas in the landscape, and some of them are described in the chapter dealing with rock garden plants (Chapter 4), although in a small yard they would fit admirably into a narrow border. The larger varieties, however, need space if they are not to be spoiled by constriction. *Daphne odora* 'Aureomarginata' is both strongly scented and appealing to the eye, with pale purple flowers from midwinter to mid-spring and shiny, mid-green leaves with edges lined with creamy-white. It is evergreen and therefore retains an attractive quality throughout the year.

The semi-evergreen hybrid *Daphne* x *burkwoodii* is even more fragrantly flowered, but often not until mid-spring at the earliest and then into early summer. Slightly earlier-flowering, the evergreen *Daphne pontica* is a scented gem, with spider-like, yellow-green flowers emitting a somewhat nutty and lemony aroma that pervades the air at night as well as during the day. It has the virtue of being suitable for growing under trees and in heavy soils.

The Christmas Box, *Sarcococca humilis* (also known as *S. hookeriana* var. *humilis*), unfolds strongly fragrant, small white flowers in late winter and early spring amid evergreen, glossy green leaves. Its neat, somewhat tufted habit and tendency to colonize bare soil by sending up new stems makes it a superb ground-covering plant. However, like many other undemanding and tolerant plants, by surviving in inferior soils it is seldom given the more fertile, slightly alkaline soil that it needs for maximum growth and flowering.

Spring

In spring the viburnums continue to play a major role in the scented garden. *Viburnum* x *burkwoodii* is a superb hybrid with a sweet and penetrating fragrance that pervades the garden from early spring to early summer. It is later in flowering than *Viburnum* x *bodnantense*. *Viburnum* x *carlcephalum* is another sweetly scented type with glorious heads of creamy-white flowers up to 4 inches (10cm) wide during spring and early summer.

A further spring-flowering type, and one of the most popular of all shrubs, is the daphne-scented *Viburnum carlesii*. Its name derives from William Richard Carles, the British Vice-Consul in Korea from 1883 to 1885, who sent dried specimens of it to Kew Gardens. At the same time, a Korean lady sent a living specimen of it to a nursery in Japan, progeny from which were sent to Kew for identification. The superb fragrance of the flowers and the moderate stature of the shrub make it an ideal choice for planting in a small yard. Another small-yard type is the sweetly fragrant *Viburnum* x *juddii*, which has a bushy habit and is free-flowering, with scented white heads during late spring and early summer.

Viburnum 'Anne Russell' has a very penetratingly sweet scent from early spring to early summer, displaying white flowers that emerge from pink buds. The size of this shrub makes it suitable for even the smallest yard.

For a rich fragrance, sweet and like lily-of-the-valley, *Skimmia japonica* 'Fragrans' must head the list of late spring-flowering shrubs. It has creamy-white, star-like flowers. The form *Skimmia japonica* 'Rubella' is also richly fragrant, with a delightful perfume from its white flowers with yellow anthers. The flowers of *Skimmia laureola* also have a sweet fragrance, although the rich green leaves have a rather pungent aroma when crushed. However, their smell cannot be too abhorrent, as in the plant's native habitat of the north-

The strongly fragrant Daphne odora 'Aureomarginata' *is a double-value shrub, with a lovely scent and variegated leaves for year-round attractiveness.*

west Himalayas the leaves are burnt as incense, while an oil distilled from them is used for scenting soap.

During mid- to late spring the glorious magnolias flood the garden with scent and color. For a rich and fruity fragrance, the evergreen *Magnolia grandiflora* 'Exmouth' is well worth planting, but it does need a large area or, preferably, a position against a west- or south-facing wall. The globular, creamy-white flowers, often up to 8 inches (20cm) wide, soon dominate the garden.

The strongly sweet and eye-catching flowers of *Magnolia* x *soulangiana* 'Alba Superba' never fail to bring pleasure. It is a deciduous tree or large shrub that looks superb on a lawn, where its pure-white, chalice-shaped flowers soon attract visitors. Do not plant it too close to a house or patio, as the shrub's shape – with the scented flowers appearing at first on naked branches – is a picture that needs to be absorbed at a single glance. The later flowers appear amid leaves that develop after the flowers first open.

The Star Magnolia, *Magnolia stellata*, has sweet, demurely fragrant star-shaped, white flowers, and a size that enables it to be planted in most yards. With its scented, decorative flowers, it is such a good plant for the landscape that it seems strange that in its native Japan the wood was cut to make matches and kitchen utensils.

The aromatic qualities of *Magnolia salicifolia* are twofold: the star-shaped, white flowers are sweet, and the leaves, wood and bark emit a delightful lemon scent when bruised.

During mid- to late spring, a wealth of different scents pervades the garden. The vanilla-scented, yellow flowers of the semitropical evergreen shrub *Azara microphylla* create an aura of scent for yards around it. The tiny flowers are borne in dense clusters from the leaf joints. It is best grown against a south- or west-facing wall.

The cowslip-scented, pale primrose-yellow flowers of *Corylopsis pauciflora* appear daintily as small bells that hang from the bare shoots. As well as their glorious scent, they are visually extremely attractive when framed by the blue sky of spring. The bare stems tend to be a reminder of winter, yet the bright flowers give the impression that a new season has arrived. The slightly larger shrub *Corylopsis willmottiae* has flowers with a similar scent.

The sweetly scented, honey-like flowers of the Common Gorse, *Ulex europaeus*, are dominantly golden-yellow and, *en masse*, create a strong focal point. In landscapes it is the double-flowered form that makes the best plant, with a compact and smaller stature and glorious pea-shaped flowers that smother the prickly stems. It looks best when combined with a piece of rustic fencing, perhaps a split-rail fence or unpainted pickets, so that it brings radiant color along what could otherwise be a bare area; it is not a shrub

that looks at its best when planted as a specimen in a shrub border, as it has a distinctly rural appearance – it can be seen creating large drifts of color in the British countryside and has been widely used to feed cattle and to provide fuel for heating bakers' ovens. Unfortunately, it has often been neglected as a garden plant, perhaps because it is uncommon outside of Europe. If you are willing to make the extra effort to locate Common Gorse in a nursery or mail-order catalog, you will be delighted with its rich scent and bright, dominant color.

Ornamental flowering cherry trees epitomise the wealth of scent and color available during spring and into early summer. The Yoshino Cherry, *Prunus* x *yedoensis*, has almond-scented white flowers on arching branches that make the tree slightly wider than it is high. *Prunus* 'Shirotae' also has a wide-spreading habit, with drooping branches bearing sweetly fragrant, semi-double, snow-white flowers. It forms an eye-catching focal point at the front of a lawn. Like all wide-spreading and pendulous flowering cherry trees, it should not be crammed into a border with other trees and shrubs or its beautiful outlines will be ruined.

Prunus 'Amanogawa', forms an erect column, with semi-double, soft pink flowers in spring. With age the tree does broaden, but initially it is very slender and therefore well suited to planting in small yards and for creating a burst of scent and color near paths and front gates.

The almond-scented white flowers of the Bird Cherry, *Prunus padus* 'Grandiflora', do not appear until late spring and early summer. Unlike most ornamental cherries, they are borne tightly packed in long, drooping tassels up to 8 inches (20cm) long. The delicate scent of the flowers contrasts with the strong and rather acrid-smelling bark, although the wood polishes so well that it has been used in furniture-making and for walking sticks.

Flowering crabs are another joy as the season progresses. *Malus floribunda* has flowers that are sweetly scented and creates one of the best displays of any flowering crab. The blossoms are single, pale pink becoming white, but deep red when in bud. It is, perhaps, at its best when some of the flowers are half to fully open and the rest are still in bud, creating a cascade of scent and color. It is small enough to be planted in most yards, and is especially attractive in front yards, where it can be planted so that branches cascade over paths – but remove any of the cherry-like fruits that fall on hard surfaces or they will make them slippery. It is, by the way, one of the earliest crabs to bear flowers.

The scent of Corylopsis pauciflora *is sweet and cowslip-like.*

Early summer

Many flowering crabs fill early summer with scented blossoms. *Malus coronaria* 'Charlottae' bears a profusion of violet-scented, semi-double, shell-pink flowers in large clusters. It comes from North America, the original plant being found growing wild near Waukegan, Lake Michigan, Illinois, by Mrs. Charlotte de Wolf in 1902. It has the further blessing of displaying yellow and orange-tinted leaves in autumn.

Malus 'Profusion' has sweet but subtly fragrant single, deep purple flowers that fade to pink. Its upright and rather open habit makes it better suited than many other flowering crabs to growing in a border with other trees and shrubs. The small, oxblood-colored fruits are an added attraction.

The fragrant, single white flowers – soft pink when in bud – of *Malus hupehensis*, often known as the Chinese Crab Apple, create a pleasing, fragrant picture. It eventually forms a large tree that precludes its planting in small yards. However, if space is available it is well worth planting, as it has the virtue of producing yellow fruits, tinged red, in addition to the scented flowers. The Chinese use the leaves in an infusion known as 'Red Tea'.

The evergreen osmanthus shrubs produce a mass of sweetly scented flowers in early summer. *Osmanthus x burkwoodii*, correctly known as X *Osmarea burkwoodii*, produces clusters of tubular white flowers during late spring and into early summer. A related species, *Osmanthus delavayi*, is slightly earlier with its freely produced, scented white flowers. The fragrance of these flowers is delightful and is indicated by their botanical name: *osme* means fragrance, *anthos* flower. The flowers of *Osmanthus fragrans* are used by the Chinese to scent tea.

Few shrubs are as richly scented and colored during late spring and early summer as the deciduous azaleas. A woodland garden or a naturalized setting where branches from deciduous trees give protection from spring frosts is ideal. These shrubs certainly need a rustic setting, and should be planted in large groups so that their scent and color almost overwhelm you. Another plant with a penetratingly sweet aroma is the yellow-flowered *Rhododendron luteum*. It is larger and more dominant than the deciduous azaleas, and if you are fortunate enough to have a large yard and a stream, it takes to such a position with the same enthusiasm as ducks to water. Do not, however, plant it in the bottom of a ditch or with its roots directly in water; position it along the top of a bank, in light, leafmold-rich soil. It can

Many flowering crabs (Malus) create a rich and dominant burst of scent and color in early summer. There are forms to suit yards of all sizes.

even be planted to create an early-summer screen of scent and color.

With a completely different form and style, and bearing orange-blossom-scented flowers, is the Japanese Bitter Orange, *Poncirus trifoliata*. The stout spines on its green stems will certainly repel any invader from molesting its pure white flowers, which bring a welcome fragrance to early summer. It can be a difficult plant to position in the landscape, as it needs to be kept out of reach of small children, but if you can find a warm corner with well-drained soil it is a rewarding shrub to grow.

'Go down to Kew in lilac-time, in lilac-time, in lilac-time', run the lines from *The Barrel Organ*, by Alfred Noyes. Whether or not you are within reach of Kew, the wonderful fragrance of lilac is not hard to find. The Common Lilac, *Syringa vulgaris*, has produced many superbly scented flowers, in single, semi-double and double-flowered forms and in a wide color range. The richly sweet, white and double-flowered 'Madame Lemoine' is unsurpassable for early summer scent. If space is limited, plant a standard form with a single trunk and perhaps in a lawn; they are also superb city-lot shrubs.

There are several other species of lilac that create wonderful oases of scent during early summer and that are compact shrubs well suited to small yards. The Persian Lilac, *Syringa x persica*, has sweet, penetratingly fragrant, lilac-colored, broadly erect, pyramidal spires of flowers. This bushy, deciduous shrub, native to a wide area from Iran to China, is said to have been grown in Europe since before 1614, and was cultivated in Indian and Persian gardens long before then.

Syringa microphylla is another superbly scented lilac, with purplish-lilac flowers borne in erect pyramids during early summer and often again later in the season. Indeed, the Chinese know this shrub as the Four Seasons Lilac because it flowers several times in one year. For a greater display of blooms, select the form 'Superba', which has masses of rosy-pink flowers. The Chinese Lilac, *Syringa x chinensis*, is a taller plant, with soft lavender to purple flowers borne in erect pyramids during early summer. It eventually forms a large shrub, and is ideal for creating scent in a large corner. It gains one common name, Rouen Lilac, from being raised in the botanic garden in Rouen, France, in about 1777.

As if to lend confusion to the so-called "meanings of flowers," in Persia (now Iran) lilac was said to stand for "the forsaken," and to have been given by lovers on parting from their mistresses, but in Britain it is the garden anemone and laburnum that mean 'forsaken'. However, in both Britain and America it was common at one time for a spray of lilac to be sent to a fiancé when an engagement was to be broken. Judging from the relatively limited flowering time of

lilac, one must assume that broken engagements happened mainly in early summer.

For a lemony tang to the air during early to late summer try *Magnolia sieboldii;* it is deciduous, with white flowers, cup-shaped at first, which bear beautiful claret-colored stamens. It does not create a dominant display of scented flowers all at the same time; instead, the flowers are produced over several months.

Few heads are not turned by the late spring and early summer flowers of *Fothergilla major,* with its sweet, upright and bottle-brush-like white flowers. The related species *Fothergilla monticola* has similar flowers, with the bonus of richly colored leaves in autumn. Both are ideal for a small yard and can be planted quite close to a path.

Early summer brings forth a richly fragrant daphne, *Daphne x burkwoodii.* Its small stature, 3ft (90cm) or so high and wide, makes it ideal even for small yards. Popular varieties include 'Carol Mackie' and 'Somerset'.

The same season produces a wealth of sweet flowers from deutzias, so reliable and floriferous in a shrub border that they are sometimes ignored. The richly scented, arching clusters of white flowers on *Deutzia* 'Avalanche' are a delight during early summer – the slender branches are often weighed down with the weight of the flowers. *Deutzia* x *elegantissima,* with star-like, rose-purple flowers, also is richly fragrant. There are also several lovely scented forms of it, among them 'Fasciculata', with bright rose-pink flowers, and the beautiful 'Rosalind', deep carmine-pink.

Deutzias are especially welcome in colder areas (to zone 5), where they appear to do better than in warm climates. This is because they mostly come from cold regions that restrict winter activity and encourage a strong burst of color in spring. In warmer areas, the winters are so mild that they often encourage the development of buds and flowers that are subsequently damaged by spring frosts.

The Buffalo Currant, *Ribes aureum,* also known as *Ribes tenuifolium,* has a spicy clove scent. The bright yellow, tubular flowers are borne in drooping clusters during late spring. It has the bonus of the pale green leaves turning yellow, with an orange and gold flush, during autumn. It gained the name Buffalo Currant from the way the North American Indians used the berries to flavor pemmican – lean, dried strips of meat, usually from buffalo, that were pounded into a paste and mixed with fat and berries from the plant. The paste was then pressed into small cakes.

Late spring and early summer is the time for the sweetly scented, golden-yellow flowers of the Scotch Laburnum, *Laburnum alpinum.* However, for even larger clusters of golden-yellow flowers, frequently over 12 inches (30cm) long, *Laburnum* x *watereri* 'Vossii' is unsurpassable.

The Common Snowball, *Viburnum opulus,* is a delight in late spring and early summer when it bears sweetly and heavily scented white flowers in flat heads. The flowers are followed in autumn by translucent red berries. These have been used in jellies as a substitute for cranberries, and in North America it is known as the European Cranberry Bush Viburnum.

The extremely hardy Ornamental Hawthorn, *Crataegus monogyna* 'Stricta', is superb for bringing scent to exposed and cold areas and makes a very decorative windbreak. The strongly sweet-scented white flowers are borne in clusters during early summer and are followed by red berries called haws.

The ordinary form *Crataegus monogyna* is the well-known Common Hawthorn, May or Quick (known as the English Hawthorn in North America). It gained the name May because at one time it used to flower early that month and enrich May festivals with its scent. However, that was under the old Julian calen-

dar which was replaced in 1582 by the Gregorian calendar. Under the 'new' calendar the May is rarely in flower on the first of May!

One of the broom family, *Cytisus* 'Porlock', produces a wealth of richly sweet-scented, butter-yellow flowers during late spring and early summer. It is not cold-hardy, however, making it unsuitable for exposed areas, and in any case it does best against a south- or west-facing wall. Hardier, and creating a mass of heavy, perhaps rather acrid flowers, is *Cytisus* x *praecox*, the Warminster Broom. The scent is not to everyone's liking, but some people do find that the aroma grows on them and the creamy-white, pea-shaped flowers which bloom during late spring and early summer have great appeal. Several forms are available including 'Albus', with white flowers, and 'Allgold', a rich sulphur yellow. The latter's cascading shoots become densely packed with flowers, creating a large glow of color.

The almond-scented flowers of the Yoshino Cherry (Prunus x yedoenis) create a wonderful aura in spring.

The Moroccan Broom, *Cytisus battandieri*, is a gem among scented plants in early to midsummer. Its pineapple-scented, large, upright heads of pea-shaped, golden-yellow flowers are borne amid silvery, three-lobed leaves that act as a superb foil for its strong coloring. If you live in the deep South, try growing it against a south or west facing wall.

The Black Broom, *Cytisus nigricans*, flowers later in the year, from mid- to late summer, with sweetly scented, bright yellow and helmet-shaped flowers. Why it is called the Black Broom is difficult to understand, as it is not black. The only possible clue is that the flowers turn black on drying – but this applies to other plants too.

The Orange Ball Tree, *Buddleia globosa*, produces a wealth of sweetly scented flowers in small, tangerine-like heads during early summer. The eye-catching globes of flowers are attractively displayed in rather loose heads amid wrinkled dark green leaves. It is very tender, and in winter the evergreen leaves may be damaged, turning the plant into a semi-evergreen with a straggly appearance. It is therefore best grown in areas no colder than zone 9.

Buddleia alternifolia also bears scented flowers at this time, although they are rather more reserved in their fragrance than most other buddleias. They are small and lavender-blue, and clustered along arching branches that bear narrow, lance-shaped leaves in a manner reminiscent of the cascading nature of willows. Often it is grown as a shrub in a border, but when planted as a standard tree in a lawn it creates a stunningly attractive focal point.

Midsummer

Few midsummer scented plants are as well known as the Mock Oranges, often also known (erroneously) as Syringa. They were first introduced to Europe along with the lilac. Initially they both shared the same name because superficially they had features in common – both have wood which is hollow and pithy and can be made into pipes. Indeed, 'syringa' is derived from the Greek *surigx*, a reed or pipe. Syringa was known as Blew Pipe, philadelphus as White Pipe Tree. During the early 1600s the White Pipe Tree gained the name philadelphus, but some gardeners persisted with the name syringa, creating unnecessary confusion right up to the present time.

Philadelphus coronarius is a superbly scented shrub, with orange-blossom-like, sweetly scented flowers. Cup-shaped and borne terminally in clusters, the yellowish-white flowers are a joy. The form 'Aureus' brings further pleasure, with bright golden-yellow foliage that slowly turns greenish-yellow as the season progresses. *Philadelphus microphyllus* is smaller in stature but just as rich in scent, and is an asset in any landscape, whatever its size. Slightly larger are the named hybrids, such as 'Avalanche', 'Belle Etoile', 'Etoile Rose', 'Sybille' and 'Virginal'. All are strongly fragrant.

The attraction of butterflies to *Buddleia davidii* is well-known; the long, tapering and richly scented spires of lilac flowers soon attract Red Admiral and Monarch butterflies. Many varieties of Buddleia are available, in a color range that includes white, dark purple, violet-blue and lilac-pink.

From mid- to late summer *Buddleia fallowiana* displays large, plume-like clusters of pale lavender-blue flowers which have a strongly sweet and pervasive fragrance. It can only be grown through zone 9. For slightly more hardiness the form 'Alba', which has creamy-white flowers, can be planted.

The olearias, known as Tree Daisies or Daisy Bushes, bring a musk-like fragrance to the landscape during midsummer. All of these shrubs come from Australia, New Zealand or Tasmania, and they are too frost-sensitive to survive in the U.S. outside of California. However, these ornamental evergreen shrubs create a superb display of daisy-like flowers which, to some people, have a hawthorn-like scent. It is the leaves and stems which have the musk-like quality. *Olearia macrodonta,* often known as the New Zealand Holly, displays daisy-like white flowers in clustered heads. Unfortunately, the description white is, as with other olearias, used too generously, as the white is dirty like unlaundered sheets rather than brilliant and fresh.

The Maori Holly, *Olearia ilicifolia,* has coarsely toothed edges on its evergreen leaves, which have white and felted undersides. Daisy-like flowers appear in large heads during midsummer. Again, the plant has a musky aroma. *Olearia* x *haastii* has a rounded shape, with whitish flowers a little later than the previous two species.

Mid- to late summer triggers the flowering of the Curry Plant, *Helichrysum angustifolium,* well-known for its strong, curry-like aroma. It is the down which covers the stems and needle-like, silvery-gray leaves that produces the extremely strong curry aroma, while the mustard-yellow flowers catch the eye.

The scent, color and habit of the deciduous *Ceanothus* 'Gloire de Versailles' is in direct contrast to the Curry Plant. The fragrance of the ceanothus is demurely sweet, with terminal spires of soft powder-blue flowers borne at the ends of long, arching stems from mid- to late summer. It merges into a mixed border with consummate ease, but space must be left around it for the stems to spread under the weight of the flower heads, especially after a shower of rain. For the same reason, do not plant it within a yard or so of a path.

A shrubby herbaceous perennial that harmonizes well with the ceanothus is the sweetly scented Tree Poppy, *Romneya coulteri,* also frequently known as the Matilija Poppy, California Bush Poppy or California Tree Poppy. From mid- to late summer it unfolds sweetly scented, satiny-white flowers with eye-catching golden-yellow centers amid deeply lobed, bluish-green, glaucous leaves. A related species, *Romneya trichocalyx,* is similar, with grayer leaves and a more upright habit, but with less sweetly scented flowers. 'White Cloud', an American hybrid between these two species, has extra large, fragrant flowers

The penetratingly sweet flowers of many azaleas create a riot of color in late spring and early summer. The shrubs are superb in an informal woodland landscape.

amid intensely glaucous leaves. Too formal a position does not seem to suit these shrubs, and a warm, relatively dry and sunny place where they can be left undisturbed suits them admirably.

Late summer
The Mount Etna Broom, *Genista aetnensis*, emits a penetratingly sweet fragrance in late summer, with a mass of golden-yellow, pea-shaped flowers in loose clusters. It gains its common name from Mount Etna, where it grows in profusion. Two other genistas are known for their sweet and pervasive scent, although they bloom slightly earlier in the year. The Madeira Broom, *Genista virgata,* has been described as 'twelve feet of splendor', which is not surprising since when it is viewed during midsummer it is covered with bright yellow, pea-shaped flowers. *Genista cinerea* is slightly smaller, with midsummer, sweetly scented yellow flowers borne on slightly arching stems that appear to throw the flowers outwards.

The unusual, greenish-white flowers of *Itea ilicifolia* are sweetly fragrant and borne in trailing, catkin-like arrangements in late summer. It is evergreen, having a bushy habit and somewhat holly-like, but thinner and more oval, leaves.

A combination of shrubs and vines can create a rich pageant of scent and color. Above are genista (left) and senecio, backed by honeysuckle and roses.

For a sweet and carrying scent that attracts bees, the Black Locust, *Robinia pseudoacacia*, is superb during midsummer. It is also known as the Common Acacia and False Acacia. The creamy-white, pea-shaped flowers appear in pendulous clusters amid leaves formed of many leaflets. For extra visual appeal, the golden-leaved 'Frisia' is superb. Both forms are ideal for planting in a sunny border, where they can be used to soften a stark line of fences.

With both a sweet and a rather unpleasant, fetid aroma, *Clerodendron trichotomum* is an interesting deciduous shrub to plant in a border. Jasmine-scented, star-shaped, pinkish-white flowers appear during late summer and early autumn. Each flower is enclosed by a maroon calyx. It is the leaves which, when bruised, have a heavy and rather unpleasant odor. By way of compensation for this characteristic, the flowers are followed in autumn by bright blue, pea-sized berries.

SHRUBS WITH AROMATIC FOLIAGE

PLANT	SCENT	COLOR	SITUATION	CULTIVATION
CHAMOMILE				
Santolina chamaecyparissus (syn. *S. incana*) Lavender Cotton	Chamomile-like.	Bright, lemon-yellow flowers during midsummer. Woolly, thread-like, silvery foliage.	Its neat, mount-forming habit allows it to be planted at the corners and edges of borders.	Height: 1½-2ft (45-60cm) Spread: 1½-2ft (45-60cm) **Hardy shrub:** Well-drained soil in full sun. No regular pruning is needed, other than cutting back overgrown and straggly plants in spring.
Santolina neapolitana Lavender Cotton	Chamomile-like.	Bright, lemon-yellow flowers during midsummer amid feathery gray leaves. 'Sulphurea' has gray-green leaves and pale, primrose-yellow flowers.	It has a more open and lax habit than *S. chamaecyparissus* and is therefore best positioned slightly back from the front of a border or path edge.	Height: 2ft (60cm) Spread: 2ft (60cm) **Hardy shrub:** Well-drained soil and plenty of sun. Cut back straggly plants in spring.
GUM				
Cistus ladanifer Gum Cistus	Richly gum-like.	Eye-catching white flowers, 2½ inches (6cm) wide, with chocolate-maroon blotches at each petal's base, during midsummer. Leathery, dull green leaves.	In a mixed or shrub border, near a corner or towards the back of the border.	Height: 5ft (1.5m) Spread: 4-5ft (1.2-1.5m) **Very tender evergreen shrub:** Well-drained light soil and a sheltered and sunny position. No regular pruning is needed, but during spring cut out dead and straggly shoots.
LAVENDER				
Lavandula angustifolia (often listed as *L. spica* or *L. officinalis*) Old English Lavender	Air-drenching lavender aroma.	Grayish-blue flowers from midsummer to autumn. Narrow, silvery-gray leaves. Many superb forms, in colors including white, lavender-blue and pale pink.	Adaptable plant ideal for planting between roses, forming a low hedge or nestling around old brick walls. Grows in coastal regions.	Height: 3-4ft (0.9-1.2m) Spread: 3-4ft (0.9-1.2m) **Evergreen shrubby perennial:** Well-drained soil and a sunny position. Remove dead flowers in autumn and prune straggly plants in spring to encourage new growth.
Lavandula stoechas French Lavender	Intense lavender fragrance.	Dark purple flowers in long spikes during midsummer. Narrow, grayish-green leaves.	Ideal as an edging for a border or in a narrow border against a well-weathered brick wall.	Height: 1½-2ft (45-60cm) Spread: 1½-2ft (45-60cm) **Evergreen shrubby perennial:** Light, well-drained soil and a warm, sunny position. Remove dead flowers in late summer and trim straggly plants in spring.
ORANGE				
Choisya ternata Mexican Orange Blossom	Leaves emit a pungent, orange-like aroma when crushed. Sweetly scented flowers.	Glossy-green leaves. Orange-blossom-like flowers during late spring and early summer, and often intermittently until autumn.	Ideal for a corner position against a south- or west-facing wall. It is especially attractive when nestling against a wrought-iron gate.	Height: 5-6ft (1.5-1.8m) Spread: 5-6ft (1.5-1.8m) **Fairly tender evergreen shrub:** Well-drained soil and a sheltered, sunny position. In spring, cut out shoots damaged by frost and thin out straggly growths.
PUNGENT				
Caryopteris x *clandonensis* Blue Spiraea/Blue Mist Shrub	Strong, pungent aroma when leaves are bruised.	Bright blue, tubular flowers during late summer and into early autumn, amid narrow, gray-green leaves.	Place towards the front of a border, where the foliage can be harmonized with other plants – it is especially attractive in front of yellow-leaved plants.	Height: 2-2½ft (60-75cm) Spread: 2-2½ft (60-75cm) **Half-hardy shrub:** Well-drained soil and a sunny position. Does well on limy soil. In spring, cut back the previous season's growth to just above soil level.
PUNGENT AND BITTER				
Ruta graveolens Rue/Herb of Grace	Pungent, acrid aroma.	Small, mustard-yellow flowers from mid to late summer. Fern-like, glaucous, bluish-green foliage. The variety 'Jackman's Blue' has deeper bluish-gray leaves.	Ideal along border edges and especially at corners, where the hummock-forming nature neatly fills awkward areas.	Height: 2-2½ft (60-75cm) Spread: 1½-2ft (45-60cm) **Hardy evergreen shrub:** Well-drained soil and plenty of sun. Pinch out the tips of young shoots to encourage bushiness.

SHRUBS WITH AROMATIC FOLIAGE

PLANT	SCENT	COLOR	SITUATION	CULTIVATION
ROSEMARY				
Rosmarinus officinalis Common Rosemary	Highly aromatic.	Mauve flowers during early summer, amid narrow, green or grayish-green leaves with white undersides. Flowering sometimes continues spasmodically until late summer.	Ideal near lawn edges as well as alongside paths. Also looks good against weathered brick walls and at the bottom of steps.	Height: 6-7ft (1.8-2.1m) Spread: 5-6ft (1.5-1.8m) **Evergreen shrubby perennial:** Well-drained soil and a sunny position. Cut out straggly shoots in spring, and if old plants become bare cut back at the same time.
SAGE				
Perovskia atriplicifolia Russian Sage	Sage-like.	Lavender-blue flowers from mid- to late summer amid gray-green leaves. The variety 'Blue Spire' has larger flowers amid deeply cut foliage.	Ideal in a mixed border when used as a foil for plants with light yellow flowers or foliage.	Height: 3-5ft (0.9-1.5m) Spread: 1½-2½ft (45-75cm) **Hardy, shrubby, perennial plant:** Light, well-drained soil and a sunny position are essential. In spring, cut down the stems to about 12 inches (30cm) above soil level to encourage the development of fresh shoots.
SHARP				
Artemisia absinthium Common Wormwood	Pleasantly sharp.	Small, round, yellow, mimosa-like flowers during mid- to late summer, amid finely divided, slender, silvery-gray leaves. The variety 'Lambrook Silver' is even more attractive, with brighter, more silvery leaves.	Plant towards the middle or front of a mixed border, with tone-contrasting foliage plants behind.	Height: 2½-3ft (75-90cm) Spread: 2½-3ft (75-90cm) **Evergreen or semi-deciduous shrub:** Well-drained soil and a sunny position. By late autumn and early winter the foliage often becomes rotty and unattractive, so plants are best cut back to within 6 inches (15cm) of the ground in mid-spring.
SWEET				
Artemisia abrotanum Southernwood/Lad's Love/Old Man	Sweet.	Dull yellow, nodding flowers during late summer and into autumn, but the plant is mainly grown for its finely divided, downy, gray leaves that give a cottage-garden feel.	Plant towards the front or middle of mixed borders, where the foliage creates superb color and contrasts with flowering perennials.	Height: 2-3ft (60-90cm) Spread: 2½-3½ft (0.75-1m) **Soft-wooded, deciduous or semi-evergreen shrub:** Well-drained soil and a sunny position. Remove faded flowers. Cut back shoots to within about 1 inch (2.5cm) of the base of the previous season's growth during spring. This creates a wealth of fresh shoots during summer.
Artemisia tridentata Sage Brush	Leaves emit an intense fragrance, especially pervasive after a shower of rain.	Inconspicuous yellow flowers in late summer and autumn, amid wedge-shaped and tapering leaves covered with silver-gray felt.	Its spreading nature demands a dominant position, so plant it towards the back or middle of a border.	Height: 6-8ft (1.8-2.4m) Spread: 6-8ft (1.8-2.4m) **Evergreen shrub:** Well-drained soil and a sunny position. Remove faded flowers and prune it to shape in spring, removing dead wood.
Myrtus communis Common Myrtle	Sweet.	Saucer-shaped, 1 inch (2.5cm) wide, fragrant white flowers borne during midsummer amid highly aromatic, lance-shaped, deep green leaves.	Ideal against a warm wall. Does well in warm, coastal areas. It is not hardy and is often grown in a pot in a greenhouse, where it reaches up to 3ft (90cm) high.	Height: 7-9ft (2.1-2.7m) Spread: 6-8ft (1.8-2.4m) **Tender, half-hardy evergreen shrub:** Plant in light, well-drained soil against a south- or west-facing wall. It is only possible to grow it outside in warm areas. Cut out straggly shoots in spring.

PLANT	SCENT	COLOR	SITUATION	CULTIVATION
SCENTED FLOWERING TREES AND SHRUBS				
BITTER				
Cytisus x *praecox* Warminster Broom	Heavy, bitter aroma, sometimes considered to be unpleasant.	Creamy-white, pea-shaped flowers borne along slender, arching stems during late spring and early summer. The variety 'Albus' bears white flowers; those of 'Allgold' are rich sulphur-yellow and long-lasting.	Ideal alongside paths or as a focal point in a border with low-growing plants.	Height: 5-6ft (1.5-1.8m) Spread: 5-6ft (1.5-1.8m) **Deciduous shrub:** Light, rather poor soil and a sunny position. To keep the shrub bushy, use shears to reduce the length of the shoots by half to two-thirds when the flowers fade.
ALMOND				
Prunus padus 'Grandiflora' (syn. *P. p. 'Watereri'*) Bird Cherry	Almond-scented.	Small white flowers borne in slender, drooping tassels up to 8 inches (20cm) long during early summer.	Superb as a specimen tree in a lawn or along a boundary, where it softens the line of fencing.	Height: 20-30ft (6-9m) Spread: 15-20ft (4.5-6m) **Deciduous tree:** Treat as for *Prunus* 'Amanogawa' (see p.153).
Prunus x *yedoensis* Yoshino Cherry	Almond-scented.	White flowers borne in pendulous clusters during mid- to late spring.	Wide-spreading tree, ideal as a focal point at the bottom of a wide lawn.	Height: 20-25ft (6-7.5m) Spread: 25-30ft (7.5-9m) **Deciduous tree:** Treat as for *Prunus* 'Amanogawa' (see p.153).
COWSLIP				
Corylopsis pauciflora	Very sweet and cowslip-like.	Pale primrose-yellow, bell-shaped flowers in drooping clusters on bare, slender stems during mid- and late spring.	Plant alongside a path so that the scent can be readily appreciated. A high canopy of deciduous trees affords protection from spring frosts.	Height: 4-6ft (1.2-1.8m) Spread: 5-8ft (1.5-2.4m) **Somewhat hardy deciduous shrub:** Lime-free soil or one enriched with peat and leaf mould and a position in dappled light or full sun. No regular pruning is needed, other than the initial shaping of the bush and the cutting out of damaged or weak shoots to ground level each year after the flowers fade.
Corylopsis willmottiae	Very sweet and cowslip-like.	Soft, greenish-yellow flowers in pendulous clusters up to 3 inches (7.5cm) long during mid- to late spring.	Plant alongside a path, preferably under a high canopy of deciduous trees that afford protection from late spring frosts.	Height: 7-10ft (2.1-3m) Spread: 5-8ft (1.5-2.4m) **Somewhat hardy deciduous shrub:** Treat as for *C. pauciflora*.
CURRY				
Helichrysum angustifolium Curry Plant	Strongly curry-scented.	Silvery-gray, needle-like leaves covered with a down. Mustard-yellow flowers from mid- to late summer.	Ideal alongside a path, where the strong scent and dominantly colored flowers create a distinctive display.	Height: 8-15 inches (20-38cm) Spread: 1½-2ft (45-60cm) **Tender shrubby perennial:** Well-drained soil and full sun. Trim shoots back to near the old wood in spring.
HONEY				
Spartium junceum Spanish Broom	Honey-scented.	Bright, golden-yellow, pea-shaped flowers borne along almost leafless, rush-like stems from mid- to late summer.	Creates a dominant splash of color at the front of a lawn for most of summer.	Height: 7-9ft (2.1-2.7m) Spread: 6-8ft (1.8-2.4m) **Deciduous shrub:** Well-drained soil and a sunny position. Remove dead flower heads to prevent the development of seeds, and lightly trim over the plant in autumn to encourage early flowering the following year.
Ulex europaeus Common Gorse, Furze, Whin	Sweet and honey-like.	Golden-yellow, pea-like flowers crowded along spiny branches during late spring and early summer, and intermittently throughout the rest of the year. The variety 'Plenus' has double flowers and is more compact than the normal type.	Ideal for covering dry banks; if grown as a single plant, choose the double form and position against a wall or post and rail fence.	Height: 5-8ft (1.5-2.4m) Spread: 5-8ft (1.5-2.4m) **Evergreen shrub:** Well-drained, light soil and a sunny position. No regular pruning needed, but leggy plants can be cut down in early spring to 6 inches (15cm) above ground level to encourage new growth from the base.
LEMON				
Magnolia sieboldii (syn. *M. parviflora*)	Lemony bouquet.	Cup-shaped, pendant, white flowers, 3 inches (7.5cm) wide, with claret-colored stamens, from early to late summer.	In a shrub border or alongside a path.	Height: 10-15ft (3-4.5m) Spread: 10-15ft (3-4.5m) **Deciduous shrub:** Well-drained but moisture-retentive neutral or acid soil and a position in light shade. No regular pruning is needed.

SCENTED FLOWERING TREES AND SHRUBS

PLANT	SCENT	COLOR	SITUATION	CULTIVATION
LILY-OF-THE-VALLEY				
Mahonia japonica	Lily-of-the-valley bouquet.	Lemon-yellow flowers in drooping clusters 6-9 inches (15-23cm) long from midwinter to mid-spring.	Plant close to a path where the winter fragrance can be fully appreciated.	Height: 7-9ft (2.1-2.7m) Spread: 8-10ft (2.4-3m) **Evergreen shrub:** Moisture-retentive garden soil in light shade. No regular pruning is needed.
Skimmia japonica 'Fragrans'	Sweet, lily-of-the-valley fragrance.	Dense clusters of small, star-like white flowers at the end of shoots during late spring. This is a male form and does not bear berries.	In a woodland setting, alongside paths.	Height: 3-5ft (0.9-1.5m) Spread: 5-6ft (1.5-1.8m) **Evergreen shrub:** Well-drained soil in light shade. No pruning is needed.
MUSK				
Olearia ilicifolia Maori Holly	The whole plant has a musky odor.	Small, white, daisy-like flowers borne in clusters up to 4 inches (10cm) wide during early to midsummer.	In a shrub border.	Height: 8-10ft (2.4-3m) Spread: 8-10ft (2.4-3m) **Evergreen shrub:** Well-drained soil in a sunny and sheltered position. Ideal for planting in coastal areas. No regular pruning is needed, other than cutting out dead shoots in spring.
Olearia macrodonta Daisy Bush/New Zealand Holly	The whole plant has a musky odor.	White, daisy-like flowers borne in clusters up to 6 inches (15cm) wide during midsummer.	In a shrub border.	Height: 8-10ft (2.4-3m) Spread: 6-8ft (1.8-2.4m) **Evergreen shrub:** Well-drained soil in a sunny and sheltered position. Ideal for planting in coastal areas. No regular pruning is needed, other than cutting out dead shoots in spring.
ORANGE BLOSSOM				
Philadelphus 'Avalanche'	Orange blossom-like and richly sweet.	White, cup-shaped flowers borne so prolifically that they weigh down the branches during early to midsummer.	Ideal in a mixed or shrub border.	Height: 3-5ft (0.9-1.5m) Spread: 4-6ft (1.2-1.8m) **Deciduous shrub:** Well-drained soil in light shade or full sun. Thin out overcrowded shoots after the flowers fade, but do not remove young shoots as they will bear flowers during the following year.
Philadelphus coronarius Mock Orange	Orange blossom-like and sweet.	Yellowish-white, cup-shaped flowers borne terminally in clusters of five to nine in early to midsummer. The variety 'Aureus' has bright golden-yellow foliage that slowly turns greenish-yellow.	Plant in a shrub border, where the strong fragrance can be readily appreciated.	Height: 6-9ft (1.8-2.7m) Spread: 6-8ft (1.8-2.4m) **Deciduous shrub:** Well-drained soil in light shade or full sun. Do not plant 'Aureus' in full sun. After flowering, cut out overcrowded shoots, but make sure young ones are left to bear flowers the following year.
Philadelphus microphyllus	Orange blossom-like and richly sweet.	Pure white, cup-shaped flowers borne singly or in small clusters at the ends of shoots in early to midsummer.	Ideal for a small garden, alongside a path or in a narrow border.	Height: 2-3ft (60-90cm) Spread: 2-3ft (60-90cm) **Deciduous shrub:** Well-drained soil in light shade or full sun. Thin out overcrowded shoots after the flowers fade, but do not remove young shoots as these will bear flowers during the following year.
Poncirus trifoliata Japanese Bitter Orange	Orange blossom-like and sweet.	Pure white flowers 1½-2 inches (4-5cm) wide, along green stems armed with stout spines, during late spring.	Avoid a position where the spines may hurt children.	Height: 6-10ft (1.8-3m) Spread: 5-7ft (1.5-2.1m) **Deciduous shrub or small tree:** Well-drained soil in full sun. No regular pruning needed, other than to shape the shrub initially.

SCENTED FLOWERING TREES AND SHRUBS

PLANT	SCENT	COLOR	SITUATION	CULTIVATION
PINEAPPLE				
Cytisus battandieri Moroccan Broom	Pineapple aroma.	Golden-yellow, pea-shaped flowers in upright heads up to 4 inches (10cm) long during early and mid summer.	Ideal as a specimen shrub in a lawn, but in cold areas plant against a south- or west-facing wall.	Height: 12-15ft (3.6-4.5m) Spread: 8-12ft (2.4-3.6m) **Deciduous shrub:** Well-drained, light soil and plenty of sun. No regular pruning is needed, other than to occasionally remove a damaged branch.
SPICY				
Chimonanthus praecox (syn. *C. fragrans*) Winter Sweet	Heavy and spicy.	Cup-shaped, claw-like flowers with ivory-colored petals and purple centers during midwinter. They appear on leafless shoots. The long, dark leaves also have a spicy aroma. The variety 'Grandiflorus' has deep yellow flowers, but is not so fragrant.	Plant against a warm wall or in a sheltered border. However, in a shrub border expect it to be smaller than when grown against a wall.	Height: 8-10ft (2.4-3m) – against a wall Spread: 6-8ft (1.8-2.4m) – against a wall **Bushy deciduous shrub:** Ideal in well-drained soil and when planted against a south- or west-facing wall in full sun. When grown against a wall, cut back all flowered shoots to within a few inches of their base in mid-spring. If grown as a bush in a border, no pruning is needed, other than cutting out dead wood and thinning overcrowded shoots.
Clethra alnifolia Sweet Pepper Bush	Sweet and spicy.	Bell-shaped, creamy-white flowers in upright clusters 6 inches (15cm) high during late summer and early autumn. The best variety is 'Paniculata', which is slightly hardier, with larger flowers on arching branches.	In a corner of a border, where it can arch and fill a large area.	Height: 6-7ft (1.8-2.1m) Spread: 6ft (1.8m) **Bushy deciduous shrub:** Moisture-retentive, lime-free soil and a lightly shaded position. No regular pruning is needed.
Magnolia grandiflora 'Exmouth'	Richly spicy or fruity bouquet.	Globular, creamy-white flowers 5-8 inches (13-20cm) wide, from mid- to late summer.	Creates a massive shrub, often with a pyramidal outline. Ideal for filling a large corner, or can be grown against a warm wall.	Height: 10-18ft (3-5.4m) Spread: 8-12ft (2.4-3.6m) **Evergreen tree or large shrub:** Treat as for *Magnolia denudata* (see p.151).
Ribes aureum (syn. *R. tenuifolium*) Buffalo Currant	Spicily clove-scented.	Bright yellow, tubular flowers in drooping clusters during late spring.	In a shrub border.	Height: 5-7ft (1.5-2.1m) Spread: 3-5ft (0.9-1.5m) **Deciduous shrub:** Well-drained but moisture-retentive soil in light shade or full sun. After the flowers fade, cut out old wood to ground level.
VANILLA				
Azara microphylla	Strongly vanilla-scented.	Small yellow flowers in dense clusters from leaf joints during late spring.	In the northern part of its range, plant near a south- or west-facing wall.	Height: 10-12ft (3-3.6m) Spread: 5-6ft (1.5-1.8m) **Evergreen shrub or small tree:** Well-drained soil and slight protection are needed. Grows through zone 9.
VIOLET				
Malus coronaria 'Charlottae' Flowering Crabapple	Violet-scented.	Large, semi-double, shell-pink flowers borne in clusters during early summer.	Superb as a specimen tree in a lawn.	Height: 15-18ft (4.5-5.4m) Spread: 10-20ft (3-6m) **Deciduous tree:** Well-drained, fertile soil in full sun or light shade. No regular pruning is needed, other than shaping the tree in spring during its formative years.

SCENTED FLOWERING TREES AND SHRUBS				
PLANT	SCENT	COLOR	SITUATION	CULTIVATION
SWEET				
Abelia chinensis (syn. *A. rupestris*)	Very sweet.	Clusters of white, tubular flowers from leaf joints during summer.	In shrub borders, preferably near to a path edge; also against a sheltered wall.	Height: 3-5ft (0.9-1.5m) Spread: 4-5ft (1.2-1.5m) **Deciduous shrub:** Well-drained loamy soil and protection from a south- or west-facing wall are essential. It is not hardy north of zone 7. No regular pruning is needed, other than initially trimming it to shape.
Azalea (deciduous) Also see Rhododendron	Strongly sweet and penetrating.	Wide range, including 'Altaclarense' (orange-yellow with a darker flash); 'Balzac' (nasturtium-red with an orange flash); 'Exquisitum' (pink, with orange flare and frilled edges); 'Magnificum' (creamy-white, blushed pink and with an orange flare); 'Superbum' (pink with apricot blotch and fringed petals). Flowering in late spring and early summer.	In a woodland setting or naturalized garden. Especially attractive when alongside a path or stream.	Height: 4-8ft (1.2-2.4m) depending on variety Spread: 3-5ft (0.9-1.5m) depending on variety **Deciduous shrub:** Well-drained but moisture-retentive acid soil in light, dappled shade. No regular pruning needed.
Buddleia alternifolia Fountain Buddleia	Sweet and delicate.	Small, lavender-blue flowers borne in rounded clusters on arching branches during early summer.	When grown as a shrub, plant in a border. As a small tree it is ideal as a focal point in a lawn.	Height: 12-18ft (3.6-5.4m) Spread: 12-15ft (3.6-4.5m) **Deciduous shrub or small tree:** Loamy soil and a sunny position are essential. Prune by removing the top two-thirds of stems after flowering.
Buddleia davidii Butterfly Bush	Very sweet.	Tapering, 10-12 inch (25-50cm) long plume-like spires packed with lilac-purple flowers from mid- to late summer. Many varieties, in colors including white, dark purple, rich purple-red, violet-blue and lilac-pink are available; all attract butterflies.	Ideal in a mixed or shrub border, but remember that arching branches can bend almost to ground level when bearing flowers, especially after a shower of rain.	Height: 7-9ft (2.1-2.7m) Spread: 6-8ft (1.6-2.4m) **Deciduous shrub:** Rich, light to medium soil and a sunny position. Prune in early to mid-spring by cutting back the previous season's growth to within 3 inches (7.5cm) of the old wood.
Buddleia fallowiana	Sweet and penetrating.	Small, pale, lavender-blue flowers borne in terminal, plume-like clusters up to 10 inches (25cm) long from mid- to late summer.	Plant in a shrub border, in full sun and in the shelter of a south- or west-facing wall.	Height: 5-10ft (1.5-3m) Spread: 4-6ft (1.2-1.8m) **Tender deciduous shrub:** Rich, light to medium soil and a sunny position. Prune back hard in early to mid-spring to encourage new growth on which the new season's flowers will be borne.
Buddleia globosa Orange Ball Tree	Very sweet.	Orange-yellow flowers borne in tangerine-like balls are displayed in clusters of eight to ten during early summer.	Ideal for filling a large corner area at the junction of two walls.	Height: 10-12ft (3-3.6m) Spread: 10ft (3m) **Tender evergreen or semi-evergreen shrub:** Plant in the protection of a south- or west-facing wall, in loamy soil in full sun. Prune lightly after flowering, removing faded flower clusters and about 3 inches (7.5cm) of stem.
Ceanothus 'Gloire de Versailles'	Demurely sweet.	Soft powder-blue flowers borne in terminal spires up to 8 inches (20cm) long from mid- to late summer and often into early autumn.	Ideal in a shrub border, where the long stems can arch freely.	Height: 6-8ft (1.8-2.4m) Spread: 6-8ft (1.8-2.4m) **Deciduous shrub:** Light, neutral or slightly acid soil in full sun; in zone 8 it benefits from the protection of a south- or west-facing wall. Prune in mid-spring by cutting back the previous season's shoots to within about 3 inches (7.5cm) of the old wood.

SCENTED FLOWERING TREES AND SHRUBS				
PLANT	SCENT	COLOR	SITUATION	CULTIVATION
SWEET				
Clerodendron trichotomum	Very fragrant, sweet and like jasmine. Although the flowers are fragrant, the leaves when bruised have an unpleasant foetid aroma.	Star-shaped, pinkish-white flowers borne in erect heads up to 9 inches (23cm) wide during late summer and early autumn. Each flower is enclosed by a maroon calyx. The flowers are followed by bright blue, pea-sized berries.	Plant in a shrub border.	Height: 8-12ft (2.4-3.6m) Spread: 8-10ft (2.4-3m) **Bushy, slow-growing deciduous shrub:** Well-drained, fertile soil in a sunny position, preferably sheltered from cold wind. No regular pruning is needed, but large shrubs can be cut back in mid-spring.
Crataegus monogyna 'Stricta' (syn. *C. m.* 'Fastigiata') English Hawthorn	Strongly sweet.	White flowers in clusters 2-3 inches (5-7.5cm) wide during early summer, followed by red berries.	Ideal for creating a decorative windbreak or for planting in a border – a hardy tree.	Height: 15-20ft (4.5-6m) Spread: 10-15ft (3-4.5m) **Deciduous tree:** Ordinary soil in full sun or a lightly shaded position. No regular pruning is needed.
Cytisus nigricans	Sweet.	Bright yellow, helmet-shaped flowers at the ends of stems from mid- to late summer.	Ideal for creating scent and color in a small shrub border during late summer.	Height: 3-4ft (0.9-1.2m) Spread: 3ft (90cm) **Deciduous shrub:** Light, rather poor soil and a sunny position. To keep the shrub bushy, clip the shoots with shears in early spring.
Cytisus 'Porlock'	Richly sweet.	Butter-yellow, pea-shaped flowers borne in clusters at the ends of stems during late spring and early summer.	Sheltered position in a shrub border or against a warm wall.	Height: 6-9ft (1.8-2.7m) Spread: 4-5ft (1.2-1.5m) **Tender semi-evergreen shrub:** Well-drained soil in full sun, sheltered from cold north and east winds. No regular pruning is needed.
Daphne x *burkwoodii* Burkwood Daphne	Deliciously sweet.	Pale, soft pink flowers in dense terminal clusters during early summer. Available varieties include 'Somerset' and 'Carol Mackie'.	Plant in a shrub border, alongside paths or in a large rock garden.	Height: 3-4ft (0.9-1.2m) Spread: 3-4ft (0.9-1.2m) **Semi-evergreen shrub:** Ordinary garden soil, moisture-retentive but well-drained and in sun or partial shade. No regular pruning is needed.
Daphne odora 'Aureomarginata' Fragrant Daphne/ Winter Daphne	Strongly fragrant.	Pale purple flowers in clustered terminal heads from midwinter to mid-spring. The edges of the shiny, medium-green leaves are creamy-white.	Position at the edges of paths, where the scent can be readily appreciated.	Height: 5-6ft (1.2-1.8m) Spread: 5-6ft (1.2-1.8m) **Evergreen shrub:** Ordinary garden soil, moisture-retentive but not water-logged. No regular pruning is needed.
Deutzia x *maliflora* 'Avalanche'	Sweet.	Clusters of white flowers on arching branches during early summer.	In a shrub or mixed border.	Height: 6-8ft (1.8-2.4m) Spread: 5-7ft (1.5-2.1m) **Hardy deciduous shrub:** Ordinary well-drained soil in full sun or light shade. After the flowers fade, cut all stems that have borne flowers to soil level.
Deutzia x *elegantissima*	Sweet.	Rose-purple, star-like flowers in clusters on arching branches during early summer.	In a shrub or mixed border. Several superb varieties, including 'Fasciculata', bright rose-pink, and 'Rosalind', deep carmine-pink.	Height: 4-5ft (1.2-1.5m) Spread: 4-5ft (1.2-1.5m) **Hardy deciduous shrub:** Ordinary well-drained soil in full sun or light shade. After the flowers fade, cut all stems that have borne flowers to soil level.
Fothergilla major Large Fothergilla	Sweet.	White flowers in 1-2 inch-(2.5-5cm) long bottle-brush heads borne on bare stems during spring. *F. monticola* is similar, but wider-spreading and with brighter autumn-colored leaves.	At the corners or junctions of shrub borders.	Height: 6-8ft (1.6-2.4m) Spread: 4-6ft (1.2-1.8m) **Deciduous shrub:** Moisture-retentive, lime-free soil to which leafmold or peat has been added. Position in full sun or light shade. No regular pruning is needed.

SCENTED FLOWERING TREES AND SHRUBS

PLANT	SCENT	COLOR	SITUATION	CULTIVATION
SWEET				
Genista aetnensis Mount Etna Broom	Sweet and penetrating.	Golden-yellow, pea-shaped flowers in loose clusters during late summer.	In a shrub border, where it can create a focal point.	Height: 15-20ft (4.5-6m) Spread: 15-18ft (4.5-5.4m) **Deciduous shrub:** Light, well-drained soil and a sunny position. No regular pruning is needed, other than occasionally cutting out badly placed and crowded shoots after the flowers fade.
Genista cinerea	Sweet and penetrating.	Yellow, pea-shaped flowers in loose terminal clusters during midsummer.	Dominant when in bloom and ideal for planting against an old wall or building.	Height: 8-10ft (2.4-3m) Spread: 5-8ft (1.5-2.4m) **Deciduous shrub:** Light, well-drained soil and a sunny position. No regular pruning is needed, other than occasionally cutting out badly placed and crowded shoots after the flowers fade.
Genista virgata Madeira Broom	Sweet and penetrating.	Bright yellow, pea-shaped flowers in terminal clusters during midsummer.	Dominant when in bloom and ideal for planting against an old wall or building.	Height: 10-12ft (3-3.6m) Spread: 10-12ft (3-3.6m) **Deciduous shrub:** Light, well-drained soil and a sunny position. No regular pruning is needed, other than occasionally cutting out badly placed and crowded shoots after the flowers fade.
Hamamelis mollis Chinese Witch Hazel	Sweet.	Golden-yellow flowers with strap-like, twisted petals in clusters on bare branches in midwinter.	Plant in a shrub border, but close to a path from which the plant can be enjoyed.	Height: 6-8ft (1.8-2.4m) Spread: 6-8ft (1.8-2.4m) **Deciduous shrub or small tree:** Moisture-retentive, neutral or acid, medium-textured soils. No regular pruning is needed, other than cutting out badly placed branches after the flowers fade.
Itea ilicifolia	Sweet.	Greenish-white flowers in catkin-like trails up to 10 inches (25cm) long in late summer.	In the shelter of a wall, but make sure that the soil does not become dry.	Height: 6-8ft (1.8-2.4m) Spread: 5-7ft (1.5-2.1m) **Bushy, evergreen shrub:** Moisture-retentive soil in light shade. No regular pruning is needed.
Laburnum alpinum Scotch Laburnum	Sweet.	Golden-yellow, pea-like flowers borne in 10-inch-(25cm) long pendulous clusters during late spring and early summer.	Ideal alongside a path or lawn, but avoid positions near a pond or where children might pick up the bean-like, poisonous seeds.	Height: 15-20ft (4.5-6m) Spread: 10-15ft (3-4.5m) **Deciduous tree:** Well-drained soil in light shade or full sun. No regular pruning needed.
Laburnum x watereri Golden-Chain Tree	Sweet.	Golden-yellow, pea-like flowers borne in pendulous clusters up to 12 inches (30cm) long. The widely-grown form 'Vossii' (also known as *Laburnum* x *vossii*) has even longer clusters of flowers.	As for *Laburnum alpinum* or grow to form an arch over a pathway.	Height: 10-18ft (3.5-4m) Spread: 8-12ft (2.4-3.6m) **Deciduous tree:** Treat as for *Laburnum alpinum* (see above).
Lonicera fragrantissima Winter Honeysuckle	Penetratingly sweet.	Creamy-white flowers from midwinter to early spring.	Plant where the scented winter flowers can be appreciated.	Height: 5-6ft (1.5-1.8m) Spread: 5-6ft (1.5-1.8m) **Partially evergreen shrub:** Well-drained but moisture-retentive soil in full sun or light shade. No regular pruning is needed.
Lonicera standishii	Penetratingly sweet.	Creamy-white flowers from early winter to early spring. It flowers more prolifically than *L. fragrantissima*.	Plant where the scented winter flowers can be appreciated, perhaps alongside a path.	Height: 4-5ft (1.2-1.5m) Spread: 4-5ft (1.2-1.5m) **Deciduous shrub:** Well-drained but moisture-retentive soil in full sun or light shade. No regular pruning is needed.

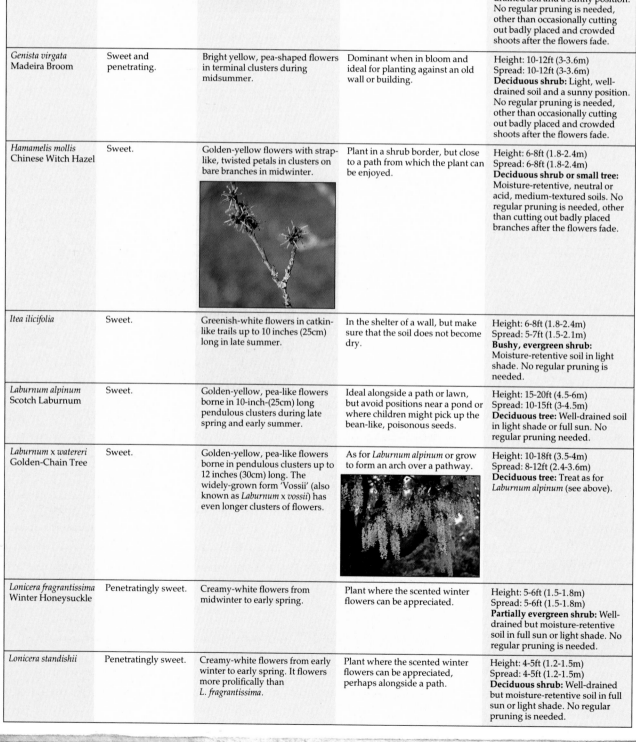

	SCENTED FLOWERING TREES AND SHRUBS			
PLANT	**SCENT**	**COLOR**	**SITUATION**	**CULTIVATION**
		SWEET		
Magnolia heptapeta (syn. *M. conspicua*) Yulan Magnolia	Sweet and subdued.	Pure white, chalice-shaped flowers, up to 6 inches (15cm) wide, borne during mid-spring and early summer.	Plant near a path, or as a feature in a bed in a lawn.	Height: 10-15ft (3-4.5m) Spread: 10-15ft (3-4.5m) **Deciduous tree:** Well-drained but moisture-retentive loamy soil and light shade. Plant in a sheltered area away from cold winds. No regular pruning is needed.
Magnolia salicifolia	Sweet.	Star-shaped, white flowers, 3-4 inches (7.5-10cm) wide, during mid- to late spring. The leaves emit a pleasant lemon scent when bruised.	Plant in a shrub border or alongside a path.	Height: 15-20ft (4.5-6m) Spread: 8-10ft (2.4-3m) **Deciduous tree or large shrub:** Treat as for *Magnolia denudata* (see above).
Magnolia x *soulangiana* 'Alba Superba' Saucer Magnolia	Strongly sweet.	Chalice-shaped, pure white and waxy flowers, 5-7 inches (13-18cm) wide, during mid- to late spring.	As a specimen shrub in a lawn.	Height: 6-10ft (1.8-3m) Spread: 6-8ft (1.8-2.4m) **Deciduous tree or large shrub:** Treat as for *M. sieboldii* (see p.145).
Magnolia stellata (syn. *M. kobus stellata*) Star Magnolia	Sweet and demure.	Star-shaped, white flowers 3-4 inches (7.5-10cm) wide, during mid- to late spring.	Plant near a path or as a specimen shrub in a lawn.	Height: 8-10ft (2.4-3m) Spread: 8-12ft (2.4-3.6m) **Deciduous shrub:** Treat as for *M. denudata* (see above).
Mahonia 'Charity'	Sweet and rich.	Deep yellow flowers in tapering, cascading spires up to 12 inches (30cm) long, from early to late winter.	Plant near to a path, where the winter fragrance can be fully appreciated.	Height: 6-8ft (1.8-2.4m) Spread: 5-7ft (1.5-2.1m) **Evergreen shrub:** Moisture-retentive garden soil in light shade. No regular pruning is needed.
Mahonia lomariifolia	Sweet and penetrating.	Deep yellow flowers borne in erect, tapering spires up to 10 inches (25cm) long from midwinter to late spring.	Plant near to a path, where the winter fragrance can be fully appreciated.	Height: 8-10ft (2.4-3m) Spread: 5-6ft (1.5-1.8m) **Evergreen shrub:** Moisture-retentive garden soil in light shade. No regular pruning is needed.
Malus floribunda Flowering Crabapple	Sweet.	Deep red buds opening to single, pale pink flowers becoming white, borne in clusters during late spring and early summer. Flowers followed by cherry-like fruits.	Ideal as a specimen tree on a lawn, or as a focal point towards the front of the yard.	Height: 12-15ft (3.6-4.5m) Spread: 10-15ft (3-4.5m) **Deciduous tree:** Well-drained, fertile soil in full sun or light shade. No regular pruning is needed, other than shaping the tree in spring during its formative years.

SCENTED FLOWERING TREES AND SHRUBS

PLANT	SCENT	COLOR	SITUATION	CULTIVATION
SWEET				
Malus hupehensis Flowering Crabapple	Sweet.	Single white flowers tinged rose-pink borne in clusters during early summer, followed by yellow fruits tinged red.	Forms a large tree; best positioned towards the front of the yard.	Height: 25-30ft (7.5-9m) Spread: 15-20ft (4.5-6m) **Deciduous tree:** Well-drained, fertile soil in full sun or light shade. No regular pruning is needed, other than shaping the tree in spring during its formative years.
Malus 'Profusion' Flowering Crabapple	Light, sweet scent.	Single, deep purple flowers paling to pink, borne in clusters during early summer. Small, oxblood-red fruits.	Ideal as a specimen tree in a lawn, or plant in a border.	Height: 15-20ft (4.5-6m) Spread: 8-15ft (2.4-3.5m) **Deciduous tree:** Well-drained, fertile soil in full sun or light shade. No regular pruning is needed, other than shaping the tree in spring during its formative years.
Osmanthus delavayi	Sweet.	White, jasmine-like flowers in clusters during spring.	Plant in a shrub border, perhaps near a corner, where the shrub's rounded shape will neatly fill the area.	Height: 6-8ft (1.8-2.4m) Spread: 6-8ft (1.8-2.4m) **Evergreen shrub:** Well-drained garden soil in light shade or full sun. No regular pruning is needed.
Osmanthus heterophyllus Holly Osmanthus	Very sweet.	White, tubular flowers in dense clusters along the branches during late summer and early autumn.	Plant in a shrub border.	Height: 6-9ft (1.8-2.7m) Spread: 6-9ft (1.8-2.7m) **Evergreen shrub:** Well-drained soil in light shade or full sun. No regular pruning required unless grown as a hedge, when it is clipped in spring. However, this does diminish the number of flowers it produces.
X Osmarea burkwoodii	Sweet.	Tubular, white flowers borne in small clusters during late spring.	Against a wall or for growing as a hedge.	Height: 6-10ft (1.8-3m) Spread: 6-10ft (1.8-3m) **Hardy evergreen shrub:** Well-drained soil in full sun or light shade. No regular pruning is needed. If grown as a hedge, position the plants 18 inches (45cm) apart and clip to shape in early summer after the flowers have faded.
Philadelphus 'Belle Etoile' Mock Orange	Penetratingly sweet.	Single white flowers, flushed maroon at their centers, during early to midsummer.	Ideal in a mixed or shrub border.	Height: 5-7ft (1.5-2.1m) Spread: 5-6ft (1.5-1.8m) **Deciduous shrub:** Well-drained soil in light shade or full sun. Thin out overcrowded shoots after the flowers fade, but do not remove young shoots, as they will bear flowers during the following year.
Philadelphus 'Virginal' Mock Orange	Sweet, rich fragrance.	White, cup-shaped, 2-inch-(5cm) wide, double or semi-double flowers during early and midsummer.	In a shrub or mixed border.	Height: 8-9ft (2.4-2.7m) Spread: 6-8ft (1.8-2.4m) **Deciduous shrub:** Well-drained soil in light shade or full sun. Thin out overcrowded shoots after flowers fade, but do not remove young shoots, as they will bear flowers during the following year.

PLANT	SCENT	COLOR	SITUATION	CULTIVATION
SCENTED FLOWERING TREES AND SHRUBS				
SWEET				
Prunus 'Amanogawa' Lombardy Poplar Cherry	Sweet and demure.	Semi-double, soft pink flowers borne in dense clusters during late spring and early summer.	It is initially very slender when young, so it is ideal where space is limited.	Height: 20-25ft (6-7.5m) Spread: 6-8ft (1.8-2.4m) **Deciduous tree:** Well-drained but moisture-retentive, neutral or slightly alkaline soil in full sun or light shade. No regular pruning is needed, but if it is necessary to shape a tree during its formative years, prune it in early summer when the sap is rising.
Prunus 'Shirotae' (syn. *P.* 'Kojima') Flowering Cherry	Sweet.	Semi-double, snow-white flowers in pendant clusters during late spring.	Ideal as a spring focal point at the front of a lawn.	Height: 18-25ft (5.4-7.5m) Spread: 25-30ft (7.5-9m) **Deciduous tree:** Treat as for *Prunus* 'Amanogawa' (see above).
Rhododendron luteum Pontic Azalea	Rich and penetratingly sweet.	Clusters of rich, bright yellow flowers, each 1½-2 inches (4-5cm) wide, during late spring and early summer.	In a woodland or naturalized garden, especially alongside a stream. It creates a wall of color alongside paths.	Height: 6-10ft (1.8-3m) Spread: 4-6ft (1.2-1.8m) **Deciduous shrub:** Well-drained but moisture-retentive acid soil in light, dappled shade. No regular pruning needed.
Robinia pseudoacacia Black Locust/ Common Acacia/ False Acacia	Sweet and penetrating, and very attractive to bees.	Creamy-white, pea-like flowers borne in pendulous clusters up to 7 inches (18cm) long during midsummer.	Ideal for planting in a border or near a boundary, where it can soften a fence.	Height: 25-30ft (7.5-9m) Spread: 10-15ft (3-4.5m) **Deciduous tree:** Well-drained soil and a sunny position. No regular pruning is needed.
Romneya coulteri Tree Poppy	Sweet.	Satiny-white flowers 4-5 inches (10-13cm) wide and with golden-yellow, dome-shaped centers, from mid- to late summer.	Superb in a shrub border or alongside paths.	Height: 4-6ft (1.2-1.8m) Spread: 4-5ft (1.2-1.5m) **Shrubby herbaceous perennial:** Light, well-drained soil in a sunny, sheltered position. Once established, do not move, as it dislikes root disturbance. In autumn, cut down all stems to within a few inches of the ground. It is often too invasive in a flower border, and is therefore usually planted with shrubs.
Skimmia japonica 'Rubella' Japanese Skimmia	Strongly and sweetly fragrant.	White, yellow-centered flowers, pink when in bud, borne in large, terminal heads during late spring. This is a male form and does not bear berries.	Plant in a woodland setting, alongside paths.	Height: 2-4ft (0.6-1.2m) Spread: 3-4ft (0.9-1.2m) **Evergreen shrub:** Well-drained, slightly acid or neutral soil in light shade. No pruning is needed.
Skimmia laureola	Very sweet; leaves are pungent when crushed.	Creamy-white, star-like flowers in loose, pyramidal clusters up to 4 inches (10cm) long during late spring.	In a woodland setting, alongside paths.	Height: 2½-3ft (75-90cm) Spread: 2½-3ft (75-90cm) **Evergreen shrub:** Well-drained soil in light shade. No pruning is needed.

PLANT	SCENT	COLOR	SITUATION	CULTIVATION
SWEET				
Syringa x *chinensis* Chinese Lilac/Rouen Lilac	Penetratingly sweet and lilac-like.	Soft lavender to purple flowers borne in 6-8-inch-(15-20cm) high erect pyramids during early summer.	Ideal for positioning along the edge of a lawn.	Height: 8-10ft (2.4-3m) Spread: 6ft (1.8m) **Deciduous shrub:** Fertile garden soil and a position in full sun or light shade. Remove dead flowers and thin out crowded and weak shoots in autumn.
Syringa microphylla Littleleaf Lilac	Penetratingly sweet and lilac-like.	Purplish-lilac flowers borne in erect, 3-4-inch-(7.5-10cm) long pyramids during early summer and often again in late summer. The variety 'Superba' is even more floriferous, with rosy-pink flowers in early summer and intermittently until autumn.	Ideal for a small garden, at the junction of paths.	Height: 4-5ft (1.2-1.5m) Spread: 4-5ft (1.2-1.5m) **Deciduous shrub:** Fertile garden soil and a position in full sun or light shade. Remove dead flowers and thin out crowded and weak shoots in autumn.
Syringa x *persica* Persian Lilac	Penetratingly sweet.	Lilac-colored flowers in 3-4-inch-(7.5-10cm) high erect pyramids during early summer.	Plant so that it borders a lawn.	Height: 5-7ft (1.5-2.1m) Spread: 5-6ft (1.5-1.8m) **Deciduous shrub:** Fertile garden soil and a position in full sun or light shade. Remove dead flowers and thin out crowded and weak shoots in autumn.
Syringa vulgaris Common Lilac	Penetratingly sweet.	Wide color range of flowers borne in 6-10 inch-(15-25cm) long pyramids during early summer. Varieties include: 'Congo' (single, dark lilac-red); 'Firmament' (single, sky-blue flowers, pinkish-mauve in bud); 'Katherine Havemeyer' (double, deep purple-lavender); 'Madame Lemoine' (double, white); 'Madame A. Buchner' (semi-double, rose-shaded, pinkish-mauve); 'Massena' (single, glowing purple); 'Michael Buchner' (double, clear lilac); 'Mrs. Edward Harding (semi-double, red); 'Souvenir d'Alice Harding (double, alabaster-white); 'Souvenir de Louis Späth' (single, deep wine-red); 'Vestale' (single, pure white).	In a border, preferably near to a path.	Height: 8-12ft (2.4-3.6m) Spread: 6-10ft (1.6-3m) **Deciduous shrub:** Fertile soil in full sun or slight shade. Remove dead flowers, especially when the plant is young, and cut out overcrowded or weak shoots.
Viburnum x *bodnantense* 'Dawn'	Richly sweet and penetrating.	White flowers, flushed pink – rich rose-red when in bud – in small clusters on bare stems from late autumn to late winter. The variety 'Deben' has white flowers, shell-pink when in bud, from late autumn to early spring.	Position close to a firm-surfaced path so that the scent can be readily appreciated.	Height: 8-10ft (2.4-3m) Spread: 8-10ft (2.4-3m) **Deciduous shrub:** Moisture-retentive soil, full sun and a position sheltered from cold winds is essential. No regular pruning is needed, other than occasionally cutting out dead shoots in spring.
Viburnum x *burkwoodii* Burkwood Viburnum	Sweet and penetrating.	White flowers, pink in bud, borne in flat heads up to 3½ inches (8cm) wide from early spring to early summer. The variety 'Park Farm Hybrid' has larger flowers and a more spreading habit. 'Anne Russell' is another related variety, with strongly fragrant white flowers, pink when in bud. Its habit is slightly smaller and it is better suited to small yards than the larger varieties.	Position close to a firm-surfaced path so that the scent can be readily appreciated.	Height: 6-8ft (1.8-2.4m) Spread: 7-10ft (2.1-3m) **Evergreen shrub:** Moisture-retentive soil and full sun. In cold areas, position in the shelter of a wall, and avoid places where early morning sunlight falls on flowers coated with frost. No regular pruning is needed, but cut out dead and overcrowded shoots after the flowers fade.

SCENTED FLOWERING TREES AND SHRUBS

PLANT	SCENT	COLOR	SITUATION	CULTIVATION
SWEET				
Viburnum x *carlcephalum* Carlcephalum Viburnum	Sweet.	Creamy-white flowers, pink when in bud, borne in heads up to 4 inches (10cm) wide during spring and early summer.	Position close to a firm-surfaced path where the scent can be readily appreciated. In autumn, the leaves of this fast-growing and compact shrub are often richly colored. Therefore, try to position it so that the colors can be appreciated and are not hidden by evergreen shrubs planted too close.	Height: 6-8ft (1.8-2.4m) Spread: 5-7ft (1.5-2.1m) **Deciduous shrub:** Treat in the same way as *Viburnum* x *bodnantense* (see opposite).
Viburnum carlesii Koreanspice Viburnum	Sweet, jasmine-like and penetrating fragrance.	Waxy-white flowers borne in rounded heads up to 3 inches (7.5cm) wide during spring and early summer. There are several superb varieties, including 'Aurora' (pink flowers, red when in bud) and 'Diana' (light pink flowers, red when in bud).	Position close to a firm-surfaced path where the scent can be readily appreciated.	Height: 4-6ft (1.2-1.8m) Spread: 4-5ft (1.2-1.5m) **Deciduous shrub:** Treat in the same way as *Viburnum* x *bodnantense* (see opposite).
Viburnum farreri (syn. *Viburnum fragrans*)	Richly sweet and penetrating.	White flowers, pink-tinged when in bud, borne in clusters up to 2 inches (5cm) wide from early to late winter.	Position close to a firm-surfaced path where the scent can be readily appreciated. Fragrant bulbs such as the sweet, honey-scented *Crocus chrysanthus* can be naturalized around this shrub to create further interest. Other useful bulbous plants include the sweetly fragrant *Iris danfordiae* and the violet-scented *Iris reticulata.*	Height: 8-12 ft(2.4-3.6m) Spread: 8-10ft (2.4-3m) **Deciduous shrub:** Treat in the same way as *Viburnum* x *bodnantense* (see opposite).
Viburnum grandiflorum	Sweet.	Deep pink flowers, fading slightly but carmine-red when in bud, borne in clusters from midwinter to spring.	Position close to a firm-surfaced path where the scent can be readily appreciated.	Height: 7-10ft (2.1-3m) Spread: 5-6ft (1.5-1.8m) **Deciduous shrub:** Treat in the same way as *Viburnum* x *bodnantense* (see opposite).
Viburnum x *juddii* Judd Viburnum	Sweet and very penetrating.	White flowers, pink when in bud, in clustered heads up to 3 inches (7.5cm) wide during late spring and early summer.	Position close to a firm-surfaced path where the scent can be readily appreciated.	Height: 5-6ft (1.5-1.8m) Spread: 6-8ft (1.8-2.4m) **Deciduous shrub:** Treat in the same way as *Viburnum* x *bodnantense* (see opposite).
Viburnum opulus European Cranberry-bush Viburnum/ Guelder Rose	Heavily sweet.	White flowers borne in flat heads up to 3 inches (7.5cm) wide during late spring and early summer, followed by translucent berries in autumn. The variety 'Roseum', the Snowball Bush, displays round, snow-white flower heads.	In a shrub border.	Height: 8-12ft (2.4-3.6m) Spread: 10-12ft (3-3.6m) **Deciduous shrub:** Treat in the same way as *Viburnum* x *bodnantense* (see opposite).

CHAPTER TEN

Scented Indoor Plants

*The charm of an indoor garden will be greatly
enhanced with the addition of a variety of
deliciously scented plants.*

THERE ARE few homes that do not have a houseplant. Surveys reveal that nearly half of all homes have a cactus or succulent, while geraniums are the next most popular plant, followed by African violets, rubber plants, tradescantias and chrysanthemums. Regrettably, it is not until one reaches bulbs in pots – which include the exquisitely scented hyacinths – that a large number of richly fragrant plants appear.

Homes benefit from rich and varied fragrances as much as from the visual interest of the color of flowers and the varied shapes and textures of leaves. Indeed, the search for pleasant odors in the home is indicated by the range of scented polishes and air-fresheners sold in their millions each year. The old London street cry, 'Who'll buy my lavender, fresh lavender, sweet blooming lavenders, who'll buy', proves that although times change, time-tested customs remain.

The problem of keeping food fresh has long since been solved by refrigerators and deep freezers, but there is still a need to mask cooking smells. The richly sweet flowers of the Pink Jasmine, *Jasminum polyanthum*, are better than air fresheners, helping to bring excitement to the dull winter months. Hyacinths, with their upright, soldier-like spires of flowers, are also superb at that time of year.

Scented geranium leaves offer a wonderful variety of delightful aromas. The Lemon-scented Geranium, *Pelargonium crispum*, is remarkable. Rub your fingers over the deeply lobed leaves and they will emit a strong, lemony scent for several hours. *P.* x *fragrans*, on the other hand, has a nutmeg and rather pine-like aroma that creates a superb freshness in kitchens. The range of other scents is just as exciting, including almond (*P. quericifolium*), peppermint (*P. tomentosum*), and rose (*P. graveolens*). Catalogues from specialist pelargonium nurseries offer even further exciting fragrances, including 'Endsleigh' (pepper-scented leaves), *P. odoratissimum* (strongly apple-scented leaves), 'Prince of Orange' (orange-scented leaves), and 'Clorinda' (a eucalyptus scent).

In addition to the Pink Jasmine, there are other indoor climbing plants with exquisite scents. The Miniature Wax Plant, *Hoya bella*, has deliciously perfumed, star-shaped flowers decoratively borne in pendulous, umbrella-like heads about 2 inches (5cm) wide from late spring to late summer. It is ideal for growing in a pot with a small framework of wire over which it can climb, or for planting in an indoor hanging basket. It will create a rich, sweet fragrance at any time from late spring to late summer. Its big brother, *Hoya carnosa*, grows 8-12ft (2.4-3.6m) high and is best grown over a permanent framework of wires in a sunroom or greenhouse. Its white to pink, star-shaped flowers are also borne in inverted, umbrella-like heads. When grown near to the entrance of a sunroom, its rich perfume can be immediately appreciated. The Madagascar Jasmine, *Stephanotis floribunda* (also known as the Wax Flower), is another sweetly scented, vigorous climber, although it is also amenable enough during its younger days to life in a small pot, with its stems twisted around a support of hooped wires. Its beautiful, white, star-shaped flowers are borne in clusters from late spring to early autumn.

Few plants are as acclaimed as the Gardenia, *Gardenia jasminoides*, for soaking the air in greenhouses with a heavy, richly sweet fragrance. The plant bears richly sweet, white, waxy flowers, which appear from mid- to late summer. As well as being used in boutonnieres, it has also been added to wreaths, while the leaves of certain species of gardenia are used to flavor tea.

Many scented houseplants are ideal for adding fragrance to dining rooms and coffee tables. The Fairy Primrose, *Primula malacoides*, has tiered whorls of flowers with a delicate and primrose-like fragrance. Its flowering period, from midwinter to late spring, makes it ideal for creating interest through fragrance in the dark and often dreary months. *Primula* x *kewensis* has a similar aroma, again flowering from midwinter to late spring. This time of the year is rich in scented plants, and many homes also have a cyclamen in flower at Christmas and the New Year. Some cyclamens have a strong fragrance – look for the Puppet, Kaori and Symphony strains.

The Persian Violet, *Exacum affine*, is another plant ideal for brightening tables. It is wonderful, with

The Persian Violet (Exacum affine) *has yellow-centered, purple flowers that fill rooms with a sweet, lily-of-the-valley fragrance during midsummer.*

Hyacinths can fill rooms with their very sweet and penetrating bouquet. 'Ostara', with its purple-blue spires, makes a dominant picture.

sweetly scented flowers that emit a fragrance reminiscent of lily-of-the-valley. Its long bloom time, from late spring to late summer, makes it ideal for providing fragrance over a long period.

For a heavy and fruity aroma Heliotrope, *Heliotropium* x *hybridum*, cannot be surpassed. One of its other common names, Cherry Pie, testifies to the scent of its Forget-me-not-like flowers, which are borne in clusters from early summer to autumn. In gardens in warm areas, it is often planted as part of a summer bedding scheme. Its curious common name Turnsole is derived from the old French *tournesol*, and Latin *tornare*, describing the nature of the flowers which turn to meet the sun.

FLOWERS FOR ARRANGING INDOORS

The art of arranging flowers is a skill that has been practised throughout the world for many centuries, and while styles may change from place to place and from one century to another, the pleasure which flowers give is immeasurable. Some ideas for displaying scented plants are given in Chapter 11. Plants that are particularly useful in flower arranging are discussed below.

The range of scented foliage for use in flower arrangements is wide, and many of the plants described in Chapter 9 will also provide interest indoors. These include the beautiful orange-scented leaves of the Mexican Orange Blossom (*Choisya ternata*), which has the bonus of sweetly scented flowers. Southernwood (*Artemisia abrotanum*), with its finely divided, sweet-scented leaves, is another, as well as Common Wormwood (*Artemisia absinthium*), which is pleasantly sharp and has silvery-gray leaves that create a superb backdrop for many flowers.

A number of evergreen conifers are beautifully scented, and a stroll through a group of them after a shower of rain or on a warm sunny day is the best way to appreciate their aromas. As usual when gathering plants for use in flower arrangements, cut them so that the loss is not readily apparent.

Some of the following scented conifers are well-known, while others are less so. The Californian Nutmeg, *Torreya californica*, resembles Yew, with foliage which, when crushed, emits a strong, heavy, sage-like aroma. Its close relative, the Japanese Nutmeg, *Torreya nucifera*, is similar in scent. The Incense Cedar, *Calocedrus decurrens*, has an upright habit with foliage which, when bruised, gives off a strong turpentine aroma.

For a fragrance of parsley enriched with a tinge of resin, choose one of the many forms of Lawson Cypress, *Chamaecyparis lawsoniana*. There are many types of it, in a range of sizes and shapes as well as colors: 'Lutea', golden-yellow; 'Ellwoodii', gray-green;

The Gardenia (Gardenia jasminoides) *emits a heavy, sweet scent from its white, waxy flowers from mid- to late summer. It is ideal in a greenhouse.*

The foliage of the arborvitae conifers also emits superb aromas when crushed. The well-known Western Red Cedar, *Thuja plicata*, has a pineapple fragrance, the Japanese Thuja, *Thuja standishii*, that of eucalyptus and lemon, and the Korean Thuja, *Thuja koraiensis*, a glorious mixture of lemons and almonds. Two Silver Firs have foliage that is citrus-scented when crushed: the Cascade Fir, *Abies amabilis*, and the Giant Fir, *Abies grandis*.

Few flower arrangements can ignore the intensely sweet flowers of the deciduous shrub Mock Orange, a common name used for a wide range of shrubs that belong to the philadelphus family. The large, clustered flowers are superb for filling a room with a rich fragrance, and if you need added color for the flower arrangement, then choose *Philadelphus coronarius* 'Aureus', which has golden-yellow leaves and fragrant, yellow-white flowers.

'Stewartii', golden-yellow changing to yellow-green in winter; 'Pottenii', sea-green; and 'Pembury Blue', silvery-blue. Other chamaecyparis species are also scented, such as the Hinoki Cypress, *Chamaecyparis obtusa*, with foliage which, when crushed, emits a somewhat sweet aroma, while the Sawara Cypress, *Chamaecyparis pisifera*, has a resinous smell. The crushed foliage of the Formosan Cypress, *Chamaecyparis formosensis*, smells of seaweed, the White Cedar, *Chamaecyparis thyoides*, has a warm gingery scent, and the Nootka Cypress, *Chamaecyparis nootkatensis*, smells of turpentine.

The true cypresses have a wonderful range of aromas. The Monterey Cypress, *Cupressus macrocarpa*, has foliage which is lemon-scented, *Cupressus goveniana* is a fusion of lemon and thyme, *Cupressus glabra* has a grapefruit fragrance, while the Bhutan Cypress, *Cupressus torulosa*, smells like mowed grass.

Junipers are also well endowed with scent. The Common Juniper, *Juniperus communis*, has foliage which, when crushed, has the aroma of apples, but unless you like a sour, catty smell, avoid the Chinese Juniper, *Juniperus chinensis*. For a strongly soapy fragrance fused with resin go for the Red Cedar, *Juniperus virginiana*.

Few homes look fully decorated at Christmas without a bowl of hyacinths. There is a wide color range, including white, yellow, pink, red and blue.

The distinctive spikes of lavender are essential for country-style displays, where their strongly aromatic flowers and upright heads have a nostalgic charm. As well as the Old English Lavender, variously known as *Lavandula spica, L. angustifolia* and *L. officinalis*, there is the highly fragrant French Lavender, *L. stoechas*, which has different flower heads from the other lavenders – each one has a large tuft of bracts resembling petals at its top that remain long after the real flowers have faded. As well as creating a rich aroma, it also produces an oil (Stoechas Oil) which is used in Spain in the treatment of asthma, cramps and lung diseases.

The large heads of lilac have a scented spring charm unmatched by other plants. Pyramidal clusters of waxy flowers in colors from pure white to purple create superb focal points in any arrangement. Another excellent plant is the dominantly yellow-colored Spanish Broom, *Spartium junceum*, which has a wealth of stems bearing deliciously honey-scented flowers. The flowers need to be displayed in a loose cluster, so that although they appear *en masse* each pea-like flower can be seen.

Winter-flowering scented shrubs are a good cure for the dull-season blues. The range is wide, but the viburnums are unrivalled. Cutting blooms from the floriferous shrubs, however, can soon spoil them, and so it is best done discreetly from the back of the shrub. Mahonias also offer flowers that can be used in floral arrangements, but here again the plants can

Rhipsalidopsis rosea *is superb in an indoor hanging basket, where its rose or pink, trumpet-shaped flowers have a sweet scent from early to midsummer.*

soon be damaged by repeated shearings. Of all the mahonias, *Mahonia japonica* appears to suffer least from this practice, provided it is carried out sensibly.

The Chinese Witch Hazel, *Hamamelis mollis*, also reveals its charms during winter, with sweetly scented, spider-like flowers along naked branches. Many flower arrangers recommend this shrub in midwinter flower arrangements, but its charms are best left outside. The growth pattern of most of these winter-flowering plants means that the repeated cutting of branches bearing flowers soon destroys their appearance. Conversely, the growth habit of some roses, such as Hybrid Teas and Floribundas, lends itself to their being repeatedly cut year after year with no detrimental effect.

There are also large numbers of herbaceous perennials, biennials, annuals and bulbs with rich bouquets that are ideal as cut flowers. Some of the best of these are the annuals. They are best grown in an out-of-the-way patch so that when the flowers are cut an essential area of the garden is not left bare of color. Heliotrope, Sweet Rocket, Wallflowers, Sweet Williams, Sweet Scabious and Sweet Mignonette all bring delightful scents into the house.

PLANT	SCENT	COLOR	SITUATION	CULTIVATION
ALMOND				
Pelargonium quericifolium Almond-scented Geranium.	Almond-scented leaves.	Rose-colored flowers with large, purple-red spots and veins.	On a kitchen windowsill or in a cool room.	Height: 2½-4ft (0.75-1.2m) Spread: 1½-2ft (45-60cm) **Tender, shrubby perennial:** Keep at 45-50°F (7-10°C) during winter, with shade from direct sunlight in summer. Repot in spring when roots fill the pot.
LEMON AND BALM				
Pelargonium crispum Lemon-scented Geranium	Lemon and balm-like leaves.	Hairy, green, deeply lobed leaves revealing an appealing fragrance when crushed. Rose-pink flowers, ¾-1 inch (18-25mm) wide, in umbrella-like heads from early to late summer.	On a kitchen windowsill or in a cool room.	Height: 1½-2ft (45-60cm) Spread: 15 inches (38cm) **Tender, shrubby perennial:** Keep at 45-50°F (7-10°C) during winter. Shade from direct sunlight in summer. Repot in spring when roots fill the pot.
NUTMEG AND PINE				
Pelargonium x *fragrans* Nutmeg Geranium	Nutmeg and pine-scented leaves.	White, prominently spotted and veined with red.	On a kitchen windowsill or in a cool room.	Height: 3-4ft (0.9-1.2m) Spread: 1½-2ft (45-60cm) **Tender, shrubby perennial:** Keep at 45-50°F (7-10°C) during winter, with shade from direct sunlight in summer. Repot in spring when roots fill the pot.
PEPPERMINT				
Pelargonium tomentosum Peppermint Geranium/Mint Geranium	Strongly peppermint leaves.	Pale green, softly hairy leaves.	On a kitchen windowsill or in a cool room.	Height: 1-2ft (30-60cm) Spread: 15-18 inches (38-45cm) **Tender, shrubby perennial:** Keep at 45-50°F (7-10°C) during winter, with shade from direct sunlight in summer. Repot in spring when roots fill the pot.
PRIMROSE				
Primula x *kewensis*	Delicate and primrose-like.	Loose, tiered whorls of yellow, ¾-inch-(18mm) wide flowers from midwinter to late spring. Spoon-shaped leaves covered with a white, waxy powder.	Superb on dining and coffee tables.	Height: 12-15 inches (30-38cm) Spread: 10-12 inches (25-30cm) **Greenhouse perennial, usually grown as an annual:** Keep at 50-55°F (10-13°C) and position in bright, indirect sunlight. While in flower, apply a weak liquid fertilizer such as seaweed extract or fish emulsion every two weeks. Plants are usually discarded when they cease to flower.

PLANT	SCENT	COLOR	SITUATION	CULTIVATION
PRIMROSE				
Primula malacoides Fairy Primrose	Delicate and primrose-like.	Tiered whorls of star-like flowers, ½ inch (12mm) wide, in a color range from pale purple through to red and white from midwinter to late spring.	Superb on dining and coffee tables. 	Height: 12-15 inches (30-38cm) Spread: 12-15 inches (30-38cm) **Greenhouse perennial, usually grown as an annual:** Keep at 55-60°F (13-15°C) and position in bright, indirect sunlight. While in flower, apply a weak liquid fertilizer every two weeks. Plants are usually discarded when they cease to flower.
ROSE				
Pelargonium graveolens Rose-scented Geranium	Rose-scented leaves.	Hairy, green, deeply lobed leaves revealing an appealing fragrance when crushed. Rose-pink flowers, 1 inch (2.5cm) wide, with dark purple spots borne in umbrella-like heads from mid- to late summer.	On a kitchen windowsill or in a cool room.	Height: 2-2½ft (60-75cm) Spread: 18 inches (45cm) **Tender, shrubby perennial:** Keep at 45-50°F (7-10°C) during winter, with shade from direct sunlight in summer. Repot in spring when roots fill the pot.
SWEET				
Ardisia crenata (syn. *A. crispa*)	Very sweet.	Creamy-white, star-shaped flowers, ½ inch (12mm) wide, in clusters during midsummer. These are followed by round, scarlet berries that often remain until midsummer of the following year.	When small, position on a side table, later in a corner where it cannot be knocked. It looks best against a white or light-colored wall, where the wavy-edged green leaves and bright berries are highlighted.	Height: 2-3ft (60-90cm) Spread: 12-18 inches (30-45cm) **Tender evergreen shrub:** Keep at 45-50°F (7-10°C) in winter and position out of direct sunlight during summer. From spring to late summer, feed every week with a weak liquid fertilizer and repot in spring when the roots fill the pot (usually every two years).
Cyclamen persicum Cyclamen/Sowbread	Delicately sweet.	Shuttlecock-shaped flowers – some varieties scented – from late autumn to early spring. The Puppet, Kaori and Symphony Strains have a beautiful bouquet.	In a cool room during winter.	Height: 6-9 inches (15-23cm) Spread: 6-9 inches (15-23cm) **Hardy corm:** 50-60°F (10-15°C) during winter and in bright, indirect sunlight. Apply a weak liquid fertilizer every two weeks during the growing and flowering period. Plants can be kept from year to year, but most are discarded and fresh ones bought during the following year.
Exacum affine Persian Violet	Sweet, resembling lily-of-the-valley.	Purple, shallowly saucer-shaped, ½-¾ inch (12-18mm) wide flowers with yellow stamens from mid- to late summer.	Position on a dining room or coffee table.	Height: 8-10 inches (20-25cm) Spread: 8-10 inches (20-25cm) **Greenhouse annual or biennial:** 55-61°F (13-16°C) in light shade. From midsummer to late summer, feed every 10 days with a weak liquid fertilizer. Most plants are bought when the flowers are just opening; to raise your own plants, sow seeds in late winter or early spring ¼ inch (3mm) deep in temperatures of 68-78°F (20-25°C). To raise larger plants that flower slightly earlier, sow seeds in autumn of the previous year.

PLANT	SCENT	COLOR	SITUATION	CULTIVATION
SWEET				
Gardenia jasminoides Gardenia/Cape Jasmine	Heavy and sweet.	White, waxy flowers, 3 inches (7.5cm) wide, from mid- to late summer. The forms most usually grown are the double-flowered 'Florida', or the even better 'Fortuniana'.	In a greenhouse or sunroom, or in a border or large tub.	Height: 2-4ft (0.60-1.2m) Spread: 2-4ft (0.60-1.2m) **Tender evergreen shrub:** Keep at 54°F (12°C) during winter and in light shade from direct sunlight during summer. Small plants need repotting every spring; topdress those in large tubs with fresh potting soil. After the flowers fade, shorten all growths by half to two-thirds. Pinch out the tips of shoots on small plants to encourage bushiness.
Heliotropium x *hybridum* Heliotrope/Cherry Pie/Turnsole	Sweet, fruity and heavy, resembling that of cherry pie.	Wide color range from dark violet through lavender to white. Forget-me-not-like flowers in clustered heads from early summer to autumn.	In pots indoors, or for use in summer bedding schemes outdoors.	Height: 12-18 inches (30-45cm) – in a pot Spread: 12-18 inches (30-45cm) – in a pot **Half-hardy perennial usually treated as a half-hardy annual:** Sow seeds ¼ inch (6mm) deep in early spring and keep at 60-68°F (15-20°C). Transfer seedlings to pots or boxes, repotting those plants for use indoors into progressively larger pots. Plant out summer bedding plants in early June.
Hoya bella Miniature Wax Plant	Sweet.	White, waxy, star-shaped flowers borne in 2-inch-(5cm) wide, pendulous, umbrella-like heads at any time from late spring to late summer. Each flower has a purple or rosy-crimson center.	On a side table or in an indoor hanging basket.	Height: 10-12 inches (25-30cm) Spread: 15-18 inches (38-45cm) **Tender evergreen shrub:** Keep at 55°F (13°C) during winter, although it will survive at a few degrees lower. Position in moderate to heavy shade during summer, but give more light in winter. From late spring to late summer apply a weak liquid fertilizer every three weeks.
Hoya carnosa Wax Plant	Penetrating and sweet.	White to flesh-pink, star-shaped flowers borne in 3-inch-(7.5cm) wide, pendulous, umbrella-like heads from late spring to late summer.	Its climbing habit makes it suitable for growing in a sunroom or greenhouse, where it can be trained along a permanent framework of wire. Established plants can easily exceed 12ft (3.6m).	Height: 8-12ft (2.4-3.6m) Spread: Climbing **Tender, vigorous, evergreen vine:** Keep at 50°F (10°C) during winter, although it will tolerate a few degrees lower. During summer give it slight shade, but allow it more light during winter. From late spring to late summer apply a weak liquid fertilizer every three weeks.

PLANT	SCENT	COLOR	SITUATION	CULTIVATION
SWEET				
Hyacinthus orientalis Common Hyacinth	Very sweet and penetrating.	Wax-like, five-petalled flowers tightly clustered in spire-like heads from midwinter to late spring. Wide color range, including white, yellow, pink, red, mauve and blue. The true species is seldom grown, being represented by the large-flowered Dutch hybrids.	In a pot on a table in a cool room.	Height: 6-9 inches (15-23cm) Spread: 4-6 inches (10-15cm) **Hardy bulb:** Keep at 50°F (10°C) after the shoots appear, raising to 65°F (18°C) after the flower buds open and display color. Position in light shade. After the flowers fade, place the container in a cool, dry position and plant the bulbs under shrubs in the garden in early summer. Buy fresh bulbs each year for flowering indoors.
Jasminum polyanthum Pink Jasmine	Sweet and penetrating.	White or pale pink, tubular, star-shaped flowers in loose clusters, 2-5 inches (5-13cm) wide, from midwinter to spring.	Usually grown in a 5-inch-(13cm) wide pot and trained over a 15-18 inch (38-45cm) high hoop of split canes. Can also be grown in a greenhouse border or a large pot in a sunroom and trained along wires. In mild areas it grows outdoors, flowering from late spring to midsummer.	Height: 5-8ft (1.5-2.4m) Spread: Climbing **Tender evergreen vine (semi-evergreen if grown outdoors):** Keep at 45-50°F (7-10°C) during winter, although it will survive at 40°F (5°C). Keep the potting soil moist during summer and place in full sun. In warm areas, stand the plant in full sun outdoors during summer, feeding it every 2-3 weeks with a weak fertilizer from spring to late summer.
Senecio rowleyanus String of Beads	Sweet.	White flowers, with purple stigmas, on stalks 2 inches (5cm) long from late summer to early winter.	In an indoor hanging basket or trailing from a high shelf.	Height: 2 inches (5cm) Spread: Trailing or mat-forming to 2-3ft (60-90cm) **Succulent indoor plant:** Keep at 50°F (10°C) during winter and in a position in full or slight shade. From late spring to late summer feed every two to three weeks with a weak liquid fertilizer. Repot in spring when the roots fill their pot.
Stephanotis floribunda Wax Flower/ Madagascar Jasmine	Very heavy and sweet.	White, waxy, tubular, star-shaped flowers with rounded, spreading lobes, borne in clusters from late spring to early autumn.	Best in a sunroom or greenhouse, where it can be trained along wires above head height. However, it is often sold for growing indoors, in a small pot with stems twined around a wire hoop.	Height: 7-10ft (2.1-3m) Spread: Climbing **Tender evergreen vine:** Keep at 55°F (13°C) during winter, although it will survive at a few degrees lower. Position in light shade during summer and feed with a weak liquid fertilizer every two weeks from late spring to late summer.

CHAPTER ELEVEN

Working with Scented Plants

A treasure trove of irresistible ideas for filling
the home with the fragrance of fresh and
dried flowers.

The art of bringing fragrance indoors from the garden is an old idea passed down from generation to generation, one born out of the need originally to mask unpleasant household smells and ward off insect pests and germs. In the last decade or so there has been a great revival of interest in all the old-fashioned skills of growing and using scented plants for their ability to evoke summer all the year round by their fragrance.

It is now possible to buy scoops of wonderfully pungent potpourri in herb or flower shops, natural herbal cosmetics abound, and the choice of cut flowers and indoor plants has never been better. It seems that, as we speed up the pace of our lives and embrace high technology as part of everyday life, we still crave simple, natural things and the need to be close to them. Scent has a powerful relaxing and therapeutic value for many people, and as the source of the fragrance is often beautiful to look at as well, it satisfies an aesthetic need, too.

If you have your own garden, then a few plants grown specially for their use indoors are a must. Among the most useful are lavender in all its varieties, roses – particularly red and crimson, strongly scented old types such as the Apothecary's Rose (Rosa gallica officinalis) *– jasmine, sweet peas, all the herbs, and Lemon Verbena* (Lippia citriodora) *for its leaves. All these are useful for making potpourris and scented sachets. The range of scented flowers for picking for the house is vast, and what you grow will depend very much on the space you have available. If you already grow vegetables, then consider sowing a row or two of flowers among them specially for cutting. Try Sweet Mignonette* (Reseda odorata), *phlox, nicotiana, sweet peas, sweet rocket and all the lovely scented dianthus varieties. Many other flowers which are not particularly scented are useful for the color and texture they add to potpourris. For example, cornflowers and marigolds hold their colors well, and peony and larkspur petals add bulk.*

Every room in the house can benefit from some form of subtle fragrance, whether it be from a posy of Lily-of-the-Valley (Convallaria majalis) *in spring or from a brimming bowlful of garden roses in summer. Spicy herb sachets or traditional bags of lavender, astringent and clean-smelling, are a delight when placed among clothes or freshly laundered linen.*

In this chapter we provide a whole host of ideas to help you bring the gardens and fields indoors, ideas which are fun to put into practice and mostly quite simple. A few are sheer indulgence, and these make superb gifts or personal treats. The first part concentrates on fresh flowers and foliage, and the second part shows how to make the most of the wealth of dried flowers, herbs and leaves available either bought or homegrown, for making endless scented delights.

P osies are just one of the lovely
things that can be made with
scented flowers. The posy on the
right includes lilac, yellow roses
and freesias. More posies are
featured on the following pages.

PERFECT POSIES

A charming way to present scented flowers is to make small posies, or tussie-mussies as they were once known, which make perfect gifts for birthdays, anniversaries and other occasions. Once they have been admired and enjoyed, they can simply be stood in water just as they are, either in a special posy vase or in any small container.

There is no great skill required to putting them together, though if you wish you can arrange circles of single types or colors of flowers concentrically, or frame the outer edge in leaves with pretty shapes. If you are using a single type of flower, simply gather a handful and make them into a bunch. With a mixed collection, begin with a central flower such as a perfect rose and build around it. Tie a small piece of thread or wire around the stems and cut them off to an equal length. A paper doily makes a pretty frame, either in traditional white or in a pale pastel to enhance the flower color. Cut the doily once into the center and remove a small circle in the middle to accommodate the stems. Pull the cut edges together to make a cone, drop the posy into this, and staple or glue the overlapping edges together. Wrap the stems with florist's tape or ribbon.

Suitable flowers for this treatment include primroses, small roses and rosebuds, lily-of-the-valley, freesias, hyacinths, lilac and mixed bunches of summer flowers, with herbs such as thyme, rosemary and lavender added. You can make these posies on a miniature scale if you wish or any size you like, but bear in mind that they should be easy to hold, neat, compact and not too loose or floppy.

Left: A selection of fresh flower posies. Below, from left to right: Lilac and rose posy; Lily-of-the- valley posy; Anemone and rose posy.

FRESH FLOWER ARRANGEMENTS

*U*sing scented flowers in the house to make arrangements and decorations poses no special problems, but there are a few points to remember. If you want the fragrance to be really noticeable, then you will need to be generous with your flowers. While as few as five freesias will scent a whole room, other flowers may need to be in a mass. The warmer the room, the stronger the scent.

It is best to aim for an abundant and dense arrangement of scented flowers, without necessarily being too concerned with achieving a perfect outline or overall shape, as one might be with an arrangement concentrating on color or form alone. Aim for something which invites people to bend down and drink in the fragrance. For table settings, think about placing a personal scented decoration beside each plate, perhaps a tiny stemmed glass filled with violets or a single perfect scented rose. Other larger table decorations are best made low and simple: a large shallow bowl filled with pale pink hyacinth flowers would be beautiful, as would brilliant, clashing sweet peas mixed with lavender spikes.

If you need to support flowers rather than simply stand them informally in a vase, then use the expanded foam available from florists. It absorbs water, and is available in many different shapes or can be cut to the shape you require, either free-form or in a container. Try making a round ball from foam to hang from a doorway as a welcome based on the Christmas kissing ball idea. Simply wrap the foam roughly in chicken wire and attach a piece of wire or string to hang it by later. Keeping the flower stems quite short, work all around the ball, filling it with flowers; keep the surface at the same level all over and leave no gaps between the blooms. You can, of course, include foliage with the flowers to avoid using quite so many blooms.

Small rustic baskets make superb containers for arrangements of scented flowers and make perfect gifts, since they can be re-used once the flowers are finished. Other shapes to try are pyramidal or conical arrangements of thickly packed, mixed scented flower heads. Stand them in front of a mirror and increase the impact even more.

A̶bove, left: Heart-shaped basket
filled with an assortment of
fragrant flowers. Above, right:
Mixed scented flowers in a ball.
Far right: Pyramid flower arrangement
with lilies, roses and stock.

Above: Primroses in wooden basket. Left: Hyacinths in blue-and-white china containers.

POTTING UP FRAGRANCE

Traditionally, bulbs and other plants have always been grown for their ability to cheer and scent the house during the long winter months, when there is little growing outside. Bulbs have been bred which stand being forced so that they flower under cover many weeks before they might outside.

Hyacinths are some of the most successful and pleasing bulbs to grow, simply because of their lovely scent. Do not simply plant in the usual plastic containers, but think of how you can create a picture. Grouped together, blue hyacinths in a collection of mixed blue-and-white china, white ones in cool green china containers, or yellow or cream planted into rough terra-cotta pots of different heights and shapes make a spectacular display. You can always start the bulbs off in ordinary pots or buy them about to flower, and then move them at the last minute into their chosen containers.

Many of the miniature bulbs have a slight scent. Snowdrops, some of the iris species and, of course, many of the small narcissi are all fragrant and deserve to be more commonly grown for indoor displays. Once they have finished flowering, they can be planted outdoors to flower naturally the following year.

Match your plants' colors to their containers, and make use of paints and stains to turn pale baskets any color you wish. Search out unlikely and unusual items to plant things in, and remember that you can always line a precious basket or trug with foil or plastic first before transplanting the plants inside. The finishing touches are always important, so use green moss around hyacinth bulbs, and smooth pebbles or horticultural sand in a planting of narcissi or crocus.

Certain scented plants such as jasmine and scented geraniums can be clipped into special shapes like a kind of indoor topiary. And for the summer months, be sure to plant some of the highly scented lily varieties for a spectacular display and unbeatable scent.

POTPOURRIS

*T*here are two basic ways to make potpourri – the moist method and the dry method. It is possible to make both kinds yourself at home using garden-grown or bought flowers, and the spices, oils and fixatives (such as orris root or gum benzoin) are all easy to obtain these days. Essential oil, which you buy ready prepared and is the pure essence of a flower scent obtained by distillation, is used in all potpourris. Pounds of flowers are used to obtain one drop of essential oil.

A good basic recipe for a moist potpourri is:

MOIST POTPOURRI

10 cups partially dried rose petals
3 cups coarse salt
2 tablespoons ground cinnamon
2 tablespoons ground allspice
2 tablespoons ground nutmeg
1 tablespoon ground cloves
5 tablespoons powdered orris root
Few drops essential oil, such as rose oil

Layer petals and salt in a crock or large bowl. Weight down and stir every day. When the mixture is dry, from three to six weeks later, crumble it and add the spices and, if you wish, other dried flowers, and then the drops of oil. Cover, seal and cure for several more weeks, then use.

A moist potpourri can be made throughout one summer, and it will keep its scent for several years if well made. The only drawback is that it is a not very pretty muddy brown color, so it is best kept covered when possible. In early times, special ceramic

Moist potpourris topped with dried red and yellow roses for decoration.

containers in the shape of a jar with a lid were used to hold potpourri. These were stood by an open fire with the lid removed to warm up and release the scent and, when finished with, closed and taken away from the heat.

DRY POTPOURRIS

*T*he popularity of potpourri made by the dry method is due to the fact that it can be used decoratively and displayed in attractive containers. It does tend to lose its scent quite quickly, but can be revived periodically with an essential oil or special reviver. Many commercial potpourris are simply dried flower petals and heads, often not scented to begin with, which have just had essential oils added to them. A properly made potpourri will be characteristically dusty from the ground spices and fixatives used in the recipe. Try to make your own, even if you follow this easy way by simply using dried flowers and oils and spices as you can, then create the color you want and a fragrance you really like. You can also make a version for each season. If you have a gardenful of flowers to pick, then you can collect things throughout the year, dry them, and add them to your potpourri, or else collect bags of petals to mix later. Even if you do not grow your own, simply keep and dry petals from bought flowers such as daffodils, roses and tulips: you will be surprised how quickly your bowl will fill up over the months.

Be experimental and add larger pieces to the potpourri such as scented bark, dried moss, various leaves, and whole spices such as nutmeg, cinnamon and allspice. These add texture as well as scent and make the finished result much more exciting than simply flowers used alone.

Recipes for potpourri can be adapted to suit the ingredients you have, and you can safely adjust proportions of various flowers quite happily. Once the ingredients

have been mixed, though, you must seal the potpourri in a paper bag, shake it well, and leave it in a warm dark place for six weeks to cure. Drying flower petals and leaves to make your own potpourri is easily done in a hot summer by simply spreading a single layer on a tray or mesh surface and letting the sun do the work. Drying flowers in a very low oven is also possible, or try placing them in a warm attic.

This is a recipe for a simple summer potpourri:

DRY POTPOURRI

2 cups dried rose petals
1 cup larkspur/cornflower petals
for color
2 cups dried lavender flowers
1 cup lemon verbena leaves
½ cup powdered orris root
1 tablespoon ground allspice
1 tablespoon ground cinnamon
1 tablespoon ground cloves
Few drops rose essential oil

Combine all the dry ingredients in a large bowl. Add drops of essential oil until scent is strong enough. Seal in a paper bag, shake and leave for six weeks.

A potpourri for the winter months could be quite different in character. It could contain more of the sweet spices such as nutmeg and cinnamon, and dark flowers such as hibiscus and deep red roses. Dried ground orange or lemon peel is a good addition, as is a dark green leaf or two, used for enhancing the festive color theme. If you like, top the potpourri off with brilliant whole red roses and small bundles of cinnamon twigs.

Left, from the top: Autumn, Summer and Winter dry potpourris. Right: Spring dry potpourri.

SCENTS ON SHOW

*T*he different ways of displaying and using potpourris are endless, and the first thing you are likely to want to do with some you have made is simply to have a large bowlful to enjoy in a living room, bedroom or hall. Large, shallow containers made from wood, metal or ceramic are all suitable, as you can spread out the ingredients and appreciate all the different flowers and leaves. Old wooden boxes such as shaker boxes make good containers, and so do antique or new baskets, lined to stop debris from sifting on to the furniture.

Clear glass containers are not generally very well suited to the texture of dried petals and leaves, but layering different-colored flowers in simple modern glass shapes such as tanks and cylinders can look wonderful, particularly in a modern setting Similarly, in a cool, simple interior, bowls containing a single-flower potpourri, such as one made from lavender or rose petals, look stunning and far more in keeping than the old-fashioned multi-flower potpourri which is right in a traditional interior.

Small, handled baskets lined with fabric and with a pretty padded lid make lovely gifts and are a perfect way to display a potpourri in a bathroom or bedroom. Other gift-wrapping ideas could include scoops of potpourri in small plain paper bags decorated with stencils or flower cutouts. A simple twist of colored tissue paper looks good tied with pretty ribbon in a bow. If you are good with scissors and glue, then try the Victorian art of découpage to cover a plain cardboard or wooden box. Simply cut out pictures of flowers from seed catalogues and magazines and glue them all over the surface of the box, building up a design as you go. Finish off with a layer of clear varnish, which mellows and ages the colors and gives a glossy sheen. Choose your cutouts to match the color of the potpourri inside, and

you have a stunning container or gift box.

Think about using potpourri with fresh flowers for a very different look. Surround a group of pot plants with the dried flowers in a similar color to the fresh ones. Try a big antique copper or brass pan with tiny scented pink cyclamen surrounded by rose potpourri, or simply place small posies of any cut flowers in a bowlful of potpourri. Place it somewhere low to enable the view to be appreciated from above.

Top: Pretty lined basket filled with potpourri. Above: Glass container layered with dried flowers. Right: Découpage box containing potpourri.

SACHETS AND HERB BAGS

*S*achets and bags of sweet-smelling flowers, herbs and spices have been used for many centuries to freshen clothes, bed linen, closets and wardrobes, and special recipes were devised for particular purposes such as keeping clothes moths at bay. Nowadays we are likely to use such things for the delightful scents they give to all manner of things, from cushions to shoe shapers. Simple potpourris can be used to stuff sachets, or you can use recipes designed for one particular job, such as a sleep mixture for a pillow. Most people are familiar with lavender bags made from scraps of fabric sewn together, containing nothing more than lavender flower heads and meant to be slipped among clothes in a drawer, or sheets in a linen closet. Larger sachets can be made using polyester padding as a stuffing with a small amount of scented potpourri added for the fragrance.

Two fairly simple recipes for a sachet mixture are:

RECIPE 1

1 cup rose petals
1 cup lavender
½ cup crushed rosemary
2 crushed sticks cinnamon
¼ cup powdered orris root
Few drops rose essential oil

Mix all the dry ingredients in a large bowl. Add drops of oil until you get the scent you want. Put the mixture in a paper bag, shake well, seal and leave in a dark place for two weeks. Use to fill sachets as required.

RECIPE 2

3 cups lavender
¼ cup powdered orris root
Few drops lavender essential oil

Make as above.

Of course, you do not have to make your own mixtures for sachets and bags: you can simply use any bought potpourri whose smell appeals to you. Choose one that is not made up from very bulky ingredients, or it will be difficult to fill small bags and the result will look lumpy and misshapen.

Natural fabrics are best for making bags and sachets, as they allow the scent to escape. Cotton and linen are good for everyday sachets, but for more luxurious ones you can use silk, net, lace and satin.

Sachets and bags can be any shape and size you like, and it is fun to coordinate fabrics and colors with the purpose the bags will be used for. Fine ticking stripes look good for linen closets and mens' shirt drawers, while creamy silk and lace sachets are a luxurious addition to a lingerie drawer.

One of the simplest scented bags needs no sewing at all. Start with either a square of fabric and pink the raw edges or use a handkerchief, preferably with a pretty lace edging. Put a small ball of padding in the center and add a scoop of scented mixture. Draw up the edges and secure them tightly with a ribbon. If you plan to hang the bag in a closet, make sure that the ends of the ribbon are long enough to make a loop.

To make a small, general-purpose, oblong bag for stuffing, cut a long strip of fabric a little wider than you want the finished bag to be. Fold it in half and sew along the two long sides. Turn it right-side out and tuck the raw-edged top

*A*bove: Striped sachets for the linen closet. Right: Lace-trimmed lingerie sachet.

Left: Selection of scented
cushions. Above: Scented sachet
affixed to embroidered tea-cosy.

down inside the bag. Fill with
your mixture, and padding if desired, then tie tightly with a ribbon
just above where the raw edges
are inside.

Little flat sachets can be made
with pinked edges, and these are
useful for slipping into pockets inside cushions or pillows, where
they will not generally be on show.
Simply cut two fabric shapes the
same size and stitch a little way in
from the edge all the way around,
but leave a little space through
which to push the filling. Insert
the mixture and stuffing and sew
across the gap.

Try adding some scent to a tea-
cosy by sewing a small pocket inside the cosy and slipping a sachet
inside this. The warmth of the tea-
pot will release the scent. Choose
a flowery, evocative scent and
match it to a summery printed
fabric, or make a spicy version
suitable for a winter tea-time. A

cool, elegant all-white cosy decorated with a single sprig of
lavender and containing lavender
sachets looks superb with the best
white china. This idea would be
lovely made up with rosemary or
thyme, too, or you could make a
citrusy version with lemon verbena,
lemon peel and citron oil. A jas-
mine- or rose-scented sachet would
be good, too, and you could serve
fragrant tea to match (see page 194).

The hot-water-bottle cover is an
old-fashioned idea worth reviving.
Use a pre-quilted fabric for the
basic shape and add a pocket in
the shape of a basket over a bunch
of appliquéd flowers. Make a
scented sachet in the shape of a
single flower to tuck into the
pocket. Try a fresh herbal blend for
the sachet or a stronger, cleaner
smell such as cedar or sandalwood.
It is sensible to make the sachets
removable in any of these projects
so that you can replenish them.

— 185 —

Scented shoe shapers for keeping shoes smelling fresh and in good shape are very easy to make and are a lovely gift idea. It is possible to buy dress patterns to cut a perfect outline, or you can approximate the shape and simply make a loose egg-shape stuffed not too tightly with the scented mixture so that it will fit most sizes and shapes of shoe. Choose a strong, clean-smelling mixture.

The theme of hearts is a lovely starting point for all sorts of flower-filled ideas. A frilled, embroidered, heart-shaped pillow would look lovely on a bed mixed with a group of plain cushions. The scent chosen for the sachet should be something romantic: perhaps it could contain a mixture of rose, lavender and oil of bergamot. Tiny heart-shaped sachets are no more difficult to make than round or square versions and look particularly pretty hanging in a wardrobe among clothes.

A pincushion can also be filled with sachet. Petit point or tapestry makes a good solid surface for the front of the cushion, while the back can be made from velvet or any other rich, plain fabric. Stuff the shape very tightly, traditionally with sawdust but these days with padding, and add potpourri in the center of the stuffing. A narrow edging of color-coordinated silky cord finishes the whole thing off beautifully.

Above: Scented tapestry pincushion. Right: Fragrant heart-shaped pillow and a selection of sachets on the same theme.

MOTH SACHETS

*S*achets designed to prevent moth damage to clothes may seem old-fashioned in these days of chemicals and aerosols, but for people living in the country where moths can be a problem, or for those who hate using artificial pesticides, a mixture of specific natural herbs and flowers can be the perfect answer. Little sachets – moth-shaped, perhaps, for fun – filled with the moth-repellent mixture can be hung from clothes hangers or hooked inside a wardrobe. They can be tucked in among wool sweaters when they are put away in storage during the summer months, or a small amount of mixture can be put into padded hangers along with the padding.

A far more traditional method of repelling insects is to hang small bunches of herbs and flowers in a closet. These can be made to look very pretty as well as being effective. Use lavender, southernwood, rosemary, cinnamon sticks and some colorful dried flowers, plus something soft and frothy such as sea lavender to make the bunch more attractive. Arrange the stems into a small posy and wire the stems tightly together. Finish off with a ribbon or yarn bow and add a loop to hang the bunch up with.

Here is a recipe for a mixture to fill sachets with for the specific purpose of keeping moths away. Southernwood with its curious pungent smell has always been used effectively for this purpose. Rue is another anti-moth herb and so are rosemary and tansy.

RECIPE FOR SACHETS AND BAGS

1 cup dried lavender
1 cup dried crumbled southernwood
½ cup dried crumbled rosemary
2 crushed sticks cinnamon

Combine all the ingredients and put into sachets and bags.

Left, clockwise from the top:
Scented hanger; Shoe shapers;
Moth-shaped sachet filled with
moth-repellent mixture. Above:
Hanging bunch of moth-repellent
herbs and flowers.

BEAUTIFUL BATHS

We all love adding fragrances, foams and oils to baths and showers, but few people realize how easy it is to make the little bath bags that soften and scent the water. You can add any ingredients to your taste and experiment until you get your own personal recipe. A small boxful of these bags makes a lovely present, as does a large glass apothecary's jar finished off with a bow and pretty label. The bags should be made from muslin or cheesecloth to allow the ingredients to permeate the bath water and can usually be used for several baths, so they are quite economical. They can be simply made and the edges just pinked with shears, as there is no need to be very fussy about the finish. String is preferable to ribbon for tying them up since it will be getting wet. Either drop the whole bag into the bath as you run the water or loop it over a tap and let the hot water flow through the contents.

The oatmeal and powdered milk in the recipe below bulk out the ingredients and soften the water beautifully. Adjust the proportions according to how many bags you wish to fill.

RECIPE FOR BATH BAGS

1 cup medium oatmeal
½ cup powdered milk
½ cup dried herbs and/or flowers
(try using chamomile, marigold, rose, lavender, rosemary, thyme, lemon balm, peppermint, sweet woodruff)
¾ cup dried cut lemon or orange peel

Mix all the ingredients together and fill the muslin sachets.

Right: Bath bag looped on to tap.
Far right: Selection of simple muslin bath bags.

FLORAL WATERS

Other bathroom ideas which include scented flowers are colognes, floral waters and hair rinses.

ROSEMARY AND LAVENDER
HAIR RINSE

1 tablespoon lavender flowers
1 tablespoon rosemary
1 cup (300ml) water
2 cups (600ml) distilled water or
rainwater
1 teaspoon lemon juice
or good wine vinegar

Bring the lavender flowers and rosemary to a boil in one cup of water. Take off the heat and allow to infuse for several hours. Strain off the liquid and add it to the distilled water or rainwater. Add the lemon juice or wine vinegar and bottle.

This rinse is excellent for dark hair, but you could make a version for blonde hair using chamomile blossom instead of the rosemary and lavender.

ROSE PETAL COLOGNE

2 cups distilled water
¾ cup alcohol (it must be odorless,
so vodka could be used)
2 cups of strongly scented rose petals

Combine the ingredients and mix thoroughly. Leave for several days, covered. Strain off the liquid and add a few drops of rose oil if you need to boost the scent.

You can adjust this recipe by using other flowers such as lavender and changing the oil, too. Bottles once filled look very pretty with a few petals or a sprig of herb added to them. Look for ornate, attractive old glass bottles, or buy simple new ones.

Assortment of prettily bottled colognes, floral waters and hair rinses made with scented flowers.

FLOWERY TEAS

Fragrant, flower-scented teas are very simple to prepare at home and make beautiful presents to give to friends and family. Find small wooden boxes to put the tea in, or improvise by wrapping a scoop of tea in a plain white or cream tissue-paper twist tied up with ribbon. Always label the tea, making a note of the flavor and the infusion method. A plain wooden box looks lovely stencilled with a flower motif to match the flower fragrance inside. Stencil plain brown bags, too, or refill old empty miniature tea chests.

Base your tea on the best-quality China large-leaf tea, then add flower heads or petals to your taste and mix well. Rose petals work very well and so does sweet summer jasmine. Use about 2 tablespoons of these to every ½lb (250g) of China tea. Others to try are hibiscus or lemon balm, but you will need a higher proportion of these to tea than with the rose or jasmine. A ratio of 4 tablespoons of hibiscus or lemon balm to every ½lb (250g) of China tea gives a deliciously aromatic tea.

BURNING BUNDLES

When you have rubbed all the lavender flower heads from their stalks, use the stems to make aromatic bundles for burning on an open fire or even on a barbecue. Other aromatic twigs include most of the herbs such as rosemary, thyme and lemon verbena. Tie up the stem bundles in the summer and store them somewhere dry and dark until the season of fires begins again in the winter. Keep a basket of twigs and other fragrant things such as pine cones beside the hearth to add to the fire when you want to scent the house. They look quite decorative, too, in their quiet, subtle greens and browns, and provide a hint of summer on long, cold, dark winter nights.

Above: Selection of gift-wrapped flower teas. Right: Aromatic stem bundles for burning on an open fire.

PERFUMED PAPERS

$\mathscr{S}$cented letter-writing or gift-wrapping paper is available ready-made in card shops, but you can produce your own.

The best way to do this is to use a large airtight plastic box big enough to hold several sheets of paper and envelopes at one time. Lay the paper inside the box and add several strongly scented sachets. Close the lid and store the box somewhere cool and dark for several weeks. Remove and use the paper as required, replacing it each time with a new batch at the bottom. If the scent is too weak, put a few drops of essential oil on a cotton ball or pad and put this inside a piece of greaseproof paper to avoid staining the writing paper. Put the perfume pad in the box as well as the sachets.

To scent large sheets of wrapping and tissue paper, roll them into a loose cylinder and secure with a rubber band. Find a plastic bag large enough to hold the roll, and add scented sachets in the same way as with the writing paper. Seal the end with a twist of wire and let it absorb the scent for however long is necessary. A faint, subtle scent is best, so do not aim for anything too strong and overpowering. Sheets of paper treated this way can be used to line drawers where clothes are stored.

Choose pale, pretty colors and flowery designs to echo and match the soft summery flower scents you use such as rose and lavender.

Fragrant stationery, including writing and wrapping paper, envelopes, gift tags and small cardboard boxes.

SCENTED CANDLES

Scented candles have been made since people first used wax candles to see by, and while it is now possible to buy them ready-made their scents are often rather crude and overpowering. With only a small amount of equipment you can make your own candles cheaply and easily and then you can control the fragrance exactly. Bayberry is a traditional scent for candles in America and other good scents are citrus, gardenia, pine and sandalwood. The aroma is added in the form of essential oils to the hot melted wax before it is poured into molds or used for dipping.

Floating candles are lovely to make or buy, and if you float them in a shallow bowl among scented petals or flower heads the whole confection makes a wonderful party or dinner-table decoration. Choose pearly, soft colors and tint the water, if you wish, with food coloring. To intensify the fragrance, a few drops of essential oil can be added to the water.

Left: Floating candles in a bowl with sweet-smelling flower petals and buds. Above: Assortment of scented candles.

Above: Scented dried flower posy attached to curtain tie-back. Right: Scented wreath made up of dried flowers on a foam ring base.

WREATHS AND OTHER DECORATIONS

Dried flowers are usually used for their decorative qualities, and any inherent scent they have is considered a bonus. Although certain flowers retain their fragrance long after drying, and more so if they have been dried fast and carefully and not stored for too long, they will always gradually lose their scent along with their color. Of course, herbs used for cooking and medicinal purposes retain the aromas of their foliage for a long time, so they are useful additions to a dried flower mixture if you want to create more than just visual interest. Lavender keeps its scent well, as do so many varieties of rose, and once you have made a dried flower arrangement you can always add a few drops of essential oil to keep it smelling as sweet as possible.

Do not simply fill your vases with dried flowers: use them to create all kinds of different decorations which you might not make with fresh flowers. Using foam bases in an assortment of shapes, you can make scented, flower-filled pyramids, balls and wreaths, as well as bunches and little posies. Swags and wreaths look marvellous on plain walls. You can take several posies and string them along a soft rope to twine through banisters or along a piece of furniture. Alternatively, you can attach a small posy to a curtain tie-back, matching the colors or flowers in the curtain fabric.

A scented wreath can be fashioned on a purchased foam ring base, which means that you can make the texture very dense and solid-looking, each flower head being cut off short and pushed into the foam, with no space left between the blooms. You can make a softer version using a straw or grapevine base to which you glue or wire single flowers or little bunches. This method is better if you are using sprigs of herbs and foliage, and allows more fluidity in the design.

Index

Figures printed in **bold** indicate illustrations

CREDITS

PHOTOGRAPHS
Unless specified below, the photographs for this book have been taken by David Squire. Credits for the remaining photographs are given below:

A-Z Collection: 44 (bottom), 45.

Angelo Hornak/Victoria and Albert Museum: 9.

Eric Crichton © Salamander Books Ltd: 40 (bottom), 46 (center), 47 (center), 54 (center), 56 (top), 58 (top), 60, 66 (top), 75 (top), 76 (top), 87 (top), 88, 89 (top), 112 (bottom), 114 (center), 146 (top) 147 (center), 158.

Eric Crichton: 14 (bottom), 24 (top), 30, 32, 38 (top, bottom), 39 (center), 40 (center), 42 (bottom), 43 (bottom), 44 (top), 47 (top), 49 (center), 56 (bottom), 59 (top), 77 (bottom), 78, 82 (top), 89 (bottom), 92, 99 (bottom), 106, 112 (center), 156, 162 (top, center), 163 (top, center), 164 (center, bottom), 165 (top, bottom).

Di Lewis © Salamander Books Ltd: 166–201.

Brian Matthew: 39 (bottom), 54 (top), 57, 59 (bottom), 82 (bottom), 90 (bottom), 114 (bottom), 115 (top).

Peter McHoy: 46 (top), 48 (center), 51, 57 (bottom), 66 (bottom), 67 (top), 75 (bottom), 83, 85, 103, 155 (bottom), 157, 162 (bottom).

Photos Horticultural: 14 (top), 40 (top), 41 (center), 42 (top), 43 (top, center), 44 (center), 46 (bottom), 47 (bottom), 48 (top), 49 (top), 50, 53, 61, 80, 99 (top), 104, 107, 111 (top), 153 (top), 162 (top, bottom, center), 163 (bottom), 164 (top).

Harry Smith Photographic Collection: 42 (center), 71, 72, 91 (top), 110 (bottom), 115 (bottom), 116 (top), 119, 120, 123, 125–127, 167.

AUTHOR'S ACKNOWLEDGEMENTS
David Squire wishes to thank the following nurseries for their help: Bennett's Water Lily Farm, Dorset; Stapeley Water Gardens, Cheshire; and Lotus Water Garden Products Ltd., Buckinghamshire. Thanks are also due to friends who have made their gardens available for 'sniffing', and who have offered their thoughts about scented plants. David Squire wishes to thank the publishers for their help during the preparation of this book, and particularly editors Krystyna Mayer and Tony Hall for their helpful and valuable suggestions.

EDITORIAL ASSISTANCE
Copy editing by Barbara Baran and Diana Vowles.
Index by David Squire.

SOURCES

BULBS

Dutch Gardens, Inc.
P.O. Box 200
Adelphia, NJ 07710
201-780-2713

John D. Lyon Co.
143 Alewife Brook Pkwy.
Cambridge, MA 02140
617-876-3705

McClure & Zimmerman
1422 W. Thorndale
Chicago, IL 60660
312-989-0557

John Scheepers, Inc.
Phillipsburg Rd., R.D. 2
Middletown, NY 10940
914-342-1135
914-342-3727
$3.00 for catalog

Van Bourgondien Bros.
P.O. Box A
245 Farmingdale Rd., Rt. 109
Babylon, NY 11702
516-669-3500

Van Engelen Inc.
Stillbrook Farm
307 Maple St.
Litchfield, CT 06759
203-567-8734
203-567-5662

Vandenberg
Black Meadow Rd.
Chester, NY 10918
914-469-2633
$2.00 for catalog

HERBS

Casa Yerba Gardens
3459 Days Creek Rd.
Days Creek, OR 97429
$1.00 for catalog

Fox Hill Farm
444 W. Michigan Ave., Box 9
Parma, MI 49269-0009
517-531-3179
$1.00 for catalog

Merry Gardens
P.O. Box 595
Camden, ME 04843
207-236-9064
$1.00 for catalog

Misty Meadow Gardens
301 E. South St.
Hillsboro, OH 45133
513-393-9606

Richter's
Box 26
GoodWood, Ontario
Canada L0C 1AO
416-640-6677
$2.50 for catalog

The Sandy Mush Herb Nursery
Rt. 2, Surrett Cove Rd.
Leicester, NC 28748
704-683-2014
$2.00 for catalog

Sunnybrook Farms
9448 Mayfield Rd.
P.O. Box 6
Chesterland, OH 44026
216-729-7232
$1.00 for catalog

Taylor's Herb Gardens, Inc.
1535 Lone Oak Rd.
Vista, CA 92084
619-727-3485

HOUSEPLANTS

Logee's Greenhouses
55 North St.
Danielson, CT 06239
203-774-8038
$3.00 for catalog

Orchids by Hausermann, Inc.
2N 134 Addison Rd.
Villa Park, IL 60181
312-543-6855
$1.25 for catalog

Shady Hill Gardens
821 Walnut
Batavia, IL 60510
$1.00 (credited toward purchase)

PERENNIALS

Bluestone Perennials
7211 Middle Ridge Rd.
Madison, OH 44057
216-428-7535
800-852-5243

Carroll Gardens
444 E. Main St.
P.O. Box 310
Westminster, MD 21157
800-638-6334
301-848-5422
301-876-7336
$2.00 for catalog

The Country Garden
Rt. 2, Box 455A
Crivitz, WI 54114
715-757-2045

Far North Gardens
16785 Harrison
Livonia, MI 48154
313-422-0747
$2.00 for catalog

International Growers' Exchange, Inc.
P.O. Box 52248
Livonia, MI 48152-0248
313-422-0747
Catalog subscription $5.00 for 3 years

Klehm Nursery
Rt. 5, Box 197
South Barrington, IL 60010
312-551-3715
$2.00 for catalog

Milaeger's Gardens
4838 Douglas Ave.
Racine, WI 53402-2498
414-639-2371
$1.00 for catalog

Andre Viette Farm & Nursery
Rt. 1, Box 16
Fishersville, VA 22939
703-943-2315
$2.00 for catalog

Wayside Gardens
Hodges, SC 29695-0001
800-845-1124
$1.00 (credit toward order)

White Flower Farm
Litchfield
CT 06759-0050
203-496-9600
203-496-1661
$5.00 per year for two catalogs

ROSES

The Antique Rose Emporium
Rt. 5, Box 143
Brenham, TX 77833
409-836-9051

Jackson and Perkins Co.
1 Rose La.
Medford, OR 97501

Roses of Yesterday and Today
802 Brown's Valley Rd.
Watsonville, CA 95076-0398
408-724-3537
$2.00 for catalog

SEEDS

W. Atlee Burpee and Co.
Warminster, PA 18974
215-674-4915

The Fragrant Path
P.O. Box 328
Fort Calhoun, NE 68023
$1.00 for catalog

Harris Seeds
Moreton Farm
3670 Buffalo Rd.
Rochester, NY 14624

Nichols Garden Nursery
1190 N. Pacific Hwy.
Albany, OR 97321
503-928-9280

Park Seed Co.
Cokesbury Rd.
Greenwood
SC 29647-0001
803-223-7333

Thompson and Morgan
P.O. Box 1308
Jackson, NJ 08527
201-363-2225

SHRUBS AND TREES

Ferris Nursery
811 Fourth St. N.E.
Hampton, 1A 50441
515-456-2563

Forest Farm
990 Tetherow Rd.
Williams, OR 97544-9599
503-846-6963
$2.00 for catalog

Gossler Farms Nursery
1200 Weaver Rd.
Springfield
OR 97478-9663
503-746-3992
503-747-0749
$1.00 for catalog

Greer Gardens
1280 Goodpasture Island Rd.
Eugene
OR 97401-1794
503-686-8266

Musser Forests
P.O. Box 340-S88M
Indiana
PA 15701-0340
412-465-5685

Roslyn Nursery
211 Burrs La.
Dix Hills, NY 11746
516-643-9347